T4-AIQ-747

XML Design Handbook

Scott Bonneau
Tammy Kohl
Jeni Tennison
Jon Duckett
Kevin Williams

Wrox Press Ltd. ®

XML Design Handbook

© 2003 Wrox Press

All rights reserved. No part of this book may be reproduced, stored in a retrieval system or transmitted in any form or by any means, without the prior written permission of the publisher, except in the case of brief quotations embodied in critical articles or reviews.

The authors and publisher have made every effort in the preparation of this book to ensure the accuracy of the information. However, the information contained in this book is sold without warranty, either express or implied. Neither the authors, Wrox Press, nor its dealers or distributors, will be held liable for any damages caused or alleged to be caused either directly or indirectly by this book.

First published March 2003

Published by Wrox Press Ltd,
Arden House, 1102 Warwick Road, Acocks Green,
Birmingham, B27 6BH
United Kingdom
Printed in the United States
ISBN 1-86100-768-X

Trademark Acknowledgments

Wrox has endeavored to provide trademark information about all the companies and products mentioned in this book by the appropriate use of capitals. However, Wrox cannot guarantee the accuracy of this information.

Credits

Author
Scott Bonneau
Tammy Kohl
Jeni Tennison
Jon Duckett
Kevin Williams

Additional Material
Nikola Ozu

Commissioning Editor
Tony Davis

Technical Editors
Niranjan Jahagirdar
Ashvin Vaidyanathan

Managing Editors
Matthew Cumberlidge
Kalpana Garde

Project Managers
Cilmara Lion
Abbas Rangwala

Technical Reviewers
Urban Bettag
Richard Bonneau
David Franke
Michael Kay
Craig McQueen
Ken Monnington

Production Coordinators
Sarah Hall
Manjiri Karande

Indexer
Andrew Criddle

Proof Readers
Jennifer Williams
Victoria Blackburn
Naomi Pereira

Cover Design
Natalie O'Donnell

About the Author

Scott Bonneau

Scott Bonneau has been involved in software development since he was fourteen years old and used his first dial-up bulletin board system. He wrote his first significant piece of code (a fully-functioning BBS in PowerBASIC) shortly thereafter and has been hooked ever since.

Scott has been developing software professionally for seven years, focusing primarily on systems-level programming and distributed systems. Scott is currently a Senior Software Engineer at MessageOne, Inc., an Austin, TX based provider of disaster recovery and business continuity solutions for corporate messaging environments (Exchange, Notes, RIM).

Scott was born and raised in Central Massachusetts and is an avid Boston sports fan. If you can't find him in front of his computer or on the couch watching the Patriots, you'll find him at the hockey rink or on a soccer field living out his dreams to someday be a goalie in either the NHL or the MLS.

Scott contributed *Chapters 2, 4*, and *Appendix A*.

I would like to thank first and foremost my wife, Amanda, who had to put up with far too many long nights of me working on the material for this book, but who never stopped supporting me.

I'd like to also thank my parents for my genes (you'll find my father Richard Bonneau as a technical reviewer for the book) and for all of the encouragement they gave me as a young geek. I think they're proud of the geek I've grown up to be.

I'd also like to thank Tony Davis, whose tireless efforts made this book possible, and without whose guidance I wouldn't have known where to start.

Tammy Kohl

Tammy R. Kohl, CEO of Concentric Spheres, Inc., has been in the software industry for nearly twenty years. As an early adopter of XML and XSLT, Ms. Kohl has applied these and other XML-related technologies in a wide range of large and small-scale commercial applications including those for customer relationship management, content management, and multi-modal rendering of rich online experiences.

She has a BS (Westfield State College) and an MS (University of Massachusetts, Amherst) in Computer Science. Ms. Kohl has worked as a senior developer, principal software engineer, product manager, and system architect for many software companies, including Dragon Systems, Healthcare Automation, Context Media, and Amerinex Applied Imaging. She has owned and operated a successful software-consulting firm.

Ms. Kohl has co-authored papers on automated feature extraction and tracking from digital imagery for predicting solar storm activity for NOAA (National Oceanic and Atmospheric Administration), and has extensive computer vision application and algorithm expertise. She has developed graduate level course materials for Computer Vision and Image Understanding at the University of Massachusetts, Amherst, and is a contributor of several articles to Macromedia's online Designer and Developer Center, on "ColdFusion MX for Java Programmers".

An authority on rapid project development, system architecture, and information transfer within human and computer systems, Ms. Kohl's current focus is on effective communication, knowledge-sharing, and metadata discovery and collection across the Internet.

Tammy contributed *Chapters 1* and *7*, and can be reached at: tkohl@concentricspheres.net.

I would like to thank Andrew Wetmore for his on-demand editorial assistance and friendship, and Charlie Kohl for everything else.

Jeni Tennison

Jeni Tennison is an independent consultant specializing in XSLT and XML Schema development. She trained as a knowledge engineer, gaining a PhD in collaborative ontology development, and since becoming an consultant has worked on using XML in a wide variety of areas, including publishing, water monitoring, and financial services.

She is the author of *XSLT and XPath On The Edge* (*Hungry Minds, 2001*) and *Beginning XSLT* (*Wrox, 2002*), one of the founders of the EXSLT initiative to standardize extensions to XSLT and XPath, and an invited expert on the W3C XSL Working Group.

She spends much of her spare time answering people's queries on XSL-List and xmlschema-dev mailing lists.

Jeni contributed *Chapter 5*.

Jon Duckett

Jon has been writing about XML since 1998 when he co-authored Wrox's first book on XML. Since then he has worked with XML on a variety of projects in the UK and Australia, and has contributed to several Wrox titles. When he is not in front of the computer, you will most likely find him playing or listening to music.

Jon contributed *Chapter 3*.

Kevin Williams

Kevin's first experience with computers was at the age of 10 (1980) when he took a BASIC class at a local community college on their PDP-9. By the time he was 12, he stayed up for 4 days straight, hand-assembling 6502 code on his Atari 400. His professional career has been focused on Windows development – first client-server and then Internet. He's done a little bit of everything, from VB to Powerbuilder to Delphi to C/C++ to MASM to ISAPI, CGI, ASP, HTML, XML, and almost any other acronym you'd care to name. But these days he's focusing on XML work.

Kevin is an established Wrox author on XML. His company (BlueOxide) is currently building XML and web services authoring tools. Some of the sites he has worked on include USA TODAY and Nasdaq Online.

Kevin contributed *Chapter 6* and provided some material for *Chapter 3*.

Nik Ozalan

Nikola Ozu is a systems and information architect who lives in Wyoming at the end of a dirt road – out where the virtual community is closer than the nearest town, but still only flows at 24kBps and doesn't deliver pizza.

Recent work has included the use of XML for both production and publishing of text and bibliographic databases, an architectural vocabulary, and a new production and delivery system for hypermedia. He designed and developed an early hypertext database, a monthly CD-ROM product called Health Reference Center in 1990, followed by advanced versions of the similar InfoTrac. Given that large text databases were involved, some intimate involvement with SGML was unavoidable. Previous work has ranged from library systems on mainframes to telecom equipment, industrial robots, games, toys, and other embedded microsystems.

Nik provided additional material for *Chapter 6*.

XML Design

Handbook

Table of Contents

Table of Contents

XML Design
Handbook
Introduction

Introduction

XML is rapidly becoming the mechanism of choice for application designers who need to share data, store data, transmit data over a network, or do just about anything else that you can do with data. The platform- and language-agnostic nature of XML makes it a natural choice for developers building cross-platform applications, and its readability and ease of use, along with the availability of several standard parsing libraries, makes it an attractive option even when platform-independence isn't a necessity.

The ubiquity of XML, and the rate at which it achieved that ubiquity, is pretty stunning. From fairly humble beginnings in the late 1990s, XML's popularity has skyrocketed to the point where major commercial software packages such as Microsoft's SQL Server and Oracle's database now support XML at their cores. Microsoft's successor to the Windows XP operating system will be almost a complete rewrite, at least in part due to Microsoft wanting to have XML at the core of the operating system as well. It's not often that we see a technology become so widely and rapidly adopted across so many platforms and applications.

Along with XML's growth came a whole host of books aimed at getting the developers of the world up to speed on all of the various facets of XML, including the core language itself, XSLT, XPath, the major parsing APIs (DOM and SAX), and nearly every other nook and cranny of the XML space that you can think of. The majority of these books take a mechanical approach to the subject; that is, they describe the "whats" and "hows" of XML, such as "what is an element," "what defines a well-formed document," and "how can I parse a document using SAX." This content is, of course, very valuable for laying the groundwork of working with XML, but is often insufficient when you sit down to design your application. This is akin to reading the Java Language Specification and then trying to build a commercial-quality Java application.

> **Simply knowing the syntax and features of the language isn't enough; you need to understand how to use the language and its features effectively in order to design and build efficient applications.**

This is where our book comes in – we assume that you're already somewhat familiar with the mechanics of XML and so we focus on how to build a well-designed XML-enabled application. Throughout the book we'll take an in-depth look at all of the critical pieces of the XML space that require careful design in order to build efficient, robust, and extensible applications. Instead of focusing on the "whats" and "hows," we'll spend most of our time on the "whys," such as "why would I want to use DOM instead of SAX in this case" or "why would I want to use an attribute instead of an element in this other case."

The goal of this book is to get developers and architects thinking about the ramifications of their XML design approach, in the same way that they do about their database design or Java class structure. It is packed with best practice tips and techniques on all aspects of XML-related design, and should prove an indispensable desktop reference.

What's Covered in this Book?

This book analyzes each of the critical pieces of the XML space that requires careful design in order to build efficient, robust, and extensible applications. Each of these subjects has a chapter devoted to it.

In Chapter 1, *XML Architecture Strategies*, we analyze various different types of systems; for example those for analyzing data, transforming data, managing data, and so on. In each case we discuss the potential use of XML in these systems, based on dataflow patterns and data usage. The chapter covers best practice techniques for tackling such issues as:

❏   Organizing data analysis functional units into Web Services components

❏   Controlling text-to-text transformations

❏   Maintaining personalization information

❏   Coding secure, reliable transactions

In Chapter 2, *Basic Document Design*, we discuss some of the more generic issues that apply across all uses of XML, such as:

❏   Narrative and data-oriented document structures: when to use what?

❏   Building blocks: elements, attributes and character data

❏   General data modeling pitfalls

In Chapter 3, *XML Schemas*, we take a look at how to design robust, flexible schemas for document validation, covering:

❑ Basic ground rules for XML Schemas and when they are advantageous over DTDs

❑ Schema re-use mechanisms

❑ Best practice advice for effective use of namespaces with your schemas

❑ Some models for schema design: benefits and flaws

In Chapter 4, *Parsing Strategies*, we dissect the major parsing APIs (SAX, DOM, and pull parsers).

❑ SAX, DOM, and pull parsers: when to prefer which?

❑ Implementation patterns for DOM and SAX

In Chapter 5, *XSLT*, we cover several best practices for XSLT design.

❑ Using the XSLT processing model: push and pull, templates, recursions, and Namespaces

❑ Speeding up the stylesheet

❑ Increasing modularity and reusability

In Chapter 6, *XML Storage and Archiving*, we discuss designing systems where XML is used for long-term archival or as a storage medium. This chapter covers:

❑ Pros and cons of Native XML, relational and hybrid repositories

❑ Critical storage system design issues

❑ Problems with XML decomposition and the advantages of hybrid XML-relational modeling

❑ Assessment of various archiving strategies

In Chapter 7, *Presentation Strategies*, we cover the major design issues involved with using XML as a presentation mechanism.

❑ Configurability

❑ Performance

❑ Using rich media

❑ Cross-platform support

❑ Working with third-party or legacy data and software

❑ Maintainability and extensibility

In Appendix A, *Parser Performance*, we examine the comparative performance, in terms of speed and memory usage, of the Apache Crimson and Xerces parsers as well as GNU's Ælfred2.

The book is designed so that you don't have to read it cover-to-cover in order to use it; we've taken great care to not only cleanly separate the content chapter-by-chapter, but also section-by-section wherever possible. This means that if you're looking for an answer to a particular question, you can narrow your reading to the specific section or sections that cover that particular material.

Who is this Book For?

This book is for developers and architects who want to learn techniques for building efficient, robust XML-enabled applications, and also what pitfalls to avoid that can turn an application into an XML-enabled disaster. In order to focus on the crucial design issues, we assume that you have at least a basic understanding of the syntax and features of base XML and related technologies such as XSLT, XML Schema, as well as DOM and SAX parsers.

Code Conventions

We have used several different typographical conventions throughout the book to differentiate between different types of information. Here are some examples of these style conventions that you'll encounter, along with descriptions of their meaning:

Advice, hints, and background information comes in this type of font.

Asides and short anecdotes appear in boxes like this. It may also contain the gist or summaries for sections.

Important words are in a bold font.

When we're referencing code in a normal text context, such as if we were to discuss the `DocumentBuilderFactory` class, it appears in a fixed-width font. When we're discussing excerpts from actual programs, the code is in a gray box:

```
public void foo()
{
    // Do something
}
```

These formats are used consistently throughout the book so that you can quickly identify the type of information that's being presented.

Tell Us What You Think

We've worked hard on this book to try to present you with a lot of valuable and useful information. However, this work would all be for naught if it weren't for readers like you who buy the book and use it. We'd love to hear your thoughts on the book – what did you like, what didn't you like, and what could we have done better? Your feedback will shape both future revisions of this book as well as future works, so please take the time to drop us a line and tell us what you think! You can reach us by email at:

feedback@wrox.com

There is a plethora of information about this book, the authors, other books by Wrox Press and many other topics available on our web site. Please point your browser to the following address to keep up with all of the great information available about this and other titles from Wrox Press:

http://www.wrox.com

For information on our Professional to Professional (P2P) series of books, including mailing lists, discussion forums, articles, and subscriptions, please point your browsers to:

http://p2p.wrox.com

Downloading the Sample Code

The sample code for this book can be found by going to the Wrox web site (http://www.wrox.com) and entering the name of the book in the search box and navigating to the homepage for the book.

Errata

We've tried very hard to ensure the accuracy and correctness of all of the material presented in the book, but unfortunately, mistakes do occur and sometimes manage to creep into the final revision of the book. We want to make sure that we're giving you the best product possible, so if you do find a mistake, please let us know by sending an email to support@wrox.com to tell us about the problem. Please include the title of the book, ISBN number, and the page the error occurs on, as well as the nature of the mistake, and we'll do our best to respond as quickly as possible.

XML Design

Handbook

1

Architecture Strategies

There are many different ways of categorizing architectures so as to explore how XML can be used to enhance the design. XML is a format for data representation, whether the data being represented is informational or instructional; this chapter focuses on how various architectures are influenced by choices involving XML based on how the system interacts with data. For example, a reporting system will analyze data, a media player will experience data, a speech recognition program will transform data, a contact management application will maintain contacts, a CAD/CAM system will control machinery using the data, and a financial system will perform transactions on data.

Software architectures can be categorized based on many different aspects. Here, we focus in particular on dataflow aspects of the system and how XML can be used when making architectural decisions. The chapter is organized along these lines, because the nature of XML will affect the architecture through methods for representing, storing, and interacting with data. While other chapters will focus on data representation and storage issues, here we will explore the following types of systems based on dataflow patterns and data usage:

- ❑ **Systems for analyzing and transforming data** – where new data is derived from processing over existing data, such as business intelligence, predictive systems, data mining and reporting tools, or where the data is converted into a different form or format, such as speech to text, Word to DocBook, or a photograph to a digital image.

- ❑ **Systems for managing data** – where data is created, modified, used, and managed according to the requirements of the application, such as for word-processing, an e-mail client, or a content management system. Transaction-based systems, such as financial and supply-chain applications, fall in this category.

❏ **Systems for experiencing and controlling with data** – where the data represents sensory information, such as video, audio, or slideshow presentations. Systems used for controlling devices, or for driving other processes, include consumer electronics, satellite telecommunications equipment, or environmental controls.

Complex systems may have aspects of most or all of the types of data interaction. Each type of system will include one or more guidelines for using XML-based technologies, as well as an example scenario of the concept put into practice.

1.1 Example Sce nario

To explore the factors that influence XML architectural strategies, we'll use a common example throughout this chapter.

The sample application is a web-based **Common Resources Exchange (CRE)** that is accessible via the Internet, and whose goal is to match those with a surplus of some item or commodity with those who have a need. Further, the system also works with shipping services, airlines, and trucking companies to coordinate the transfer of items from their source to their destination.

This system touches on many points that are relevant to the various data requirements and workflows:

❏ **Analysis and Transformations** – CRE includes features for creating and managing agents that are given a description of a need or something being offered. As matches are found, they are reported back to the agent owner. Agents can also be instructed to automate the acquisition of a resource and coordinate its delivery.

Also, since this is a multinational system, the system must provide transformations to local conventions for currency, weights and measures, date format, and social courtesies.

❏ **Data Management** – This CRE application is essentially about managing data to keep track of who has what, who needs what, who's going to get what, and how it's going to get there.

❏ **Experiences and Control Systems** – Interacting with CRE may be done through a phone by giving vocal commands, from a web page where a richer experience can occur, or through a wireless handheld device where a less rich experience is desired.

CRE coordinates the transporting of the items by interacting in an automated way with the various scheduling systems of each particular transporter. If 100 tons of grain were offered as a surplus, and a need for 50 tons of grain required by an emergency relief agency had to be met, the system could communicate by synthesized voice via telephone, by e-mail, by direct satellite communication, or through a Web Service to communicate and coordinate with transportation companies. As soon as a viable route was confirmed, all other modes of communication would stop their requests.

1.2 Systems for Analyzing and Transforming Data

Systems for analyzing data are those that create new data or meta data through the processing of existing data. The purpose of data analysis is to draw a conclusion or come to a better understanding about the nature of the data being processed, such as automated feature detection of lines and curves from an image in a computer vision application, or a **Return on Investment (ROI)** forecast from a financial application given a set of economic assumptions. Analytical results may be used as input to other systems, or may take their final form as a report.

What's important for systems that perform data analysis is that the functional pieces be organized into components that have a well-planned API so that they may be combined to create more complex algorithms. Component-based or object-oriented design has many well-researched and documented advantages over linear or procedural design approaches, the main one being that it manages complexity well. In analytical systems more than other types of systems, complexity can quickly get out of control, causing inaccurate results, and a design that is hard to extend or modify.

Another important aspect of systems that perform analysis is their ability to produce results that can be used by other systems, both analytical and otherwise. This means that a common format for expressing the data must be worked out prior to any type of data transfer, which is where XML adds tremendous value.

The following diagram shows how one component is fed data, where it may first pass through some sort of data validation process, and how the results are produced after processing:

Figure 1

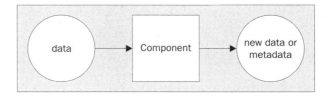

If the input and output data is organized such that the format of the input and output modules agree, then the components can be combined as building blocks to implement more complex algorithms. For example, in our CRE application, a component called SearchCommodities could take in, as arguments, the following criteria that expressed a need for "10 tons grain or 8 tons rice" and "500 liters milk and 500 liters fresh water", and would return the set of suppliers that could meet this need. Consider the following graphic representation:

Figure 2

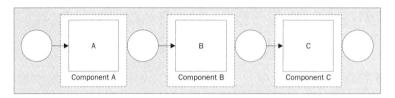

This approach means that the same components can be recombined to implement new algorithms. The output of SearchCommodities (Component A shown above), which is the set of suppliers, could be input to another component called SearchTransportRoutes (Component B), which would output the various ways that the needed items could be delivered. Furthermore, the API carries forward to all components built from other components, as shown below:

Figure 3

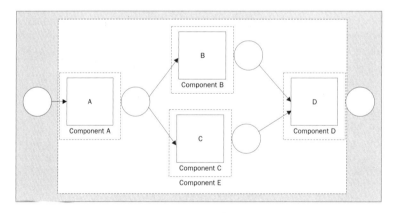

In our example, the request for ten tons of grain would be fed into Component B (a SearchCommodities component), and eight tons of rice into Component C (also SearchCommodities). Component D could have an API that accepts results of both commodities' searches, and resolves based on the transport channels which is the best approach.

Other examples of analytical systems are offline reporting tools, real-time system monitors, interactive (OLAP) tools for data mining and pattern discovering, scientific applications, predictive systems, and business intelligence systems.

1.2.1 Use an XML-based API to Provide a Common and Flexible Data Representation Among Software Components

The same way that object-oriented components can shroud complexity, XML as the mechanism for representing the API can simplify the maintenance of complex sets of input arguments and output results. If the component evolves, often only the XML Schema will need expansion, as opposed to changing function arguments. For example, our SearchCommodities component might initially require an actual item to be matched (like grain, loaves of bread, or baby clothes), whereas in a newer version, the component could also return all surplus offerings based on providing a search radius.

In our example, SearchCommodities accepts the following `cre1.xml` document as input, where an organization in Miami, Florida, is searching for ten tons of grain:

```
<CRE_ITEM>
   <need user_id="345123" deadline="2003/03/01"
        destination="Miami, Florida, USA">
     <need_detail>
       <quantity unit="tons" amount="10"/>
       <description>grain</description>
     </need_detail>
   </need>
</CRE_ITEM>
```

SearchCommodities takes the input requirements and searches its data store of currently listed surplus offerings and produces the following XML document as output. This result, `cre2.xml`, shows that there are currently two sources able to fill the need for ten tons of grain:

```
<CRE_ITEM>
   <need user_id="345123" deadline="2003/03/01"
        destination="Miami, Florida, USA">
     <need_detail>
       <quantity units="tons" amount="10"/>
       <description>grain</description>
     </need_detail>
   </need>
   <offering user_id="10020" source="New York City, NY, USA">
     <offering_detail>
       <quantity units="tons" quantity="7"/>
       <description>grain</description>
```

```
      </offering_detail>
    </offering>
    <offering user_id="34354" source="Ontario, Canada">
      <offering_detail>
          <quantity units="kilograms" quantity="12000"/>
      </offering_detail>
    </offering>
  </CRE_ITEM>
```

Next, SearchTransportRoutes takes the above XML document and searches various transportation companies for routes to produce the following output XML document, cre3.xml. The system must then determine, for each route, whether the capacity is sufficient for transporting the item; otherwise, the route is eliminated from contention. The following result shows that only the Ontario source has an available transportation route with enough capacity to connect the surplus to the need by the required deadline:

```
<CRE_ITEM>
  <need user_id="345123" deadline="2003/03/01"
        destination="Miami, Florida, USA">
    <need_detail>
      <quantity units="tons" amount="10"/>
      <description>grain</description>
    </need_detail>
  </need>
  <offering user_id="34354" source="Ontario, Canada">
    <offering_detail>
      <quantity units="kilograms" amount="12000"/>
      <description>grain</description>
    </offering_detail>
  </offering>
  <route user_id="987500" route_code="ar_20030214">
    <route_detail
        departs="Ontario 2003/02/13 6:15AM CST"
        arrives="Miami 2003/02/15 6pm EST">
      <capacity unit="kilograms" amount="20000"/>
      <description>
          Allied Railway
      </description>
    </route_detail>
  </route>
</CRE_ITEM>
```

Two components used in this example (shown in next section), SearchCommodities and SearchTransportRoutes, accept an XML document based on the same schema, and each uses only the information that it needs to perform its analytical task. This provides a flexible approach to component design. The XML document contains the current state of a CRE match – from need expressed, to sources located, to transportation routes found. As more components interact with this information, the data that's needed is contained within the XML document.

The disadvantage to this approach is that every component will be parsing the same XML document repeatedly. Also, care must be taken so that the XML Schema is not overly complex itself, as it may therefore negate any gains in simplicity that it would otherwise offer.

Users can interact with CRE in a number of possible ways, which will be explored in the *Section 1.4: Systems for Experiencing and Controlling with Data*, but here we present a web page-based user interface, as shown below:

This interface is based on CREsetup.html:

```html
<html>
 <body>
  <h1>Enter your CRE Request:</h1>
   <form action="servlets/ProcessNeedCREservlet" mode="get">
    <table>
     <tr><td>Deadline:</td>
       <td><input type="text" size="15" name="deadline"/></td></tr>
     <tr><td>User ID:</td>
       <td><input type="text" size="15" name="user_id"/></td></tr >
     <tr><td>Destination:</td>
       <td><input type="text" size="30" name="destination"/></td></tr>
     <tr><td>Amount:</td>
       <td><input type="text" size="15" name="amount"/></td></tr>
     <tr><td>Units:</td>
       <td><input type="text" size="15" name="units"/></td></tr>
     <tr><td>Description:</td>
       <td><input type="text" size="30" name="description"/></td></tr>
     <tr><td colspan="2" align="center">
       <input type="submit" value="Submit Request"/></td></tr>
    </table>
   </form>
 </body>
</html>
```

13

The architecture upon which CRE is based could take a number of forms, including
ASP/.NET, JSP, Java Servlets, or web-enabled scripting languages such as ColdFusion,
Perl, and Python. In the following example, we use Servlets to demonstrate the XML-
based API to components written as Java classes in `ProcessNeedCREservlet.java`:

```java
import java.io.*;
import javax.servlet.*;
import javax.servlet.http.*;
import javax.xml.transform.*;
import javax.xml.transform.stream.*;
import javax.xml.transform.dom.*;
import org.w3c.dom.Document;
import org.w3c.dom.DOMException;
import org.w3c.dom.Element;
       // encapsulates searching through surpluses
import org.commonresourceexchange.cre.SearchCommodities;
       // encapsulates searching transport routes
import org.commonresourceexchange.cre.SearchTransportRoutes;

public class ProcessNeedCREservlet extends HttpServlet {

   public void doGet( HttpServletRequest req, HttpServletResponse res )
           throws IOException, ServletException {

       // Variables to hold input parameterss
       String paramDeadline    = req.getParameter("deadline");
       String paramUserId      = req.getParameter("user_id");
       String paramDestination = req.getParameter("destination");
       String paramAmount      = req.getParameter("amount");
       String paramUnits       = req.getParameter("units");
       String paramDescription = req.getParameter("description");

       SearchCommodoties searchCommodities = new SearchCommodities();
       SearchTransportRoutes searchTransportRoutes =
           new SearchTransportRoutes();
       File xslStyle = "CREResults.xsl";

       // creItemDoc is initialized from the form parameters
       DocumentBuilderFactory factory =
DocumentBuilderFactory.newInstance();
       DocumentBuilder builder = factory.newDocumentBuilder();
       Document creItemDoc = builder.newDocument();

       Element root = (Element) document.createElement("CRE_ITEM");
       document.appendChild (root);

       Element need = (Element) document.createElement("need");
       root.appendChild(need);
       need.setAttribute("user_id", paramUserId);
       need.setAttribute("deadline", paramDeadline);
       need.setAttribute("destination", paramDestination);

       Element need_detail = (Element)
document.createElement("need_detail");
       need.appendChild(need_detail);
```

```
        Element quantity = (Element) document.createElement("quantity");
        need_detail.appendChild(quantity);
        quantity.setAttribute("units", paramUnits);
        quantity.setAttribute("amount", paramAmount);

        Element description = (Element)
document.createElement("description");
        need_detail.appendChild(description);

description.appendChild(document.createTextNode(paramDescription));

        // First search out for sources
        creItemDoc = searchCommodities.ProcessCRE(creItemDoc);
        // Second, seearch out a transporation route
        creItemDoc = searchTransportationRoutes.ProcessCRE(creItemDoc);

        // report results of commodities and transport route searches,
        // using an XSLT stylesheet
        TransformerFactory factory = TransformerFactory.newInstance();
        Transformer t = factory.newTransformer(new
StreamSource(xslStyle));
        t.transform(new DomSource(paramCreXml),
                    new StreamResult(res.getOutputStream()));
    }
}
```

The servlet would return the following result to the browser:

NEEDED by 2003/03/01		OFFERED:		ROUTE:	
User Id:	345123	User Id:	34354	User Id:	987500
Destination:	Miami, Florida, USA	Source:	Ontario, Canada	Route Code:	ar_20030214
Quantity Amount:	10	Quantity Amount:	12000	Departs:	Ontario 2003/02/13 6:15AM CST
Quantity Units:	tons	Quantity Units:	kilograms	Arrives:	Miami 2003/02/15 6pm EST
Description:	grain	Description:	grain	Description:	Allied Railway

1.2.2 Use XSLT for Transforming XML Markup

Transformation processes are those that take data in an XML format and create a new version where the data is represented in a different text-based format. Designing components to use a standards-based markup convention is important in order to allow processes and the resulting data to interact with third-party systems.

In the example shown in the previous section, the XML CRE results were transformed via an XSL transform engine by using the following predefined XSLT stylesheet:

```
        File xslStyle = "CREResults.xsl";
        TransformerFactory factory = TransformerFactory.newInstance();
        Transformer t = factory.newTransformer(new StreamSource(xslStyle));
        t.transform(new DomSource(paramCreXml),
                    new StreamResult(res.getOutputStream()));
```

Before returning the search results, the XML data is first transformed via the CREResults.xsl XSLT stylesheet, shown here:

```
<?xml version="1.0"?>
<xsl:stylesheet version="1.0"
xmlns:xsl="http://www.w3.org/1999/XSL/Transform">
  <xsl:output method="html"/>

<xsl:template match="/CRE_ITEM">
  <table valign="top" cellpadding="5">
    <tr>
      <td valign="top"><xsl:apply-templates select="need"/></td>
      <td valign="top"><xsl:apply-templates select="offering"/></td>
      <td valign="top"><xsl:apply-templates select="route"/></td>
    </tr>
  </table>
</xsl:template>

<xsl:template match="need">
  <table>
    <tr><td colspan="3">NEEDED by <xsl:value-of select="@deadline"/>
    </td></tr>
    <tr><td colspan="3"><hr/></td></tr>
    <tr><td>User Id:</td><td><xsl:value-of select="@user_id"/>
    </td></tr>
    <tr><td>Destination:</td><td><xsl:value-of select="@destination"/>
    </td></tr>
    <xsl:apply-templates/>
  </table>
</xsl:template>

<xsl:template match="need_detail">
  <xsl:apply-templates/>
</xsl:template>

<xsl:template match="offering">
  <table>
    <tr><td colspan="2">OFFERED:</td></tr>
    <tr><td colspan="2"><hr/></td></tr>
    <tr><td>User Id:</td><td><xsl:value-of select="@user_id"/>
    </td></tr>
    <tr><td>Source:</td><td><xsl:value-of select="@source"/></td></tr>
    <xsl:apply-templates/>
  </table>
</xsl:template>

<xsl:template match="offering_detail">
  <xsl:apply-templates/>
</xsl:template>

<xsl:template match="route">
  <table>
    <tr><td colspan="2">ROUTE:</td></tr>
    <tr><td colspan="2"><hr/></td></tr>
    <tr><td>User Id:</td><td><xsl:value-of select="@user_id"/>
    </td></tr>
    <tr><td>Route Code:</td><td><xsl:value-of select="@route_code"/>
```

```
    </td></tr>
    <xsl:apply-templates/>
  </table>
</xsl:template>

<xsl:template match="route_detail">
    <tr><td>Departs:</td><td><xsl:value-of select="@departs"/>
    </td></tr>
    <tr><td>Arrives:</td><td><xsl:value-of
select="@arrives"/></td></tr>
  <xsl:apply-templates/>
</xsl:template>

<xsl:template match="quantity">
  <tr><td>Quantity Amount:</td><td><xsl:value-of select="@amount"/>
  </td></tr>
  <tr><td>Quantity Units:</td><td><xsl:value-of select="@units"/>
  </td></tr>
</xsl:template>

<xsl:template match="description">
  <tr><td>Description:</td><td><xsl:value-of select="text()"/>
  </td></tr>
</xsl:template>

<xsl:template match="sourceRadius">
  <tr><td>Search Radius Amount:</td>
  <td><xsl:value-of select="@amount"/></td></tr>
  <tr><td>Search Radius Units:</td><td><xsl:value-of select="@units"/>
  </td></tr>
</xsl:template>

</xsl:stylesheet>
```

1.2.3 Use an XML-based API to Extend and Reuse Existing Components

XML, along with a component-based architecture, means that extending components and recombining components is easily accomplished, since the XML document that serves as the API remains the same.

For example, suppose a new group within the CRE organization wanted to provide an expanded service, where organizations could search surpluses based on a search region, and then actively seek out a need that could be filled. If the SearchCommodities component accepted an XML document that described the search radius without any specifics about what item it was looking for, the input XML document would look like the cre4.xml sample below. This example gives instructions to search all surplus offerings within a 25-kilometer radius of London:

```
<CRE_ITEM>
  <need user_id="435432"
      destination="London, England, UK" deadline="now">
```

```
      <need_detail>
        <sourceRadius units="kilometers" amount="25"/>
      </need_detail>
    </need>
  </CRE_ITEM>
```

A user interface (like the CRE setup screen) that included a field for search radius could be used. The same servlet could also be used as it is simply providing access to the SearchCommoditites component. The result would be the following cre5.xml file:

```
<CRE_ITEM>
  <need user_id="435432" destination="London, England, UK"
      deadline="now">
    <need_detail>
      <sourceRadius units="kilometers" amount="25"/>
    </need_detail>
  </need>
  <offering user_id="8898" source="London, England, UK">
    <offering_detail>
      <quantity unit="loaves" amount="45"/>
      <description>day-old bread</description>
    </offering_detail>
  </offering>
  <offering user_id="34354" source="Saint Albans, England, UK">
    <offering_detail>
      <quantity unit="pairs" amount="100"/>
      <description>irregular trousers</description>
    </offering_detail>
  </offering>
</CRE_ITEM>
```

This shows that 45 loaves of day-old bread and 100 pairs of irregular trousers are currently available as a surplus in the region, as shown in the following figure. Based on this information, a supplier might react to a known need for clothing in homeless shelters in nearby towns:

NEEDED by now		OFFERED:	
User Id:	435432	User Id:	8898
Destination:	London, England, UK	Source:	London, England, UK
Search Radius Amount:	25	Quantity Amount:	45
Search Radius Units:	kilometers	Quantity Units:	loaves
		Description:	day-old bread
		OFFERED:	
		User Id:	34354
		Source:	Saint Albans, England, UK
		Quantity Amount:	100
		Quantity Units:	pairs
		Description:	irregular trousers

This new application is based on reusing existing components, and thus benefits from a greatly reduced development schedule, both because of the object-oriented design, as well as because of its use of XML for the API.

1.2.4 Use an XML-based Network Protocol to Maximize Component Reusability and Availability

XML-based network protocols have been evolving steadily over the years. Standardized APIs have focused on easing complexities with remote execution over networks with XML-RPC (remote procedure call), **Simple Object Access Protocol (SOAP)** and most recently Web Services. These mechanisms mean that components can have access via networks that will enable developers to focus on the creative parts of software development rather than on arcane issues involving network transfer protocols.

The following example builds upon the example from the previous section. Rather than access our SerachCommodities and SearchTransportRoutes by using Java Servlets, we will now provide a SOAP interface. The following code from SearchCommodities shows a SOAP request that passes in the same XML argument embedded in a SOAP envelope:

```
POST /SearchCommoditities HTTP/1.1
Host: www.commonresourceexchange.org
Content-Type: application/soap+xml; charset=utf-8
Content-Length: 524
<?xml version="1.0"?>
<soap:Envelope
   xmlns:soap="http://www.w3.org/2001/12/soap-envelope"
   soap:encodingStyle="http://www.w3.org/2001/12/soap-encoding">
   <soap:Body
    xmlns:cre="http://www.commonresourceexchange.org/cre">
      <cre:ProcessCRE>
        <cre:CRE_ITEM>
          <cre:need user_id="435432"
                     destination="London, England, UK" deadline="now">
            <cre:need_detail>
              <cre:sourceRadius units="kilometers" amount="25"/>
            </cre:need_detail>
          </cre:need>
        </cre:CRE_ITEM>
      </cre:ProcessCRE>
   </soap:Body>
</soap:Envelope>
```

The SOAP server at www.commonresourceexchange.org would process the call to "ProcessCRE" with the given input arguments, taken from the example in the previous section, where a CRE namespace has been introduced to avoid naming collisions with other XML tags. The SOAP server would return the following SearchCommoditiesResponse.xml SOAP response message:

```
HTTP/1.1 200 OK
Content-Type: application/soap; charset=utf-8
Content-Length: 1003
<?xml version="1.0"?>
```

19

```
<soap:Envelope
  xmlns:soap="http://www.w3.org/2001/12/soap-envelope"
  soap:encodingStyle="http://www.w3.org/2001/12/soap-encoding">
  <soap:Body
      xmlns:cre="http://www.commonresourceexchange.org/cre">
      <cre:ProcessCREResponse>
      <cre:CRE_ITEM>
      <cre:need user_id="435432"
        destination="London, England, UK" deadline="now">
        <cre:need_detail>
           <cre:sourceRadius units="kilometers" amount="25"/>
        </cre:need_detail>
      </cre:need>
      <cre:offering user_id="8898" source="London, England, UK">
      <cre:offering_detail>
        <cre:quantity unit="loaves" amount="45"/>
        <cre:description>day-old bread</cre:description>
      </cre:offering_detail>
      </cre:offering>
        <cre:offering user_id="34354"
           source="Saint Albans, England, UK">
        <cre:offering_detail>
        <cre:quantity unit="pairs" amount="100"/>
        <cre:description>irregular trousers</cre:description>
      </cre:offering_detail>
    </cre:offering>
  </cre:CRE_ITEM>
      </cre:ProcessCREResponse>
  </soap:Body>
</soap:Envelope>
```

1.3 Systems for Managing Data

Systems for managing data are those that create, modify, combine, delete, and relocate data, among other types of data interactions. Some examples include word processors, integrated development environments, file managers, e-mail and web servers, content managers, contact managers, and graphics programs.

The following diagram shows how data passes through many different processes in a workflow that is directed by the user. As data passes through the various processes, it may undergo modifications, creation, or deletion. For example, in a contact manager, the processes might represent creating a new contact, importing a contact, editing the information about a contact, printing the contacts in a group, and exporting a contact:

Figure 4

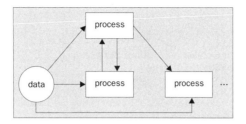

Systems that manage data usually function as tools or **Integrated Development Environments (IDEs)** for a large and diverse audience. These systems could better serve these audiences with a flexible workflow framework to accommodate the individual preferences or assigned user roles associated. A workflow framework could be devised in an XML representation. This type of approach requires an associated interpreter that would direct control from screen to screen.

1.3.1 Use XML to Represent Meta Data About the Items Being Managed

Meta data holds information about the object that may be especially specific, such as the distance between source and destination locations in a CRE_ITEM, or may describe an essential characteristic, such as the expiration date on a baked item. Since XML is self-describing, it is an ideal representation for meta data, as it has the capacity to take on any text-based description. This unfortunately can lead to a meta data strategy with no labeling consistently.

In our example just mentioned, the meta data in the first case reflects a distance in miles, and in the second case, a date. It's possible that in the next surplus search, items might include school furniture, with meta data of seat height.

The following meta1.xml XML is taken from a previous example where a number of surplus offerings were returned from a regional search. The problem is that there is too little information to make an informed decision in this information:

```
<offering user_id="8898" source="London, England, UK">
    <offering_detail>
        <quantity unit="loaves" amount="45"/>
        <description>day-old bread</description>
    </offering_detail>
</offering>
<offering user_id="34354" source="Saint Albans, England, UK">
    <offering_detail>
        <quantity unit="pairs" amount="100"/>
        <description>irregular trousers</description>
    </offering_detail>
</offering>
```

In the `meta2.xml` example that follows, meta data is added to provide a richer description:

```
<offering user_id="8898" source="London, England, UK">
    <offering_detail>
      <quantity unit="loaves" amount="45"/>
      <description>day-old bread
        <metadata name="baked on" value="2003/01/01"/>
        <metadata name="type"     value="whole wheat"/>
        <metadata name="servings" value="20 slices"/>
      </description>
    </offering_detail>
  </offering>
  <offering user_id="34354"
        source="Saint Albans, England, UK">
    <offering_detail>
      <quantity unit="pairs" amount="100"/>
      <description>irregular trousers
        <metadata name="gender" value="men's"/>
        <metadata name="waist"  value="34 inch waist"/>
        <metadata name="length" value="unfinished"/>
        <metadata name="color"  value="taupe rust plaid"/>
      </description>
    </offering_detail>
  </offering>
```

This additional information, as shown in the meta data tags, will give people seeking surpluses valuable information to make more informed decisions.

1.4 Systems for Experiencing and Controlling with Data

Systems for experiencing data are those that use the data to produce an effect that is experienced by the user, such as a media player, browser, game, or interactive learning environment. Unlike analytical and transformational systems, new data is not created in these types of systems. Although, like systems that control with data, this is some sort of effect that is based on the data that occurs, the fundamental purpose of the data for experiencing is different, and therefore the architectures will differ as well.

What's important for systems where the data is experienced by the user is that rich experiences can be created, the users can influence the experience by specifying preferences, the users can have some level of interaction with the rendering device, and that the system will be responsive to the bandwidth and other practical issues when dealing with the large sizes typical of media files. Systems must also take into account the need to support multiple modalities of the experience. For example, a video should be able to deliver just the audio if the user is accessing the media via an audio-only device, or an online game should be able to produce output that works for low-bandwidth as well as high-bandwidth networks.

Another aspect that has become an important topic is the issue of **Digital Rights Management (DRM)**, where certain media must be protected in order to rightfully compensate the owners – such as works by film creators, recording artists, and online book publishers.

The following diagram shows some of the important aspects of how data flows in this type of system. The data to be experienced may first pass through a system that verifies the digital rights accessibility. The data is rendered using user preferences, if any. Finally, there's usually some level of interaction between the user and the rendering device.

Figure 5

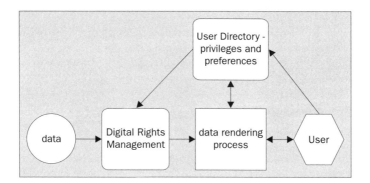

Key design factors are what type of medium and what type of rendering device will be used, and how it relates to the source repository or content management system, as well as how the approach integrates with the rich media authoring system, if such a system is used.

Control systems (systems for controlling devices and other systems with data) are systems that create some sort of measurable affect, such as a city-wide automated traffic system, where the traffic lights are the devices under control based on the measured effect of traffic waiting at red lights. Control systems are similar to systems for experiencing data; the two dataflow diagrams bear resemblance; there is an identifiable outcome from the data passing through control processes, but rather than affect the senses of a person via an experience, the effect is on equipment or third-party systems.

What's important for control systems is that they must be able to efficiently sense and react to conditions in a secure and reliable way. The following diagram shows how data flows through control systems in a feedback loop:

Figure 6

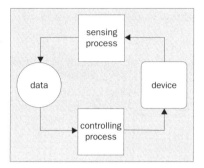

Here, the data sensed from a device can feed into processes that control the same (or some other) device. For instance, in a traffic control system, cars are sensed from devices embedded in the road, and the device affected is the traffic light.

1.4.1 Use XML and XSLT to Support Experiences for Multiple Modalities

XSLT provides a powerful way of creating a rich media experience in multiple modalities. For example, CRE could offer a number of entry points into the system, including calling via phone, using a browser to go to a web page, or using a handheld wireless device. In *Section 1.2.2: Use XSLT for Transforming XML Markup*, we show how to provide a web-based UI.

To achieve a flexible system where users can experience rich media in a modality that is appropriate or desired, we need to separate the content from the way in which it has been presented in the past. The modal1.xml example that follows describes the items that were found, and a set of possible ways to sense or experience the data. It includes an audio, a video, marked-up text, and a plain text version:

```
<offering user_id="8898" source="London, England, UK">
    <offering_detail>
       <quantity unit="loaves" amount="45"/>
       <description>day-old bread
          <metadata name="baked on" value="2003/01/01"/>
          <metadata name="type"     value="whole wheat"/>
          <metadata name="servings" value="20 slices"/>
          <media mimetype="audio/r-pm-ra"
             source="http://www.crebread.com/audio/item1001.ra"/>
          <media mimetype="video/r-pm-ra"
             source="http://www.crebread.com/video/item1001.rv"/>
          <media mimetype="text/html"
             source="http://www.crebread.com/text/item1001.html"/>
          <media mimetype="text/plain"
             source="http://www.crebread.com/text/item1001.txt"/>
       </description>
    </offering_detail>
 </offering>
```

The data in the media tags can be used to feed an audio device, a video device, an HTML render, or can be used as plain text. The following ProcessRenderCREservlet.java servlet feeds the XSLT engine with the necessary data, and returns with a rendered result:

```
import jaova.io.*;
import javax.servlet.*;
import javax.servlet.http.*;
        // encapsulates searching through surpluses
import org.commonresourceexchange.cre.RenderExperience;

public class ProcessRenderCREservlet extends HttpServlet {

   public void doGet( HttpServletRequest req, HttpServletResponse res )
        throws IOException, ServletException {

        // Variables to hold input parameterss
        String paramMimetype = req.getParameter("mimetype");
        String paramCreXml   = req.getParameter("cre_item_doc");

        RenderExperience renderExperience = new RenderExperience();

        // get the xslt stylesheet filename from the component
        File xslStyle = RenderExperience.lookupStylesheet(
    paramMimetype, paramCreXml);

        // report results of commodities and transport route searches,
        // using an XSLT stylesheet
        TransformerFactory factory = TransformerFactory.newInstance();
        Transformer t = factory.newTransformer(new
    StreamSource(xslStyle));
        t.transform(new StreamSource(paramCreXml),
                new StreamResult(res.getOutputStream()));
   }
}
```

The function takes in mimetype and cre_item_doc form arguments as strings. Using the mimetype, the RenderExperience component performs a lookup into a data store of stylesheet (a table in a database, an XML document, etc.) organized by mimetype, so as to access the XSLT stylesheet. After the stylesheet has been identified and accessed, it is applied to the XML data. For our example, the result is the information about the leftover bread in a format that is desired to the user making the HTTP request.

1.4.2 Use XML Standards-based Languages According to the Industry of the Device or System being Controlled

XML standards are appearing in most industries, and have started to venture beyond the traditional IT areas like insurance, banking, and commerce, into such fields as auto repair and human genome identification.

In our scenario, once a transportation route was selected, an ebXML message could be created from the CRE Processing XML result that would communicate with the chosen transportation company via electronic messages, to reserve the space and book the item transport. Since this is an XML-to-XML transformation, an XSLT stylesheet applied to the XML result is a low-maintenance solution.

1.5 Summary

In this chapter, we saw that categorizing systems into how their data is represented and how data flows through the application helps to illustrate how XML can be applied as part of an architectural strategy. For systems that analyze or transform, where new data or meta data is created or extrapolated, then combing an XML API and an object-oriented design gives a system that is flexible to modifications and amenable to reuse in new algorithms.

When managing data, XML can help in the overall system structure by working within a workflow framework, and more commonly, as the representation for the data being managed (such as the contacts in a contact management system). In systems where data is used to define a user experience, such as audio, video, or PowerPoint presentations, XML as the basis for data representation, paired with XSLT for the presentation, give a flexible, maintainable, and robust foundation.

XML Design

Handbook

2

2

Basic Document Design

The subject of document design is certainly not one that can be covered in its entirety in just one chapter. As such, we will stress the fundamental principles of document design, and focus on just three specific areas:

- **Narrative and Data-oriented document structures.** These two document styles comprise the vast majority of XML documents. In this section, we discuss broadly the defining characteristics of each style and look at examples of when to use each one. The majority of the rest of the chapter will deal with data-oriented document structures, but you can find good information on building narrative document structures in other books such as *XML in a Nutshell* from *O'Reilly and Associates (ISBN: 0-596-00292-0)*.

- **Building Blocks: Attributes, elements, and character data.** While there are many other features of XML documents, few of them have the kind of impact on design, readability, and parsing performance as these three can and do have. In this section, we offer advice on the appropriate use of these basic building blocks, including performance implications.

- **General data modeling pitfalls.** Data modeling is a huge subject – one that could easily fill a book of its own. So, rather than trying to cover everything, we restrict our discussion to the common pitfalls that can have very serious side effects when it comes time to use your documents.

This chapter is meant to serve as a foundation for the material that will be covered in later chapters, which strive to help you design better documents for specific purposes, such as doing XSL transforms or using XML for long-term storage.

2.1 Narrative an d Data-oriented Document Structures

XML documents are normally used to model data in one of two ways. A **narrative document** structure uses the XML content to augment some existing text-based data, in a similar way to how HTML tags are used to augment the text in web pages. In a **data-oriented document** structure, the XML content is itself the important data. In this section, we'll examine these two styles and walk through some examples of when you would want to use each. This section discusses, explicitly and briefly, ideas that are largely "common sense" but that are central to the rest of the chapter.

2.1.1 Use Data-oriented Document Structures to Model Well-structured Data

As discussed earlier, a data-oriented document structure is one in which the XML content directly describes the data in the document; in other words, the XML markup *is* the interesting data in the document. A small example illustrates this point well:

```
<shape>
  <type>octagon</type>
  <numberOfSides>8</numberOfSides>
  <numberOfDimensions>2</numberOfDimensions>
</shape>
```

This document uses XML to describe some properties of a shape. Here, the textual content (alternatively called parsed character data, or just character data; we'll use these terms interchangeably) in the document (octagon, 8, and 2) is meaningless without the XML tags. This example could also be written as follows:

```
<shape>
  <type name="octagon"/>
  <numberOfSides count="8"/>
  <numberOfDimensions count="2"/>
</shape>
```

This document encodes the same data as the first one, but instead of using character data to describe the values, it uses attributes. In this case, there is no character data at all, and it's clear that the XML content is, itself, the data in the document; if you were to remove the XML content, the document would be empty aside from white space. Note that the document style above isn't one that we'd recommend for use in practice, as we'll see in detail a bit later in the section. It's only presented here for the sake of comparison.

To continue the process, we could take this example one step further by building our XML as follows:

```
<shape type="octagon" numberOfSides="8" numberOfDimensions="2"/>
```

This document encodes the same data as the first two, but this time the type, side count, and dimension count are all data attributes of the <shape> tag. In this case, it's obvious that the XML markup is the only useful data in this document. It would easily be possible to encode this same data in many other ways, but the point is clear.

All three of these documents are simple examples of data-oriented documents in that they use XML markup to describe some well-structured data. With the data represented in these particular documents, you can imagine that the data has a one-to-one mapping with the properties of an object in our application, effectively making the XML document a serialized version of our object.

When you are encoding objects whose basic job is to communicate with software (as opposed to communicating with people), you are probably going to want to use a data-oriented document structure. The hierarchical nature of XML allows it to easily represent complicated data structures that include members that are also complicated data structures. Any data that can be encoded as text (including binary, which can be encoded using a base-64 encoding scheme or something similar) can be represented in XML.

This kind of serialization is a very common use of XML. In fact, Microsoft's .NET Framework Common Library includes functionality that can be used to automatically serialize any class to XML, and deserialize an XML stream into an object, via the XmlSerializer class in the System.Xml.Serialization namespace. At the time of writing, there was no corresponding class in the standard Java libraries, but there is an API currently under development, the functionality of which will be very similar. This API is a part of the Java XML Pack and is called the **Java API for XML Binding (JAXB)**, and provides a way of mapping from Java classes to and from XML documents, as well as validating in-memory Java objects against a DTD or an XML Schema.

> *You can find out more information about JAXB from Sun's JavaSoft website at* http://java.sun.com/xml/jaxb/index.html. *We cover the .Net* XmlSerializer *class briefly at the end of Chapter 4.*

Obviously, data-oriented documents are not limited in usefulness to holding serialized data structures. For JavaBeans and other data structures, the mapping from member variables to XML content is usually very straightforward, but XML can be used to represent other kinds of data that don't map directly to a data structure. For instance, the Ant build system from Apache uses an XML file to describe a *process*, in this case the process of building a piece of software. (In fact, Ant can be used to do more than just build software, just like makefiles. You can find out more about Ant at the Apache website: http://jakarta.apache.org/ant/index.html.) A well-defined process can be thought of as well-structured data, so an encoding of a well-defined process can be done using a data-oriented document.

An Ant build file is functionally similar to a `makefile` in that it contains build targets that in turn contain the commands (Ant calls them "tasks") necessary to build something. In a manner similar to makefiles, targets can also have interdependencies. These targets and their dependencies together define the process of building a piece of software. Ant also uses the extensibility of XML to provide some interesting functionality that makefiles cannot directly support, such as allowing for writing custom tasks in Java, that can then be used in your build files just like any of the predefined tasks.

By now, it should be clear that data-oriented documents are the best choice for representing well-structured data of virtually any flavor. Let's move on and look at narrative documents, which are better suited for less structured data.

2.1.2 Use Narrative-style Document Structures to Augment Plain-text Data

The essential difference between narrative document structures and data-oriented document structures is that narrative document structures are designed to be consumed by people, whereas data-oriented document structures are generally designed to be consumed by applications. As opposed to data-oriented structures, narrative documents are usually human-readable text that is augmented in some way with XML markup.

Specifically, the two basic characteristics that distinguish a narrative document from a data-oriented document are as follows:

❑ **The meaningful content is not defined by the markup** – the XML is generally not an integral part of the information contained in the document, but is used to enhance or augment the text data in some way instead (we'll provide examples of this throughout this section).

❑ **The markup data is highly unstructured** – whereas data-oriented documents are used to describe a set of data, and are rigidly structured, narrative-style documents comprise meaningful content in the form of free-flowing text, much like the content of any book or magazine article (hence the term "narrative"). The data in these kinds of documents can be thought of as unstructured in the sense that the markup in the document doesn't tend to follow any kind of rigid or sequential pattern. For instance, the number of tags and their order within the `<body>` tag of an HTML document is extremely flexible, and may differ from document to document.

Probably the most obvious examples of narrative-style (though not strictly XML) documents are HTML web pages, which use markup in the form of HTML tags to augment the text of the web page with presentation information. Although this presentation data is very important, and definitely affects the reader's experience of the page (for example, it may describe the size, color, and location of images and text on the page), it is fair to say that meaningful data exists separately from the HTML markup.

*Note that this is somewhat of an oversimplification. With the advances in
modern browsers and scripting languages, it is certainly possible to have
pages that contain "markup-only" content.*

In the same way that we use HTML markup in HTML documents to define presentation
characteristics, we use XML tags in our narrative documents to do things such as
annotate the text with semantic information, such as definitions of terms. Let's look at a
concrete example of how a narrative document structure might be used in practice. If
you imagined that a hospital used XML to represent the minutes that were taken during
the course of an operation, you might end up with a document structure that looks
something like this:

```
<operation>
  <preamble>
    At <time type="begin">10:04 PM</time> on <date>10/24/2002</date>,
    the procedure was begun.  The surgeons were <surgeon>Dr. Alan Law
    </surgeon> and <surgeon>Dr. Christy Smith</surgeon>, assisted by
    medical student <student>Ari Light</student>.
  </preamble>

  <minutes>
    Dr. Law used a <tool>scalpel</tool> to make an incision just below
    the <incisionPoint>left kneecap</incisionPoint>.

    ...
  </minutes>
</operation>
```

You can see from this example document that the actual useful content contained in
the document is just the plain-text description of the operation. The XML markup
serves to add some semantic information to the text, such as the time and date that the
procedure was begun, who the operating surgeons were, and other noteworthy pieces
of information.

Narrative documents are useful for a wide variety of applications, including but not
limited to:

❑ **Presentation**

XHTML is a good example of how you can use XML markup in a narrative-
style document to affect the presentation of text-based content (XHTML is a
fully XML-compliant version of HTML. You can find out more about it at
the W3C's website: http://www.w3.org/TR/xhtml1).

❑ **Indexing**

Applications can do efficient indexing of text-based documents by using
XML markup in the document to identify key sections, and then index the
documents based on that content by using a relational database or full-text
indexing software.

33

❏ **Annotation**

An application can use XML to add annotations to existing documents, allowing users to add comments to an existing piece of text without modifying the text directly, much like when a reviewer adds comments to a word document (I saw plenty of those while writing my chapters for this book!).

Let's now look at another example of how we might use XML markup in a narrative-style document to index some content. Let's say that you are a software engineer at a company that provides a news content service. Your company receives written news stories in a plain-text format from several sources, and collects them for storage as text files on a central server. The application you're responsible for building needs to provide quick access to those documents, based on queries for the key pieces of information (such as people's names, places, companies, and so on) in the documents. You realize that in order to meet the query performance requirements of the application, you need to index the documents to identify the key information. To do this you decide to encode the news articles as narrative-style XML documents and use markup to enclose the information that will be queried.

For instance, you might get a news story that looks like this:

```
Wrox Press announces new book, "XML Design Handbook"

Today, Birmingham, England-based Wrox Press announced that sales of
its new book, "XML Design Handbook," topped 1,000,000 copies.
Commissioning editor Tony Davis was quoted as saying, "We're rather
disappointed. We'd assumed it would sell at least 1.5 million copies
by the end of the first week." Nonetheless, the collaboration of
United States- and United Kingdom-based authors has become the all-
time best-selling technical book, making its authors, including
Shrewsbury, Massachusetts' own Scott Bonneau, all very rich.
```

If you had to search through this entire document (and many others like it) for the key information every time a search was executed, the performance of the application would be terrible. However, by making use of XML to markup the documents as they enter the system, you could extract the keywords and put them into a well-indexed relational database, or you could insert the XML-encoded documents themselves into a full-text indexed database, both of which would improve your application's performance.

The sample document as a narrative XML document with the appropriate content enclosed in tags, would look something like this:

```
<story id="12345">
  <organization>Wrox Press</organization> announces new book,
  "XML Design Handbook"

  Today, <city>Birmingham</city>, <country>England</country>-based
  <organization>Wrox Press</organization> announced that sales of
  its new book, "XML Design Handbook" topped 1,000,000 copies.
```

```
Commissioning editor <person>Tony Davis</person> was quoted as
saying, "We're rather disappointed. We'd assumed it would sell at
least 1.5 million copies by the end of the first week."
Nonetheless, the collaboration of <country>United States</country>
and <country>United Kingdom</country>-based authors has become the
all-time best-selling technical book, making its authors, including
<city>Shrewsbury</city>, <state>Massachusetts</state>' own
<person>Scott Bonneau</person>, all very rich.
</story>
```

As you can see in this version of the document, all the key pieces of information (the semantics of the document) are indicated by XML tags that identify them by their category. This example actually has its roots in a real application; a company called NetOwl has a product called the NetOwl Extractor, which automatically analyzes text documents and adds precisely this kind of markup to them. You can find out more about it at http://www.netowl.com.

Let's now look at the building blocks of XML document design.

2.2 Building Blocks: Attributes, Elements, and Character Data

XML documents have many features, but the three that affect document design at the most fundamental level are attributes, elements, and character data. As such, it's reasonable to think of these three as the fundamental building blocks of XML, and the key to designing good documents is learning when to use which block.

One of the most common decisions that XML document designers encounter is whether to use attributes or elements to encode certain pieces of data. There is no universally correct solution and, in many cases, it boils down to a stylistic issue. However, under certain circumstances (particularly with very large documents), making the correct decision is critical to ensure good performance when processing the documents.

It would be impossible to try to envision every possible type of data that one might want to encode in XML. Therefore, it's equally impossible to provide a fixed set of rules dictating when to use attributes and when to use elements to encode that data. However, to help you make these decisions, we will, in this section, compare and contrast the fundamental characteristics of each of these building blocks and then use this as a basis to discuss the appropriate use of each. Understanding these differences will help you make intelligent decisions for your own documents, based on the requirements and constraints of your application. The majority of the discussion will center on the distinctions between attributes and elements, but as character data plays an important role in XML design, we'll discuss that in more detail towards the end of the section.

2.2.1 For Narrative-Style Documents, Understand "The Rule"

As opposed to data-oriented document structures, there is a very simple rule when it comes to deciding when to use attributes and when to use elements: **narrative text should be text content, and all information *about* the text should be elements and attributes for those elements**. This is the concept that led to the development of XML and the rise of these concepts.

This makes sense if you think about the purpose of the markup in a narrative-style document, which is simply to add some semantic data to the text. Anything that adds semantic information to the text should appear in the form of an element (like the <time> element from our hospital example in *Section 2.1.2: Use Narrative-style Documents to Augment Plain-Text Data*); anything that describes *that* semantic value (like the type attribute on that <time> element) should appear in the form of an attribute on that element. Finally, the content whose semantic is modified by the element should then appear as text content in the context of the element.

> **The narrative text goes in element content; information about the text goes in attributes.**

2.2.2 Understand the Differentiating Characteristics of Elements and Attributes

In some cases, the decision to use an element or attribute to encode a certain piece of data is not critical. However, they have very definite differentiating characteristics and, under certain circumstances, use of one or the other can have a major impact on the performance of your application. In the following sub-sections, we'll discuss those characteristics.

2.2.2.1 Elements are More Expensive than Attributes, Both in Space and in Time

Elements tend to take more space and more time to parse than attributes do when the two are used to represent the same data. The difference in cost between using a single attribute and a single element is not great and, for most documents, the total difference in cost is negligible. However, when you're dealing with extremely large documents, or you need to keep the document size to a minimum (if, for instance, you're transmitting XML documents over a low-bandwidth pipe), this issue can come in to play. Let's look at the space and time issues separately.

2.2.2.1.1 Spatial Issues

Spatially, elements will always take up more space than attributes because the element requires at least some XML markup. Consider this example:

```
<address>
  <street>123 Main Street</street>
  <city>AnyTown</city>
  <state>TX</state>
  <country>USA</country>
</address>
```

This is a simple example of an address, which is something you might commonly see encoded in XML. If we were to define a C# class called `address`, with string members called `street`, `city`, `state`, and `country`, this is the XML that would be generated if you serialized the class using the `System.Xml.Serialization.XmlSerializer` class mentioned earlier. This particular encoding takes up 108 characters, ignoring white space. We could encode the same data using a mixture of elements and attributes, which would save us from having to have end element tags:

```
<address>
  <street v="123 Main Street"/>
  <city v="AnyTown"/>
  <state v="TX"/>
  <country v="USA"/>
</address>
```

This brings us down to 94 characters, at the cost of some readability (*I* know that that v stands for "value," but would anyone else?), and saves us some parsing complexity since we don't have to deal with any free text content (character data). (Once again, as noted earlier, this "mixed" style is not recommended for the reasons we'll cover shortly.)

We can represent this same data by exclusively using attributes:

```
<address street="123 Main Street" city="AnyTown" state="TX"
  country="USA"/>
```

This is minimal encoding, with 69 characters, ignoring white space (a 36% saving in terms of space). This is just a trivial example; for very large documents containing more data per record as well as more records, this savings can be critical, both in terms of the space the document takes up, and in terms of the sheer time it takes to read the extra text from the stream and parse it.

To illustrate this point, I generated a series of documents, all representing precisely the same data, using three different styles.

The first style uses attributes to represent all the data. A sample file looks like this:

```
<document>
  <element attribute0="attribute text" attribute1="attribute text"/>
  <element attribute0="attribute text" attribute1="attribute text"/>
  <element attribute0="attribute text" attribute1="attribute text"/>
</document>
```

The second style uses elements for all the data, and uses character data for the attribute values:

```
<document>
  <element>
    <attribute0>attribute text</attribute0>
    <attribute1>attribute text</attribute1>
  </element>
  <element>
    <attribute0>attribute text</attribute0>
    <attribute1>attribute text</attribute1>
  </element>
  <element>
    <attribute0>attribute text</attribute0>
    <attribute1>attribute text</attribute1>
  </element>
</document>
```

The third style is mixed; it uses elements for all the data, but instead of character data, it uses attributes *on* those elements to store the attribute values:

```
<document>
  <element>
    <attribute0 value="attribute text"/>
    <attribute1 value="attribute text"/>
  </element>
  <element>
    <attribute0 value="attribute text"/>
    <attribute1 value="attribute text"/>
  </element>
  <element>
    <attribute0 value="attribute text"/>
    <attribute1 value="attribute text"/>
  </element>
</document>
```

Using these styles, I generated two sets of three documents. The first set had 10,000 "elements" (top-level pieces of data), each of which had 10 "attributes" (the actual attribute values), and the second set had 50,000 elements each with 10 attributes. The first striking thing about these documents is their size. The following table demonstrates the size penalty of using elements:

38

Style	# "Elements"	# "Attributes" per "Element"	File Size
Attributes	10,000	10	2,940,025 bytes
Elements	10,000	10	4,770,025 bytes
Mixed	10,000	10	4,470,025 bytes
Attributes	50,000	10	14,700,025 bytes
Elements	50,000	10	23,850,025 bytes
Mixed	50,000	10	22,350,025 bytes

The attribute-based documents are almost 40% smaller than the element-based documents, and about 35% smaller than the mixed-style documents. In this case, the mixed-style documents only end up being about 6% smaller than element-only documents. Based on this data, it's clear that in situations where size is important you'd want to use attributes over elements wherever possible. Keep in mind that the documents don't have to approach this size all by themselves for this problem to crop up; if your application generates or consumes many smaller documents, you're going to run into precisely this same problem.

The space overhead related to elements can also extend to memory, depending on what parsing technology you use. For instance, DOM has to construct a new Node instance in its tree for every element that it encounters in your document. This in turn means constructing all of the members of the Node instance, all of which occupy memory (and take non-zero time to construct).

The overhead of creating and storing attributes in a DOM tree is much less, and furthermore, some DOM implementations optimize for attributes by not actually parsing out an element's attributes until they're accessed. This leads to savings in parsing time, and cuts down on memory overhead since the text representation of the attributes that the DOM implementation caches can take up considerably less space than that same data would in object form.

2.2.2.1.2 Parsing Time

Elements are also more expensive than attributes in terms of time because of the way that major low-level parsing technologies DOM and SAX work (we'll cover parsing and the details of DOM and SAX in *Chapter 4*). Attributes can exhibit a substantially smaller cost in optimized DOM implementations since they may not be processed until they're accessed. Moreover, you save all the overhead of the unnecessary object creation. All these things add up very quickly, and as we'll see in *Chapter 4*, they can make DOM unusable quickly as the size of the document grows to hundreds of thousands of elements. However, unless your favorite DOM implementation is extremely well documented, then short of looking at its source, there is no way to tell how optimally it handles attributes or elements unless you do some empirical testing.

With SAX, the costs of elements are a little more clear-cut. Every element in a document translates into at least two method calls: startElement() and endElement(), on your ContentHandler instance. In addition, if your document uses character content to represent its values (like the first example from above), there will be at least one additional call to the characters() method on your ContentHandler (for text areas that are large, or ones that contain entity references [like <], or even sometimes just at line breaks, SAX can break up the character data, causing multiple calls to characters()). Again, if your document has too many elements, the cost of making two or more extra method calls can be very substantial and can degrade the performance of your parsing code significantly. For attributes, SAX merely groups them into a data structure, aptly named Attributes, that is passed as an argument to a single call to startElement(). Thus, even to account for the creation and initialization of the Attributes structure itself, there is much less overhead involved.

To investigate this further, I wrote two simple programs, one using SAX and one using DOM, that simply parse any XML document, and count the number of elements and attributes that they encounter.

For the sake of completeness, let's quickly look at the code used in these tests. Here is the main method for the DOM-based code:

```
public static void main(String[] args) throws Exception
{
  if (args.length < 1)
  {
    System.err.println("Must specify filename.");
    return;
  }

  DocumentBuilderFactory factory =
    DocumentBuilderFactory.newInstance();
  DocumentBuilder builder = factory.newDocumentBuilder();

  long start = System.currentTimeMillis();

  Document document = builder.parse(new File(args[0]));
  int[] counts =
    countElementsAndAttributes(document.getDocumentElement());

  long end = System.currentTimeMillis();

  double totalTimeSeconds = (double)(end - start)/1000.0;
  System.out.println("Found " + counts[0] + " elements and " +
    counts[1] + " attributes in " + totalTimeSeconds + " seconds");
}
```

It's all very straightforward. It uses a DOM DocumentBuilder to parse the document, and then calls into another method to count the elements and attributes. At the end it catalogs the time the entire process took and outputs the count and time information. Let's look at the countElementsAndAttributes() method to see what it's doing:

```
// Returns an int array, with the first int being the element
// count (including the passed element itself), and the second
// being the attribute count.
private static int[] countElementsAndAttributes(Element element)
{
  int[] counts = new int[2];

  // Element count is at least 1, including this element
  counts[0] = 1;

  // Get attribute count from the element
  counts[1] = element.getAttributes().getLength();

  NodeList children = element.getChildNodes();
  for (int x = 0, xSize = children.getLength(); x < xSize; ++x)
  {
    Node child = children.item(x);
    if (child.getNodeType() == Node.ELEMENT_NODE)
    {
      int[] childCounts =
        countElementsAndAttributes((Element)child);
      counts[0] += childCounts[0];
      counts[1] += childCounts[1];
    }
  }

  return counts;
}
```

This simple recursive method counts the number of elements and attributes, for itself and all of its children. It initializes the `int` array that it's going to return with an element count of 1 (for itself) and the count of all of its attributes. It then iterates over all of its children, and looks for element nodes. For each element node that it finds, it calls itself recursively, and adds the counts returned by the recursive call to its own counts, which it finally returns at the end of the method.

The SAX code for doing this is a little more straightforward. Here's what the `main` method from our SAX version looks like:

```
public static void main(String[] args) throws Exception
{
  if (args.length < 1)
  {
    System.err.println("Must specify a filename.");
    return;
  }

  GenericParserSAX myParser = new GenericParserSAX();
  XMLReader reader = XMLReaderFactory.createXMLReader();
  reader.setContentHandler(myParser);

  long start = System.currentTimeMillis();
  reader.parse(new InputSource(new FileReader(args[0])));
  long end = System.currentTimeMillis();

  double totalTimeSeconds = (double)(end - start)/1000.0;

  System.out.println("Found " + myParser.m_elementCount +
                     " elements and " + myParser.m_attributeCount +
```

```
                              " attributes in " + totalTimeSeconds +
                              " secoonds");
     }
```

This method instantiates an instance of our `GenericParserSAX` class, which extends
SAX's `DefaultHandler` class, and then instantiates an `XMLReader` for the actual
parsing. It sets our class's instance (`myParser`) as the content handler for the reader,
and then tells the reader to parse. The parser code itself, as we'll see in a minute,
actually does the counting. Finally, this method outputs the time the process took as
well as the counts.

> *DocumentHandler implements* ContentHandler, *as well as*
> ErrorHandler, DTDHandler, *and* EntityResolver. *I used*
> *DocumentHandler here because it has no-op implementers of all of the*
> ContentHandler *methods (as well as those for the other interfaces as well).*
> *Since this example only uses a few of the* ContentHandler *methods,*
> *extending* DefaultHandler *rather than implementing* ContentHandler
> *directly means that we don't have to write our own implementers for the*
> ContentHandler *methods that the example doesn't use.*

Our class only implements three `ContentHandler` methods, `startElement()`,
`endElement()`, and `characters()`, all of which are overridden from
`DefaultHandler`. To simulate a real parsing application, this code maintains a stack
of `StringBuffer` instances (one per element that it encounters). The
`startElement()` method pushes a new one on the stack, `characters()` appends to
it, and `endElement()` pops it off the stack and calls `toString()` on it.

Calling `toString()` on a `StringBuffer` is almost a no-op; no copying of the internal
`char[]` is done. The `StringBuffer`'s internal `char[]` is used to construct a `String`
instance, which is then returned to you. However, it forces any further manipulation of
the `StringBuffer` to be done on a new copy of the `char[]`, since otherwise the
immutability of the `String` instance would be violated.

Here is what the code looks like:

```
     private int m_elementCount = 0;
     private int m_attributeCount = 0;
     private Stack m_buffers = new Stack();

     public void startElement(String uri, String localName,
                              String qName, Attributes attributes)
       throws SAXException
     {
       m_elementCount++;
       m_attributeCount += attributes.getLength();
       m_buffers.push(new StringBuffer(32));
     }
     public void endElement(String uri, String localName, String qName)
       throws SAXException
```

```
{
  StringBuffer buffer = (StringBuffer)m_buffers.pop();

  buffer.toString();
}

public void characters(char ch[], int start, int length)
  throws SAXException
{
  if (!m_buffers.isEmpty())
  {
    StringBuffer buffer = (StringBuffer) m_buffers.peek();
    buffer.append(ch, start, length);
  }
}
```

We ran each of the six documents listed in the previous table through both of these programs. All of the programs were run on an AMD 1.67GHz machine with 512MB of RAM, using Sun's JDK 1.4.0_01 for Windows and using a Xerces SAX2 driver and DOM DocumentBuilderFactory implementation. Here are the results:

Parser Type	# Elements / # Attributes	Attribute Style	Element Style	Mixed Style
SAX	10,000/10	0.828 seconds	0.906 seconds	1.375 seconds
DOM	10,000/10	1.063 seconds	2.297 seconds	2.516 seconds
SAX	50,000/10	2.468 seconds	3.062 seconds	3.859 seconds
DOM	50,000/10	6.703 seconds	9.765 seconds	13.844 seconds

Let's consider the first two rows in this table first. You can see that the attribute style ends up being slightly more efficient than the pure element style, which is what we'd expect given what we know about SAX. The mixed style performs the worst of the three, incurring the overhead of both the added elements and the attributes.

As for DOM, as we anticipated, using attributes ends up yielding a huge savings, by more than a factor of two. The mixed style ends up being the worst of both worlds here as well, and takes slightly more time than the pure element-based approach.

Moving on to the final two rows in the table, you'll notice a couple of interesting pieces of data. First, for SAX you'll notice that the ratios between the styles stay roughly the same, but it's clear that the mixed style is an under-performer, taking nearly twice as long as a pure attribute-based approach. By this point, it should be clear that the mixed style is not very appropriate if performance is an issue.

In the DOM row, you can see that the pure attribute-based approach yields a savings of nearly 45% over the pure element-based approach, and is more than twice as fast as the mixed approach. You'll also notice that the DOM solution is more then three times as expensive in terms of time than the corresponding SAX solution. This example illustrates the fact that DOM does not deal well with documents with exceedingly high element counts.

We have hard data indicating the relative size and time costs between elements and attributes. You might argue that the results of this test are dependent on the parser implementation used during the test, and to some extent, this is always going to be true, regardless of the context. However, the tests here are broadly applicable because they test the structure of the APIs much more than the characteristics of the implementation. Therefore, the behaviors elicited by the tests are fundamental and characteristic of the *interface* more than the underlying *implementation*. Clearly, a poorly implemented version of the API is going to behave differently than an efficient implementation. However, that doesn't change the fact that while, for instance, there is a need to make a call to both the startElement() and endElement() functions for each element in the document, this need does not exist for any attribute in the document.

To quell any potential conspiracy theories, I ran these tests with three different SAX drivers (the Apache Crimson driver that ships with JDK 1.4, the Xerces driver, and a SAX2 driver based on an XML pull parser, which we'll discuss more thoroughly in *Chapter 4*), all of which yielded similar results. The complete results are available in *Appendix A*, and you can run these tests yourself with your favorite SAX driver by downloading the example source from http://www.wrox.com.

2.2.2.2 Elements are more Flexible than Attributes

Attributes are extremely limited in terms of the data that they can represent; an attribute can only represent one string value. Attributes are not suited to holding any kind of structured data. They are intended to hold short strings. Elements, on the other hand, are obviously very well suited to representing structured data, since they can contain other nested elements as well as character data.

You may store structured data in an attribute, but then you will also be responsible for writing all of the code to parse that string value out. In some cases, this may be acceptable; for instance, it's reasonable to store a date as an attribute. Your parsing code is likely to parse out the string containing the date, into an in-memory date instance for later use. This is actually quite a prudent approach; you get the benefits of using a single attribute as opposed to several elements to represent your date value, plus the time it takes to parse out a date string is minimal, so you save the additional XML processing time as well. (Note that this approach works with dates because they have a very common set of formats when represented as a string and so they don't require a lot of *a priori* knowledge in order to parse. However, overusing this technique destroys the usefulness of the XML representation, so be careful not to overdo it.)

Note that the use of XML schemas, which we'll discuss in the next chapter, allows for some limited structuring of attribute data, such as representing sequences of decimal numbers. Beyond simple cases like this, however, attributes should be avoided when representing structured data.

It is generally unwise to try to get too creative with encoding structured data into a single string. The most extreme case I've ever seen of this had an entire additional XML-escaped (for instance ">" instead of ">", etc.) XML document as the text content of an attribute. At parsing time, that attribute was read into a string (the parser un-escaped the string during parsing), and then that string value, which was at that point a complete, well-formed XML document, was itself sent to another parser to be parsed.

This is not the best use of XML, nor is it a recommended practice, but it clearly demonstrates the lack of flexibility that attributes provide. If you are using attributes in this manner, you're most likely underutilizing the flexibility that XML provides. Attributes are great at storing relatively short and unstructured strings, and that is what they should be used for the majority of the time. If you find yourself still needing to store some relatively complicated structured text in your document, you should consider representing it as character data instead for a very good reason: performance.

In addition to the fact that very long strings in an attribute value are stylistically undesirable, they can also pose a performance problem. Since attribute values are just string instances, the parser must hold the entire value in memory at once. For very long strings, memory can become an issue if your attribute value is excessively large. In SAX, very large character data is broken up into several chunks that are passed individually to the `characters()` method of the `ContentHandler`. Thus, the entire string doesn't need to be in memory all at once (this point is debatable in DOM, since the entire document is represented in memory all the time).

2.2.2.3 Character Data versus Attributes

This is very much a stylistic issue, but there are some guidelines to consider when making a decision on this, so we'll cover them briefly here.

Consider using character data when:

❑ **The data is very long**

Attributes were not meant to store very long values, as they require the entire string to be in memory at once. From an implementation standpoint, character data can be broken up into smaller chunks that can be processed independently.

❑ **There are a large number of XML-escaped characters in the data**

If you encode the data using character data, you can use a CDATA section to avoid having to XML-escape the string. For instance, using an attribute to represent a boolean expression you might end up with something looking like this: `"a &lt; b &amp;&amp; b &gt; c"`. However, if you used character data, you could encode the same string in a much more readable fashion: `<![CDATA[a < b && b > c]]>`.

❑   **The data is short but performance is an issue and you're using SAX**

As we saw in *Section 2.2.2.1.2: Parsing Time* with the mixed-style documents, character data can be considerably less expensive than attributes in terms of parsing time when using SAX.

Consider using attributes when:

❑   **The data is short and unstructured**

This is what attributes were designed for, but be aware that performance can suffer versus character data for extremely large documents (> 100,000 elements) when using SAX.

❑   **You're using SAX to parse it, and want to keep the parsing code simple**

It's much simpler to parse out attribute data than character data, since attributes are available when you're parsing the start of an element's context. Parsing out character data is not too complicated, but it does require a few extra steps and some extra logic that can be error-prone, particularly for SAX beginners.

2.2.3 Favor Attributes for Data that Identifies the Element

In many cases, data objects have a property, or a set of properties, that is used to uniquely identify that piece of data from others of the same type. For instance, an ISBN number or the combination of the author and title may be used to uniquely identify a "book" object:

```
public class Book
{
  private String m_isbn;
  private String m_title;
  private String m_author;
  private int m_numPages;
  private String m_description;
  private String m_genre;
  private String m_format;

  public Book(String isbn)
  {
    m_isbn = isbn;
  }

  public Book(String title, String author)
  {
    m_title = title;
    m_author = author;
  }

  // Getters & Setters omitted
  // ...
}
```

This is a simple class describing a book, including a few relative properties and a couple of constructors; all of the getter and setter methods have been omitted. There is no default constructor, which is not uncommon, particularly for data classes that have some immutable members. In this case, the constructors require that you either have an ISBN number or the title and author.

Let's say you want to encode the data in this class as XML. For classes or structures like this, it usually makes sense to model that data as an attribute of the element containing that object's data for a variety of reasons; most importantly, the impact that this can have on the parsing process.

The use of attributes rather than elements can simplify the parsing process under a few different circumstances. When there is no default constructor for the object that you're deserializing, having the key data as attributes makes the construction of that object less complicated. This is so because you can construct the object in the code that handles the start of the element that contains the data describing the object. If you were to write the parsing code to handle the construction of our book object by using SAX, it would look something like this:

```
// Used to hold the current book instance during parsing.
private Book m_currentBook = null;

public void startElement(String uri, String localName,
                         String qName, Attributes attributes)
  throws SAXException
{
  if ("book".equals(qName))
  {
    // Get the relevant key values from the attribute list
    String isbn = attributes.getValue("ISBN");
    String author = attributes.getValue("author");
    String title = attributes.getValue("title");

    // Switch to see what key data exists...
    if (isbn != null)
    {
      // Construct the book based on the ISBN.
      m_currentBook = new Book(isbn);
    }
    else
    {
      // Make sure that there are both an author and a title before
      // constructing the book.  If not, throw an exception.
      if (author != null && title != null)
        m_currentBook = new Book(title, author);
      else
        throw new RuntimeException("Book requires either ISBN " +
                              "or both author and title.");
    }
  }
}
```

This is clean parsing code; it guarantees that whenever we are within the <book> tag's context, there will be a valid Book instance to be operated on. This example is slightly more complex than you might normally see, as there are two possible exclusive keys (ISBN or author and title), but it's definitely within the realm of situations that you may encounter.

If you decide to use elements instead of attributes here, writing clean, robust code gets more difficult:

```
// Used to hold the current book instance during parsing.
private Book m_currentBook = null;

// Temporary variable used to store the name of the author.
private String m_author = null;

public void startElement(String uri, String localName,
                         String qName, Attributes attributes)
    throws SAXException
{
  if ("book".equals(qName))
  {
    // Do nothing, since we can't construct a new Book without the
    // key information.
    return;
  }

  if ("isbn".equals(qName))
  {
    // We'll assume that an XML schema or DTD enforces that if there
    // is an ISBN element that it comes before the author and title.
    // We'll also assume that the value of the ISBN is stored in
    // an attribute called "value" to simplify parsing.
    m_currentBook = new Book(attributes.getValue("value"));
    return;
  }

  if ("author".equals(qName))
  {
    // We'll assume that the value for the author is in an attribute
    // called "value" to simplify parsing.
    String author = attributes.getValue("value");
    if (m_currentBook != null)
      m_currentBook.setAuthor(author);
    else
      m_author = author;
    return;
  }

  if ("title".equals(qName))
  {
    // We'll assume that the value for the title is in an attribute
    // called "value" to simplify parsing.
    String title = attributes.getValue("title");
    if (m_currentBook != null)
      m_currentBook = new Book(title, m_author);
    else
      m_currentBook.setTitle(title);
    return;
  }
}
```

This parsing code is more complex as it constantly needs to react differently, based on whether or not the m_currentBook member variable has been initialized. In contrast to the previous example, the parsing state is not clear-cut when dealing with the elements within the <book> context. This can lead to parsing code that is dirtier and harder to maintain, which brings with it innocuous parsing bugs that can be difficult to track down.

Another case where having the identifying information included with the enclosing element as attributes can simplify the parsing process is while validating the contents in a document. Occasionally, you might want to do a quick, cursory check over a document to validate its contents, before doing a more in-depth and extensive processing of the document. This is particularly useful for tiered or distributed systems; by doing some validation up front, you can eliminate unnecessary traffic to a lower tier or across a network boundary (such as an order entry system validating the format of a credit card number or an account number, before submitting an order to an order fulfillment system).

In these situations, it helps tremendously to have the identifying or key information as an attribute rather than an element. The parsing code is greatly simplified, as we saw above, and the performance is much better, since you can completely ignore the vast majority of the content in a document and often terminate the parsing process early.

Ultimately, the decision of attributes over elements in this situation is largely stylistic since you can achieve the same result using either approach. However, there *are* some situations where there are clear advantages of using attributes for identifying data; so, when designing your document structure, make sure to consider whether or not your document falls into those categories.

2.2.4 Avoid Attributes for Data where Order is Important

Unlike elements, there is no enforceable ordering for attributes; no matter how you specify attributes in a schema or DTD, there is no requirement that the attributes as they appear in a given document will actually conform to any specific order. As a quick example, look at the following DTD (we'll look at XML Schemas in *Chapter 3*, but we'll use this simple DTD for the sake of this example):

```
<!DOCTYPE doc [
  <!ELEMENT anElement (#PCDATA)>
    <!ATTLIST anElement anAttribute CDATA #REQUIRED>
    <!ATTLIST anElement anotherAttribute CDATA #REQUIRED>
]>
```

The DTD specifies a simple document with a single element, anElement, which has two required attributes, anAttribute and anotherAttribute. Consider the following two documents based on this DTD:

```
<!DOCTYPE doc [
  <!ELEMENT anElement (#PCDATA)>
    <!ATTLIST anElement anAttribute CDATA #REQUIRED>
    <!ATTLIST anElement anotherAttribute CDATA #REQUIRED>
]>

<doc>
  <anElement anAttribute="foo" anotherAttribute="bar"/>
</doc>
<!DOCTYPE doc [
  <!ELEMENT anElement (#PCDATA)>
    <!ATTLIST anElement anAttribute CDATA #REQUIRED>
    <!ATTLIST anElement anotherAttribute CDATA #REQUIRED>
]>

<doc>
  <anElement anotherAttribute="bar" anAttribute="foo"/>
</doc>
```

The only difference between these two attributes is the ordering of the attributes; in the first document, the anAttribute attribute is specified before anotherAttribute, and in the second document, the ordering is reversed. Since XML doesn't enforce any kind of attribute ordering, both of these documents are legal and conform to the DTD.

As a result, in situations where the ordering of the values is important, elements are better suited than attributes. In keeping with this example, one could easily specify a DTD where one element needs to appear before another:

```
<!DOCTYPE doc [
  <!ELEMENT anElement (aSubElement, anotherSubElement)>
  <!ELEMENT aSubElement (#PCDATA)>
  <!ELEMENT anotherSubElement (#PCDATA)>
]>
```

Using this DTD, we produced the following two documents:

```
<!DOCTYPE doc [
  <!ELEMENT anElement (aSubElement, anotherSubElement)>
  <!ELEMENT aSubElement (#PCDATA)>
  <!ELEMENT anotherSubElement (#PCDATA)>
]>

<doc>
  <anElement>
    <aSubElement>Sub Element #1</aSubElement>
    <anotherSubElement>Sub Element #2</anotherSubElement>
  </anElement>
</doc>

<!DOCTYPE doc [
  <!ELEMENT anElement (aSubElement, anotherSubElement)>
  <!ELEMENT aSubElement (#PCDATA)>
  <!ELEMENT anotherSubElement (#PCDATA)>
]>
```

50

```
<doc>
  <anElement>
    <anotherSubElement>Sub Element #2</anotherSubElement>
    <aSubElement>Sub Element #1</aSubElement>
  </anElement>
</doc>
```

As before, these two documents are identical except for the ordering of the sub-elements. In this case, however, the second document (where `anotherSubElement` comes before `aSubElement`) does not conform to the DTD. If you were to run these documents through a validating SAX parser, the first document would parse correctly, but the second one would cause the parser to throw an exception indicating that it doesn't conform to the specified DTD.

That wraps up our discussion of attributes, elements, and character data. In the next section, we'll cover some guidelines for modeling data in your XML documents.

2.3 General Data Modeling Pitfalls

The manner is which you model your data in XML dictates just about every aspect of how people and applications are going to interact with those documents. Thus, it is critical that the data be modeled to make that interaction as straightforward, efficient, and painless as possible. Thus far, we've covered modeling at a very low level, discussing which XML primitives (such as attributes and elements) are more appropriate in which situations. For the rest of the chapter, we'll discuss some guidelines that apply at a higher level.

2.3.1 Avoid Designing for a Specific Platform or Parser Implementation

A large part of the appeal of XML is that it is portable and platform-independent, which makes it a great tool for sharing data in a heterogeneous environment. When documents are used to share data and communicate externally to an application, the design of the document is extremely critical, and as a designer, you must take into account a whole host of issues relating to the fact that there will be third-party consumers of your documents. For one, the cost of making a change to the data structure once it's published and people have written code based on that structure is extremely high, potentially to the point of being prohibitive. In addition, once you expose a document structure to the outside world, you effectively lose all control over *how* documents conforming to that structure will be processed, which can be a major problem if you haven't considered that case at design time.

Note that XML certainly has found its way into places where sharing data isn't a concern, such as in situations where XML is used to represent some internal state of a closed system; (for instance, when it is used to store a configuration state that isn't accessible to end users). However, in situations like these, document design issues are usually far less critical because the cost of making a change to the document structure in the event that an issue is discovered is very low. The changes are localized to the given application and don't affect the outside world.

I would go as far as saying that it is never a good idea to design a document structure to match a particular parser implementation. This is not like designing a document structure that's appropriate for a given parsing technology (like DOM, SAX, or pull-parsers) – it's more like suggesting that you write your Java code tailored to a specific VM; it rather defeats the purpose. Parser implementations will evolve and only get better, so it doesn't make too much sense to optimize for one particular implementation. Since the nature of XML is that it is platform-parser-technology-agnostic, it's impossible to control precisely the performance characteristics of parsing a given document when you're no longer in charge of deciding how it will be processed.

As a result, the best thing that you, as a document designer, can do is to tailor your document to suit the task it's trying to serve. A document structure is a contract, and nothing more – it's an interface, not an implementation. It is therefore extremely important to have an understanding of the usage of documents conforming to *that* structure. For example, if you were building an API in your favorite programming language, you wouldn't design an interface for that API without understanding how that interface was going to be used. If you did, the result would most likely be an unusable API that doesn't suit the needs of its would-be users. This fact is as true for XML document structures as it is for programming interfaces.

To crystallize this point, think about the different design you might have for a bulk- vs. single-row-oriented database interface. If your API will be affecting hundreds or thousands of rows in a database, you would likely design it to use arrays or collections of objects as parameters, because a single database query that affects a thousand rows is significantly faster than a thousand queries that each affect a single row. You don't need to know the innards of Oracle or SQL Server to make an intelligent design decision here. Similarly, when designing document structures, it's much more important to account for the broad truisms of the technologies today, than it is to worry about the specific issues of a given implementation. To tie this point to what we discussed earlier in the chapter, understanding, for instance, the general performance characteristics of attributes versus elements, is more important than knowing if a particular parser implementation has an optimized (or sub-optimal) engine for processing large numbers of attributes.

As with anything in engineering, the designer must use some common sense to achieve a balance between the technical ideal and the current state of reality. This is why we spent so much time in the chapter discussing issues like "elements are more expensive than attributes," because it's true regardless of technology, and it can affect the document design in the context of the intended usage of the document. To continue the example from above, if you're designing a document structure that you know is going to be used to hold thousands of records, you would be well served to understand that the use of elements can cause a significant performance penalty in terms of disk space and in terms of time when those documents are parsed.

With the advent of **Simple Object Access Protocol (SOAP)**, XML-based web services, and other XML-based communication mechanisms, the need to design document structures in a platform-agnostic manner is clearer than ever. So, when your documents are not exclusively used internally to your application, be sure to design your document structures in such a way that they don't depend heavily on any kind of platform-specific or parser implementation-specific features or performance characteristics.

2.3.2 The Underlying Data Model often isn't the Best Choice as an XML Encoding

XML is often used in situations when it's not the persistent representation for the encoded data; for instance, XML-based RPC is a cornerstone of all of the new Web Service technology that's being hyped so heavily by Microsoft and the Java community. In the case of XML-based RPC, the parameters to the remote procedure, as well as its return value (if any), are encoded in XML inside a SOAP-compliant document. The XML used to consummate the remote procedure call is clearly not the primary representation of that data; it is simply a secondary representation used for marshalling data across the socket.

In situations like this where XML is used as a transient encoding of the data, it is often a good idea to rethink the structure of your data rather than just reusing the on-disk structure as your XML-based structure. Often, the underlying data model isn't the most optimal one for XML.

The rationale behind this is straightforward; most persistent storage mechanisms, such as **Relational Database Management Systems (RDBMS)**, flat files, object databases, registries, etc., were not designed with XML and its structure in mind. Each was designed with specific purposes in mind, and has strengths and weaknesses directly in line with those purposes. Many XML-based databases were designed with this problem in mind. SQL Server 2000 from Microsoft also has been designed to support XML internally.

One of the more common uses of XML is to encode data whose persistent representation is as relational data in an RDBMS. Relational databases have a flat structure that consists of discrete tables whose only relationship to one another is a logical one; namely, the relationship described by keys between tables. Using relational databases to describe hierarchical data usually means having a table of data that represents the "parent" in the hierarchical relationship, and a separate table (or tables) that represent(s) the "children" in the relationship, with the child tables having a key that links to their parent. (This is a simplification, but it doesn't omit any details pertinent to this discussion.)

If you were to mimic this table structure in an XML document, the result would be a highly inefficient document structure that adds unnecessary complications and overhead to the parsing process because it ignores one of XML's more powerful features: the ability to represent hierarchical data. We'll cover this situation in-depth in *Section 2.3.4: Avoid Pointer-heavy Documents*, but let's look at a quick example to illustrate the point.

Let's say that you were building an application that implemented an online catalog of parts, and you used a relational database to store the catalog data. Parts in the catalog have a variable number of attributes, so you build a table structure that looks like this:

Figure 1

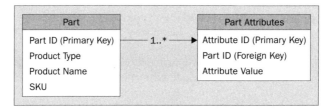

This is a sensible table structure for this data, as its separation of part data from part attribute data allows the flexibility that is required in terms of having a variable number of attributes for each part in the catalog.

If you were to take this table structure and map it directly to XML, you'd end up with a document structure that looks something like this:

```
<catalog>
    <part id="12345" sku="AZDF1023" productType="Widget" name="Gizmo"/>
    <part id="54321" sku="LKJS7892" productType="Widget" name="Foobar"/>
    <part id="98765" sku="RJSOI22" productType="Widget" name="Wizbang"/>

    <partAttribute partID="12345" attribute="Color" value="Blue"/>
    <partAttribute partID="12345" attribute="RAM" value="128MB"/>
    <partAttribute partID="12345" attribute="HDD" value="2GB"/>

    <partAttribute partID="54321" attributeID="Color" value="Red"/>
    <partAttribute partID="54321" attributeID="RAM" value="64MB"/>
```

```
      <partAttribute partID="98765" attributeID="Color" value="White"/>
      <partAttribute partID="98765" attributeID="RAM" value="512MB"/>
      <partAttribute partID="98765" attributeID="OS" value="Linux"/>
      <partAttribute partID="98765" attributeID="Office" value="Star"/>
   </catalog>
```

In this document, the catalog consists of a list of parts (mimicking the part rows in the table definition), followed by a list of part attributes (mimicking the part attribute rows). While this is a perfectly valid document structure, it's probably not the best structure for this data, mostly because it completely ignores the hierarchical nature of the data and XML's ability to represent that data hierarchically.

In this example, the hierarchy is enforced logically, using references (or pointers); each partAttribute element has a partID attribute that acts as a pointer into a part element somewhere else in the document (we'll discuss pointer-heavy document structures in-depth in *Section 2.3.4: Avoid Pointer-heavy Documents*). This certainly mimics the way that relational databases represent this data, but it doesn't take advantage of XML's strengths.

A much more natural XML structure for this type of document would be to nest the part attribute data as children of the part. It would look like this:

```
<catalog>
   <part id="12345" sku="AZDF1023" productType="Widget" name="Gizmo">
      <partAttribute attributeID="Color" value="Blue"/>
      <partAttribute attributeID="RAM" value="128MB"/>
      <partAttribute attributeID="HDD" value="2GB"/>
   </part>

   <part id="54321" sku="LKJS7892" productType="Widget" name="Foobar">
      <partAttribute attributeID="Color" value="Red"/>
      <partAttribute attributeID="RAM" value="64MB"/>
   </part>

   <part id="98765" sku="RJSOI22" productType="Widget" name="Wizbang">
      <partAttribute attributeID="Color" value="White"/>
      <partAttribute attributeID="RAM" value="512MB"/>
      <partAttribute attributeID="OS" value="Linux"/>
      <partAttribute attributeID="Office" value="Star"/>
   </part>
</catalog>
```

This document reads much more easily (both to humans and parsers) than the previous one because this one uses XML's inherent hierarchical nature to represent the data in a more natural way. Each partAttribute element is contained within the context of its owning part, which makes it obvious which part owns which attributes, and also eliminates the need for the partID attribute (which you can see has been omitted in this version of the document) on the partAttribute elements. Structuring the document in this way also makes the parsing code quite a bit simpler and more efficient for larger documents, the reasons for which we'll discuss in *Section 2.3.4: Avoid Pointer-heavy Documents*.

The key concept to keep in mind as you're designing your document structure is that it should be based on the abstract object model that best describes what you are trying to encode, not on the implementation of that model in some other technology, like the Java (or C++, etc.) class that implements the model in your application. I'm not saying that there aren't situations in which your software implementation of the model and your XML implementation won't be very similar, because for many cases, such as simple object serialization, they will be. The important thing to realize is that your XML should be a model of your data, not a model of the Java model of your data.

When designing the catalog example that we just walked through, the first thing that we did was look at the table structure that was being used in the database to store the data. The result of using this relational description of the data as a basis for the document was not a particularly good one, as we just saw. However, if we were to consider a more abstract description of the model (rather than the implementation – in this case the relational database structure), we would have arrived at the better solution immediately. To see an example of this, let's look at a UML diagram representing the catalog structure:

Figure 2

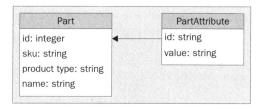

This simple UML diagram provides a basic abstract description of the relationship between parts and their attributes: namely, a part consists of an identifier, a SKU, a product type, and a name, and is associated with some number of attributes, which consist of an identifier and a value. The diagram implies that part attributes are associated with their parts in a container-containee relationship, which is precisely the structure modeled in the second document from the example.

By considering the data you're trying to model outside the context of any particular implementation, you can often arrive at a better document structure for your data than you would otherwise. This kind of analysis will usually help you model your data in a more XML-friendly structure, which will lead to more robust documents that will lend themselves to simpler parsing code, and will perform better when it comes time to parse them.

2.3.3 Avoid Over-stuffing your Documents

One of the side effects of using XML to encode data is the overhead that goes hand-in-hand with that encoding. To put it bluntly, XML is not the most efficient encoding mechanism from a signal-to-noise ratio standpoint. For every piece of data in your document, some corresponding markup takes up some space for both itself and the data it represents.

In general, it makes sense to try to keep the size of your documents as small as possible, for several reasons:

- ❏ Even though disk space is cheap, it never makes sense to waste it
- ❏ Every single bit in that file will run through an XML parser at some point; the more the data in the document, the longer it will take to parse
- ❏ If the document is going to be used as a communications mechanism, like a SOAP document for an XML-based Web Service, it's going to all have to be sent on the wire

Now, I'm not suggesting that you should take this to the extreme and end up producing a document that looks like this:

```
<a>
  <b c="Some variable">
    <d>Some text</d>
  </b>
  <e f="Some other variable/>
</a>
```

While long element and attribute names can play a part in very large documents (100K+ elements), it's also usually very valuable to make sure your documents are easily readable. As a result, while you don't necessarily want excessively long element and attribute names, it's typically not the place to cut back when you're trying to keep your documents to a reasonable size. (Keep in mind that these names will compress easily if you choose to compress your documents as well.)

It usually makes more sense to analyze the actual data that you're putting into your documents, for any unnecessary bits. There is a tendency when encoding data in XML to just "throw in the kitchen sink," so to speak.

In general, try to omit redundant data when building your document structure. A specific situation when this can crop up is when serializing classes that have attributes that are functions of other attributes. An extreme example of this is the TimeSpan class in C#. This class has a slew of public properties that allow you to access the underlying time span value, which itself is probably just an integral number representing the number of nanoseconds (or just about any other unit of time that you can think of). It has properties to represent the span in *total* years, days, etc., as well as properties that represent the *relative* number of years, days, and so forth, covered by the span. For example, for a time span of 62 total seconds, there would be just 2 relative seconds, because that is the remainder after calculating the number of minutes.

If you were to serialize this class, it would be better to just serialize the single underlying integral value rather than all the properties, since each of those other properties can be derived from *that* single underlying value. This is an extreme example, but it's not uncommon to see, say, a class that does event scheduling and calculates a next scheduled execution time, based on a previous execution time and the current time. There is no reason to serialize that value, since it can easily be recreated when the object is reconstructed.

Any field that you would mark as `transient` for regular Java serialization should probably not be serialized to XML either (for those of you who aren't familiar, fields marked with the keyword `transient` are ignored by the Java serialization code). Fields that are only used to store temporary state, such as caches or intermediate state used during long-running calculations, are good candidates for transient variables.

There will also be situations where it makes sense *not* to encode even non-transient state. For instance, suppose you're writing some code that keeps track of the differences between distributed data stores to keep those stores synchronized, and you're using XML to pass the data between the stores. If the records in your data store have many fields, of which only a few are likely to have changed since the last time the stores were synchronized, it would make a lot of sense to only encode into your XML the fields that *have* changed. For records with hundreds of fields and stores with thousands of records, this can add up to substantial savings very quickly.

It's important not to overdo it when trying to trim the amount of data in your documents; make sure that you always have the right set of data to perform the necessary function. If you look at the data in your document and realize that some of it isn't used right now, but it may be in the near future, you may consider keeping it in because the cost of making the change later on might be much greater than the cost of having some extra data floating around in the meantime. It's always a balancing act between the performance *now* and flexibility in the *future*, and you have to make decisions that make sense in the context of your own applications and its requirements. By paying a little more attention to what data is actually in your documents and comparing it against what is needed, you can end up keeping your documents smaller, making them less expensive and easier to parse.

2.3.4 Avoid Pointer-heavy Document Structures

One of the biggest pains when you write XML parsing code is realizing that the document structure that you're parsing makes heavy use of references (also referred to as pointers). For example, look at this small document:

```
<document>
  <anElement name="aParent"/>
  <anElement name="aChild" parent="aParent"/>
</document>
```

This document demonstrates a very simple use of pointers in XML. The second `anElement` element, `aChild`, has an attribute, `parent`, which references another element (in this case, the first `anElement` element, `aParent`). (Note that the pointers are simply text-based, and there are only very limited language features to support them; the resolution and management of references is normally left up to the application code.)

Pointers in XML documents can be useful in certain circumstances. For example, the Ant build system uses XML to describe the build process, and in an Ant build file, you use pointers to specify the dependencies for your target. Here's a quick example:

```
<project name="myproject" default="all" basedir=".">
  <target name="all" depends="clean,build,package"/>

  <target name="clean">
    <!-- Do the cleaning -->
  </target>

  <target name="build">
    <!-- Do the building -->
  </target>

  <target name="package">
    <!-- Do the packaging -->
  </target>
</project>
```

Here, pointers have been used in a couple of places. First, the `project` element has an attribute called `default`, which points to a target to be used when no target is specified. Second, in the target "all," the attribute `depends` points to a list of all of the other targets that must be processed before this target can be evaluated.

Pointer-heavy documents can make the parsing process quite complicated, and depending on the size of the document and how it's structured, dealing with pointers can erode the performance of the parsing code, and make it very difficult for people to follow what the document is trying to represent to a degree that would make them untenable.

The problem with parsing pointer-heavy documents is that you have to do the pointer resolution yourself. (This is at least true when parsing documents using DOM or SAX. XSLT, which sits at a higher level than DOM and SAX, has more robust mechanisms for dealing with pointer resolution.) We'll cover the topic of building efficient pointer-resolving parsing code in *Chapter 4*. Strictly speaking, pointer resolution isn't an enormously difficult technical problem; it's generally rather easy to write the code, particularly when the relationship is one-to-one or one-to-many.

To do resolution, you need to keep a certain amount of state in memory during the process; something you ordinarily wouldn't have to do. This is no big deal if the document is small, but as the size of the document grows, the amount of state that you need to keep in memory usually grows as well, and at some point that can become a problem. Note that if you're using DOM to parse the document, then this is rather a moot point, since DOM requires that the entire document be in memory anyway.

Let's look at an example. Say you're parsing a document that makes heavy use of pointers to describe a simple, non-recursive parent-child relationship. In the document, all of the parents will come first, followed by all of the children. A typical document would look like this:

```
<document>
  <parent name="parent 1">
    <!-- Some parent stuff -->
  </parent>
  <parent name="parent 2">
    <!-- Some parent stuff -->
  </parent>
  <!-- ... -->
  <parent name="parent N">
    <!-- Some parent stuff -->
  </parent>

  <!-- END parents -->
  <!-- BEGIN children -->

  <!-- "parent 1"'s children -->
  <child name="child 1 of parent 1" parent="parent 1">
    <!-- some child stuff -->
  </child>
  <child name="child 2 of parent 1" parent="parent 1">
    <!-- some child stuff -->
  </child>
  <child name="child 3 of parent 1" parent="parent 1">
    <!-- some child stuff -->
  </child>

  <!-- "parent 2"'s children -->
  <child name="child 1 of parent 2" parent="parent 2">
    <!-- some child stuff -->
  </child>
  <child name="child 2 of parent 2" parent="parent 2">
    <!-- some child stuff -->
  </child>
  <child name="child 3 of parent 2" parent="parent 2">
    <!-- some child stuff -->
  </child>

  <!-- ... -->

  <!-- "parent N"'s children -->
  <child name="child 1 of parent N" parent="parent N">
    <!-- some child stuff -->
  </child>
  <child name="child 2 of parent N" parent="parent N">
    <!-- some child stuff -->
  </child>
  <child name="child 3 of parent N" parent="parent N">
    <!-- some child stuff -->
  </child>
</document>
```

To successfully process this document, you'll need to keep some information about the parents around for processing the children elements. For example, you'll have to verify that each child has a reference to a valid parent (this is called checking for referential integrity). You may also have to access properties of the parent in order to process the children.

If the number of parents is relatively small, the amount of extra space in memory taken up by the parent data probably won't cause your system to start thrashing. It will make the SAX parsing code more complicated, though, since you'll have to write some code to manage that data.

However, a relatively large number of parents could affect the performance of your parsing code, because memory usage will increase linearly with the number of parent elements in the document. In addition, any collections that are used in the parsing code will have to be sized appropriately, otherwise they'll have to be constantly expanded (like vectors or array lists) and potentially rehashed (like hash tables and hash sets), which both takes up memory and a lot of processing time. Inappropriately sized collections can cause a serious performance bottleneck.

The problem with pointers can be aggravated if the referencing elements come before the referenced elements. For example, if you re-wrote our document such that all of the children came before any of the parents, the amount of data that you'd need to keep in memory would potentially be much greater. There are likely to be at least as many, if not more, children as parents. To process the document successfully in this case, you'd need to keep all of that child data in memory until you found and processed the parent for that child. When you find a parent, you'd want to process all of its children, which further complicates the code necessary to complete the parsing process.

You can avoid most of these issues with pointers in situations where your document models one-to-one or one-to-many relationships by using the hierarchical nature of XML. The parsing code and memory overhead of processing hierarchical data is a great deal less than when using pointers. For example, we could rewrite our example parent-child document using a hierarchical structure, which would also make the document a lot cleaner and easier to read:

```
<document>
  <parent name="parent 1">
    <!-- Some parent stuff -->

    <child name="child 1 of parent 1">
      <!-- some child stuff -->
    </child>
    <child name="child 2 of parent 1">
      <!-- some child stuff -->
    </child>
    <child name="child 3 of parent 1">
      <!-- some child stuff -->
    </child>
  </parent>

  <parent name="parent 2">
    <!-- Some parent stuff -->

    <child name="child 1 of parent 2">
      <!-- some child stuff -->
    </child>
    <child name="child 2 of parent 2">
      <!-- some child stuff -->
```

```
        </child>
        <child name="child 3 of parent 2">
          <!-- some child stuff -->
        </child>
      </parent>
      <!-- ... -->
      <parent name="parent N">
        <!-- Some parent stuff -->
        <child name="child 1 of parent N">
          <!-- some child stuff -->
        </child>
        <child name="child 2 of parent N">
          <!-- some child stuff -->
        </child>
        <child name="child 3 of parent N">
          <!-- some child stuff -->
        </child>
      </parent>
    </document>
```

When the document is structured hierarchically, the parent of a given node is implied by its context in the document. Thus, in order to process the children, the only parent you need to keep around is the one currently in context. When the parent goes out of context, there are guaranteed to be no more children for that parent, so there's no need to keep that parent's data around. This kind of structure has the additional advantage of being much more human readable.

Why doesn't Ant use a hierarchical structure? Ant models data that exhibits a many-to-many relationship; any given target can depend on any number of other targets, and any target can be a dependency of any number of other targets. In situations like these, it doesn't make sense to encode the data hierarchically, since there is no generalized ownership pattern of one target to another.

When you're designing your documents, use a hierarchical structure instead of pointers. If you have to model data that requires pointers (which you intend to have parsed using DOM or SAX, since, once again, XSLT does have more robust mechanisms for dealing with pointer resolution), try to design the documents with the parsing code in mind, so that the least possible state is required to be in memory at parsing time.

2.4 Conclusion

That wraps up our discussion on the basics of document design. We covered the two basic document styles, the characteristics of the building blocks of XML, and some important data modeling guidelines. This data has been presented in as general a fashion as possible because document design is a broad and ranging topic; it would be futile to try to cover specifics. The information that we've covered here should serve as a very solid foundation on which to make your own document design decisions based on the requirements and constraints of your own applications.

Throughout the rest of the book, we'll discuss how to design better documents for specific purposes, such as performing XSL transforms, storing data for long-term archival, and using XML as a transmission medium. The information we covered here in this chapter will serve as a basis for much of what we discuss for the rest of the book, so keep it in mind as you read on.

XML Design

Handbook

3

3

XML Schema Design

While the programming community appears to have been quick to embrace XML since its creation in 1998, the advantages of being able to share documents across platforms and between programs written in different languages require that we be able to define the vocabularies we use so that we can share this data with other programs and programmers using a schema. In this chapter, we will be looking at key schema design issues that will make your schemas more efficient and easier to adopt, therefore giving them a longer life.

In many XML design efforts, the first step is for all the involved parties to get together and define an XML vocabulary. While we can define our vocabularies using DTDs, which have been around since their inclusion in the XML 1.0 recommendation, XML Schemas can be a lot more powerful. The W3C's XML Schema specification provides a powerful technology for defining XML document structures and content.

XML Schema language isn't the easiest language to learn – anyone who's tried to read the W3C XML Schema specifications (http://www.w3.org/TR/xmlschema-1 and http://www.w3.org/TR/xmlschema-2) can attest to this. As a result, many people either learn specific approaches to schema design and reuse those approaches whenever they have a design problem they need to approach, or rely on an authoring tool to create a schema, which will not necessarily create the best schema design for the given job. Because the specifications only provide information about the behavior of XML Schemas and validation of documents, figuring out the best way to write or structure a schema can be challenging. In addition, there do exist some approaches to XML Schema that get the job done, but they aren't the best solutions when performance or reusability are taken into account.

In this chapter, we'll take a look at some common approaches to XML Schema that new developers adopt that can lead to heartache, and see some alternatives to those approaches. We will assume that you are familiar with the basic syntax of XML Schemas, and will concentrate on some of the key issues you need to be aware of when working with XML Schemas. We will look at:

❑   When XML Schemas are advantageous over DTDs

❑   Basic ground rules for schemas, such as when to validate, understanding the type of schema to be written, naming conventions, as well as consistency, order, and structure

❑   Mechanisms for creating re-usable structures including global declarations, named complex type definitions, and named model groups

❑   How the introduction of namespaces adds complexity to schema design

❑   Models for schema design, and their benefits and flaws

❑   Tightening up schemas, including occurrence constraints, value constraints with default and fixed content, representing null values in schemas, and creating your own simple types

3.1 Advantages of XML Schemas over DTDs

Although DTDs have been part of the original XML 1.0 recommendation, they do have some severe limitations. For example, they are not written in XML, they have no strong data typing, and they have limited ability to indicate sequence or occurrence of elements. Therefore, the W3C introduced XML Schemas as an alternative to DTDs, with the aim of overcoming these shortcomings and providing a more powerful XML validation language. The advantages of XML Schemas include that XML Schemas:

❑   Are written in XML, not a new syntax we have to learn before we can write a schema, and that we can therefore use existing XML tools (authoring tools, DOM, SAX, XSLT, etc.) to work with our schemas.

❑   Support datatypes that are similar to those used in most common programming languages. We can also create our own datatypes that would add further restrictions to the ones defined by XML Schema. By associating these datatypes with our element content and attribute values, we constrain the allowable structure and make sure that values in the document are of the appropriate type required by the application that will process the document.

❑   Allow schema authors to reuse markup constructs such as content models easily, and the extensible model allows us to create future iterations of schemas with greater ease.

❑   Support namespaces, allowing us to use markup from different namespaces within the same document instances.

❑   Are more powerful than DTDs at constraining content models.

Therefore, there are significant advantages to writing XML Schemas for a vocabulary when starting a new project rather than writing DTDs. If your application uses a pre-existing vocabulary with a DTD, you will need to evaluate the advantages of converting the DTD to a schema on a case-by-case basis. While there are some tools out there to help you do this, they offer more of a kick-start, which then needs refining in order to get the real advantages of XML Schemas. Therefore, this chapter will provide some useful tips in that respect. Examples of these tools include XML Authority from Tibco/Extensibility, which comes as part of TurboXML (http://www.tibco.com/solutions/products/extensibility/turbo_xml.jsp) and XML Spy (http://www.xmlspy.com).

3.2 Basic Ground Rules

Before we start looking at some specific points of schema design, we should cover some basic ground rules that apply to all the schemas that we create. We will quickly look at points concerning the following:

❑   When to validate

❑   Understanding the type of schema you have to create

❑   Naming conventions

❑   Consistency, order, and structure

3.2.1 The Role of Validation – Checking Structures of Documents

The first role of a schema is that it defines the vocabulary that we are to use, and permissible document structures. This allows different people to write instance documents that conform to the schema, and create programs that will deal with document instances.

It is only when we have document instances that have been written or created that we will validate them against a schema. If we use a schema to validate a document instance, it will ensure that:

❑   the document structure is correct

❑   the data held within elements and as the values of attributes are of the correct datatype, are within the range of allowed values, or conform to regular expressions

So, XML validation is a powerful tool. It allows incredibly complex structures (loosely typed, in the case of DTDs, or strongly typed, in the case of schemas) to be validated as they are parsed from a serialized XML document, or created using the DOM.

It should be noted that XML-level validation is not capable of checking all business rules. For example, when validating a purchase request, we will be unable to check whether an account or credit card number is valid, or whether there is enough money in an account to make a purchase.

The first question we should ask is when do we need to validate? To answer this, we need to look at whether there exists a likely risk of getting a document that would not validate against a schema, versus the cost of what happens if we do receive such a document.

3.2.2 To Validate or not to Validate?

Validation of a document instance against a schema will add to any application's load. It can take as many CPU cycles and just as long to validate a document as it does to process it (of course this will vary with different document structures and different processing methods, but is a good rule of thumb). Being aware that errors in an XML source can bring down your application or corrupt a data source, you can do a risk analysis before you start validating each document:

Risks	Costs
Risks involved in not validating XML documents that you accept	Cost in terms of processing overhead
How likely you are to receive an invalid document	Accepting documents that are not valid (the potential damage to your application)

Some applications may require that you don't reject a whole document just because you cannot understand one fragment of the otherwise useful document (such as when dealing with display of medical records). However, this will be acceptable only if the application processing the XML can handle a document with some information that it does not understand.

3.2.2.1 Always Validate Documents during Development and Testing

Validation is very useful during development and debugging; it helps point out errors in the documents you create or try to process. It will also help those who wish to adopt your vocabulary, and will help them integrate.

3.2.2.2 Turn Validation Off only if you can Trust the Source

The primary use of validation is verifying documents that arrive from **uncontrolled sources**, such as orders from business partners or articles from your XML-based web service, where the risk of getting a document that will not be valid is higher. In an exchange, be particularly wary of new participants who have not yet demonstrated an ability to create XML documents that abide by a particular set of rules. So, the first part of the assessment is whether you trust your source.

> *If you are receiving documents from a number of sources, the ability of optional validation (based upon the source of a document instance) is a powerful addition.*

Consider turning validation off when **controlled sources** are more reliable. These sources would include XML generation tools that enforce a particular DTD or schema at authoring time (like Corel's XMetaL), or systems that programmatically generate documents that match a particular schema (like a document generated from SQL Server or Oracle with the help of XML serialization mechanisms built into those platforms). In such cases, turning off validation after testing may seem a more acceptable option.

3.2.2.3 Check how Documents are Created

While you may author some XML documents manually in the development process, you should try to avoid such documents in the production environment at all costs; using authoring tools that enforce a DTD or schema is a good way of doing this.

The use of some program for creating an XML document does *not* ensure the elimination of potential errors. For example, a trading partner changing his or her data source can result in new values outside those that we can deal with, and if these values are going into a database, the value in that field (and by extension, the rest of the file) can be corrupted.

3.2.2.4 The more Complex a Schema, the Greater the Risk

The simpler the document, the easier it is to test, and the easier it is to evaluate whether a source is producing reliable data. When a schema is complicated, with possibly several valid potential document instances, the risk of getting a file that cannot be validated increases. Even if you have checked an initial set of documents from a new source, there may be an uncommon scenario that does not appear in the first tests.

3.2.2.5 Don't Validate Documents that You Create and Receive

If your application creates *and* consumes an XML, validating the document when it is created by one part of your application and received by the next creates unnecessary overhead. The standard method here is to simply validate a document when you receive it, rejecting documents that are not valid before they enter the application – as such, documents could cause the program to stop running or corrupt a data source. Just like receiving attachments with e-mails, the task of checking the file becomes the responsibility of the recipient.

3.2.2.6 Validation is a Lower Cost with Batch Processes

If you are processing documents in real-time, the issue of whether or not to *validate* would have a higher impact on the hardware performance and time taken to process the document than for batch processes. After all, at peak times, you could be doubling your server's workload as well as taking twice as long to process documents by adding validation.

Although it isn't always possible, the option of queuing all incoming XML structures for later processing would mean that you can perform validation when the system is quieter. Also, the overhead incurred for processing all documents would thus have a significantly smaller impact on your system's performance.

3.2.2.7 Summary of Validation Issues

If you have an extremely high level of confidence that the document will be correctly structured, validating the document would only waste cycles, proving what you are almost already positive about. By turning validation off, you'd be recapturing those cycles for use in other processing. In a typical design scenario for transmission, where documents that validate against a particular XML Schema are being exchanged between a closed set of partners, validation is turned on during development; all participants in the document exchange get their code ironed out in order to generate and consume those documents. However, once the code is working properly and is about to be deployed to production, validation should be turned off; the files come from a trusted source, and thus don't need to be validated. When considering validation, keep the following pointers in mind:

❑ Use validation during development, as it will help with error catching and debugging.

❑ Turn validation off only if you can trust the source.

❑ Always validate new sources of documents until you are satisfied with their reliability, even if they are using the same program as other trusted partners.

❑ Do not use handwritten XML documents. If you have to manually author documents, always try to use an authoring tool that enforces the schema.

❑ Do not repeat validation if you create *and* receive the document.

❏ If you can queue or batch process documents, the validation and processing can occur when the system is quiet. Thus, CPU resources and the time taken to process a document are not such great costs.

What's the downside to turning validation off? As I alluded to earlier in the section, attempts at processing an unvalidated document can lead to some pretty strange behavior. Effectively, any piece of code that attempts to access the document can get tripped up – whether it's a DOM or SAX parser, an XSLT stylesheet, or even another trading partner to whom the file is forwarded. These kinds of bugs can be notoriously difficult to identify and track down. Validating the document on the front-end can prevent these types of problems from occurring, but at the aforementioned price of slower processing.

3.2.3 Flexibility of Schemas Should Reflect Predictability of Data

Some schemas strictly control allowable content themselves; others give the author a greater control over how the defined markup can appear in an instance document. The main factor (in which way a schema leans) is the subject and purpose of the data being marked up. Although XML is very popular for marking up unstructured data, it is also widely used in representations of highly structured data. So, the flexibility of the schema should reflect the predictability of the data being marked up.

If you are writing a schema allowing authors to mark up books, you will need a lot of flexibility in the structure of the document (the chapters' numbers are not fixed, the numbers of paragraphs under a heading may vary, emphasized text and cross-references do not occur at the same place in a paragraph). Here, an author needs **descriptive** powers. Schemas that deal with **unpredictable** structures are sometimes know as **permissive** schemas.

However, if you were working on a project that represents account transaction information, there will be a minimum amount of information that would be required for processing the transaction, and therefore the structure would be quite **predictable**. Additional information would not be of any use even if it were collected. Therefore, the schema can be quite **prescriptive** in how it allows authors to mark up data. Furthermore, you may require a consistent structure where information appears in the same order for each document instance, so that processing applications can deal with it more efficiently. These schemas are **restrictive** or **inflexible** about how a document can be written.

> **When writing a schema, you are trying to restrict the allowable content of a document instance that can be said to conform to the schema, at the same time retaining the flexibility needed for the data at hand to be of use.**

71

In data-oriented schemas (which often represent internal data structures such as those imposed by a relational database, or properties of objects) we would want to enforce the strongest possible constraints, while still faithfully modeling the data source. XML Schemas offer us several tools for this, such as the ability to create our own simple types, value constraints, and occurrence constraints, all of which we meet in this chapter.

3.2.4 Follow Naming Conventions

By now, you should be in the practice of creating element and attribute names that are as self-describing as possible. Here are some additional pointers to remember:

❏ Element and attribute names should be **intuitive** to the user; they should reflect the experience of those who will use them.

- Be wary of regional variations that affect the domain you are working in; for example, the use of zip versus postal codes, pants versus trousers, etc.

- Use only the abbreviations that are standard abbreviations, such as Dr for Doctor, and only if they will make sense to those who use the document. With costs of storage and bandwidth constantly falling, unless you are dealing with gigabytes of data, abbreviations can cause more problems than they are worth.

❏ Do not **overload** names. For example, when representing billing and shipping addresses, do not use the same Address element for each, but rather, create separate BillingAddress and ShippingAddress elements. If you use the same element name for two different types of information, you will have to rely on a processing application to determine the element's context (this can be quite resource-intensive, especially for SAX-based applications).

❏ Wherever possible, use defined standards, such as ISBN numbers for uniquely identifying a book, or other industry-specific standards – those created by standards bodies such as ISO are ideal.

❏ Within a type, give consistency to your names by using similar names for like items. For example, you might have elements representing a supplier, customer, and employee, each requiring a unique identifier; so, using similar names such as supplierID, customerID, and employeeID for the identifiers makes it more intuitive to new users.

❏ Give your names consistency across types by using slightly different naming conventions for all elements compared with all attributes. For example, my personal preference is to use UpperCamelCase for all element names, and lowerCamelCase for all attribute names.

❏ Names that use more than one word are easier to read if all new words start with a capital letter.

❑ When creating a named complex type, use the class of information you are modeling followed by the word `Type` (for example, `AddressType`), and when creating a named model group, add the suffix `Group`.

3.2.5 Create Consistent, Ordered Structures

If two structures are similar, we should model them in a consistent manner. There are two ways in which we can apply consistency here:

❑ **Requiring the same items of information.** Whenever you have similar structures such as addresses, make sure they are consistently structured (for example, have the same element content model or carry the same attributes).

❑ **Requiring the items of information to appear in the same fixed order**. This order should fit in with the users' expectations, and their experience of similar objects in the real world.

When users expect the information to appear in a fixed order (say, in addresses), following *this* order would make the vocabulary easier to learn (note that some Scandinavian countries put the house number *after* the street name rather than before it). If there is no fixed order in the information you are marking up, you will need to ask yourself whether specifying an order will make the items easier to remember. As you can see, fitting in with users' expectations is very important.

Consistent structures simplify the writing of code for processing documents, as the same code sections can be used to process similar structures. Indeed, when ordering elements in documents, the tighter we can constrain a structure, the more we can optimize the code for that structure.

The use of the `minOccurs` and `maxOccurs` occurrence constraints in XML Schemas helps us define the number of times an element can appear in an instance document, while the sequence compositor allows us to restrict the order in which the elements can appear.

Having looked at some of the basic ground rules for writing schemas, let's look at some real examples and find out what we can do to write better schemas.

3.3 Same Constraints, Different Representations

When writing a schema, either manually or by using a schema-authoring tool, there can be many different ways of representing constraints upon a single structure. In the following section, we will introduce some of the different approaches we can take, and discuss the conditions under which each approach would be suitable. In particular, we will look at:

❑ Ways of reusing structures rather than repeating element and attribute declarations

❑ How to introduce and control the appearance of namespaces in instance documents

❑ Common models for schema design and when to use which model

❑ How to tighten up the constraints in schemas you write

By way of an introduction to some of these issues, we will look at why we should only create schemas that mirror document structures in small rigid schemas.

3.3.1 Do not Always Mirror Document Structures

The temptation when writing a schema is to simply follow the structure of instance documents. For example, suppose we were dealing with invoices like this one (eg1.xml):

```
<Invoice>
   <CustomerName>Kevin Williams</CustomerName>
   <BillingAddress>
      <AddressLine1>100 Nowhere Lane</AddressLine1>
      <City>Nowheresville</City>
      <State>VA</State>
      <Zip>24182</Zip>
   </BillingAddress>
   <ShippingAddress>
      <AddressLine1>10 Somewhere Lane</AddressLine1>
      <City>Somewheresville</City>
      <State>VA</State>
      <Zip>24361</Zip>
   </ShippingAddress>
   <Item>
      <ID>38-19273</ID>
      <Description>3-inch Grommets</Description>
      <Count>37</Count>
      <TotalCost>37.00</TotalCost>
   </Item>
   <Item>
      <ID>22-18272</ID>
      <Description>2-inch Widgets</Description>
```

```
              <Count>22</Count>
              <TotalCost>11.00</TotalCost>
         </Item>
    </Invoice>
```

Here, we are tempted to model the entire document as a single complex type, and nest other anonymous complex types inside it as follows (eg1.xsd):

```
<xs:schema xmlns:xs="http://www.w3.org/2001/XMLSchema">
   <xs:element name="Invoice">
      <xs:complexType>
         <xs:sequence>
            <xs:element name="CustomerName" type="xs:string" />
            <xs:element name="BillingAddress">
               <xs:complexType>
                  <xs:sequence>
                     <xs:element name="AddressLine1" type="xs:string" />
                     <xs:element name="City" type="xs:string" />
                     <xs:element name="State" type="xs:string" />
                     <xs:element name="Zip" type="xs:string" />
                  </xs:sequence>
               </xs:complexType>
            </xs:element>
            <xs:element name="ShippingAddress">
               <xs:complexType>
                  <xs:sequence>
                     <xs:element name="AddressLine1" type="xs:string" />
                     <xs:element name="City" type="xs:string" />
                     <xs:element name="State" type="xs:string" />
                     <xs:element name="Zip" type="xs:string" />
                  </xs:sequence>
               </xs:complexType>
            </xs:element>
            <xs:element name="Item" maxOccurs="unbounded">
               <xs:complexType>
                  <xs:sequence>
                     <xs:element name="ID" type="xs:string" />
                     <xs:element name="Description" type="xs:string" />
                     <xs:element name="Count" type="xs:unsignedShort" />
                     <xs:element name="TotalCost" type="xs:decimal" />
                  </xs:sequence>
               </xs:complexType>
            </xs:element>
         </xs:sequence>
      </xs:complexType>
   </xs:element>
</xs:schema>
```

This approach is actually known as the **Russian Doll Design** because of the way child elements are declared inside their parents' declarations like Russian Dolls. However, you might notice a couple of drawbacks with this design.

3.3.1.1 Look for Reuse when you have Repeating Structures

The child elements (or content model) for the BillingAddress and ShippingAddress elements are the same, but we have repeated their declarations for each type of address. When we have repeating structures, we should look at reuse mechanisms (discussed later).

3.3.1.2 Deeply Nested Complex Types are not Flexible

As a side issue of reusability, this design is not very flexible. If we went international with our application, we would have to add country codes wherever there is an instance of an address – you can imagine in a more typical system the headache this would cause, finding a dozen or more places in the structure where Country needed to be added.

3.3.1.3 Mirror Document Structures only when Writing Small Rigid Schemas

Nesting anonymous complex types inside a complex type associated with the root element's declaration is fine for fairly rigid small documents, such as acknowledgements of receipt of a document in a messaging application. Where little flexibility is required and less data is involved, declarations can neatly sit inside the declaration for their parent element.

However, as the structures get larger and less predictable, the schema gets much harder to read. Also, we will not get any of the benefits of reuse. The Russian Doll approach is thus far from ideal when marking up very flexible data such as books or papers, or data with class-like information where a number of elements share the same content model.

We will re-visit the Russian Doll Design along with other models later in the chapter. Having taken a look at one example of how structure can affect our design, we need to look at the topics of reuse and namespaces so as to fully understand the issues that each design will raise.

3.4 How and Why to Reuse

The way in which we can reuse XML Schema constructs is very powerful. In DTDs, we were largely limited to reusing element content already defined in content models and parameter entities if we wanted to represent reusable constructs. Within XML Schema, however, we can use a number of mechanisms.

There are two available types of reuse:

❑   **Internal reuse**, where we reuse schema components that we have already defined in the schema with which we are working

❑   **Cross schema reuse**, where we make use of schema components that have been globally defined in other schemas

By internally reusing constructs, we can use the following features of XML Schema:

❑   Reference elements and attributes that we have already declared (including element content models).

❑ Define named complex types for representing element content models that represent structures for classes of elements.

❑ Define named model groups to help define content models by grouping together related elements.

❑ Create new complex types by extending and restricting the named complex types that we have already defined. Note that if you are extending a complex type, you are limited in that you can only add to the end of the structure (not at the beginning or middle), and also that restriction involves declaring all elements again.

❑ Employ attribute groups where several attributes apply to the same elements.

❑ Use substitution groups to reuse the definition of the context in which an element can be reused (unfortunately, we do not have space to cover this point in this chapter).

As we will see throughout the chapter, there are several issues regarding when to use named complex types, and when to use named model groups. As a general rule of thumb, however:

❑ use a complex type for defining class-like information

❑ use a named model group when you are just defining a re-usable structure

3.4.1 Reuse Mechanisms

One of the prime reasons for not mirroring a document structure when creating a schema (as in the example above, which used the Russian Doll method) is that you will not make use of the excellent reusable features of XML Schemas. In this section, we will look at three features in particular:

❑ Globally Declared Elements and Attributes

❑ Named Complex Types

❑ Named Model Groups

Having looked at these, we then need to address some namespace issues before coming back to schema design models that employ these techniques.

3.4.1.1 Globally Declared Elements – Reusing Elements and their Content Model by Reference

It is important to distinguish between global and local element declarations:

❑ Global element declarations are children of the root schema element

❑ Local element declarations are nested further inside the schema structure, and are not direct children of the root schema element

77

Once elements have been declared globally, any other complex type can use that element declaration by creating a reference to it (they are even available to other schemas). This is especially helpful when an element and its content model are used in other element declarations and complex type definitions, since they enable us to reuse the content model.

> *You should be aware that if your instance documents make use of namespaces, there are greater differences between global and local element declarations, because globally declared elements must be explicitly qualified in the instance document, whereas local definitions should not always be qualified. We look at this in Section 3.5: Namespaces, which follows our initial discussion on reuse.*

In the following example of a classifieds application using XML, you can see that the ClassifiedAd element is repeated in each category of the ad (eg2.xml):

```
<ClassifiedAdListings>

   <MusicalInstruments>

      <ClassifiedAd>
         <Item>Gibson Les Paul Guitar</Item>
         <Description>Black, 1975, great condition,
                       plays beautifully.</Description>
         <Price>850.00</Price>
         <TelNo>02084419229</TelNo>
      </ClassifiedAd>

      <ClassifiedAd>...</ClassifiedAd>

   </MusicalInstruments>

   <Computers>
      <ClassifiedAd>...</ClassifiedAd>
   </Computers>

</ClassifiedAdListings>
```

So, in the schema, if we declare the ClassifiedAd element globally, we can reuse it in the elements representing each category of the ad, rather than having to repeat the declarations (eg2.xsd):

```
<?xml version="1.0" ?>

<xs:schema xmlns:xs = "http://www.w3.org/2001/XMLSchema">
   <xs:element name="ClassifiedAd">
      <xs:complexType>
         <xs:sequence>
            <xs:element name="Item" type="xs:string" />
            <xs:element name="Description" type="xs:string" />
            <xs:element name="Price" type="xs:decimal" />
            <xs:element name="TelNo" type="xs:integer" />
         </xs:sequence>
      </xs:complexType>
```

```
        </xs:element>

        <xs:element name="ClassifiedAdListings">
           <xs:complexType>
              <xs:sequence>

                 <xs:element name="MusicalInstruments">
                    <xs:complexType>
                       <xs:sequence>
                          <xs:element ref="ClassifiedAd"
                                    minOccurs="0" maxOccurs="unbounded" />
                       </xs:sequence>
                    </xs:complexType>
                 </xs:element>

                 <xs:element name="Computers">
                    <xs:complexType>
                       <xs:sequence>
                          <xs:element ref="ClassifiedAd"
                                    minOccurs="0" maxOccurs="unbounded" />
                       </xs:sequence>
                    </xs:complexType>
                 </xs:element>

              </xs:sequence>
           </xs:complexType>
        </xs:element>

     </xs:schema>
```

Having defined the ClassifiedAd element globally, it can be reused easily with the ref attribute on the element declaration. Here is the key line that allows us to do this:

```
<xs:element ref="ClassifiedAd" minOccurs="0" maxOccurs="unbounded" />
```

With this mechanism, we do not have to repeat the element declarations inside each element.

This approach is very helpful when you have an element that can appear in more than one place in a document instance, such as a paragraph in a chapter. If you just want to repeat the content model for the element, and not the element itself (in instances such as using the same address structure for BillingAddress and ShippingAddress elements), you should look at creating a named complex type or a named model group, which we will deal with next.

Remember that element declarations carrying the ref attribute will never have a name attribute, since they are referring to a named item, and they will always be empty elements because it cannot contain a complex type definition.

3.4.1.1.1 Occurrence Constraints cannot be used on Global Declarations

Note that you cannot declare minOccurs and maxOccurs on global elements, only on the local element declarations, as shown in the previous example.

79

3.4.1.1.2 Globally Declared Elements can be used as the Root Element of a Schema

A side effect of declaring an element globally is that it can be used as the root element of a document. Therefore, the following fragment could be validated using this schema:

```
<ClassifiedAd>
    <Item>Gibson Les Paul Guitar</Item>
    <Description>Black, 1975, great condition,
                 plays beautifully.</Description>
    <Price>850.00</Price>
    <TelNo>02084419229</TelNo>
</ClassifiedAd>
```

The only way to enforce having only one root element in a document is to have only one globally defined element, and carefully nest other element declarations inside complex type definitions.

This does not mean that the side effect is always bad; sometimes it is actually helpful because you can create a structure that can be used to validate fragments of documents without having to define separate schemas for each fragment. For example, when working on some schemas representing documents, such as a book schema, you might want to globally declare the Chapter elements so that one chapter is a valid document instance, and the whole book does not need to be sent or validated when only one chapter is required.

3.4.1.2 Complex Type Definitions – for Class-like Definitions

In XML Schema, an element declaration is the association of a name with a type. If we are dealing with text-only element content, we can associate the name of the element with one of the built-in simple types, or with a simple type that we may have defined ourselves. However, every time we want an element to carry attributes or create a content model with child elements within the element, we must create a complex type.

The complex types we have seen so far in this chapter have all been **anonymous complex types** – they were created within the complexType element nested inside the element declaration. For example:

```
<xs:element name="Address">
    <xs:complexType>
        <xs:sequence>
            <xs:element name="Address1" type="xs:string" />
            <xs:element name="Address2" type="xs:string" />
            <xs:element name="Town" type="xs:string" />
            <xs:element name="City" type="xs:string" />
            <xs:element name="State" type="xs:string" />
            <xs:element name="ZipCode" type="xs:string" />
        </xs:sequence>
    </xs:complexType>
</xs:element>
```

We can also create **named complex types** by defining the complex types globally (as a child of the root schema element) and giving them a name:

```
<xs:schema xmlns:xs="http://www.w3.org/2001/XMLSchema">
...
    <xs:complexType name="AddressType">
        <xs:sequence>
            <xs:element name="Address1" type="xs:string" />
            <xs:element name="Address2" type="xs:string" />
            <xs:element name="Town" type="xs:string" />
            <xs:element name="City" type="xs:string" />
            <xs:element name="State" type="xs:string" />
            <xs:element name="ZipCode" type="xs:string" />
        </xs:sequence>
    </xs:complexType>
...
</xs:schema>
```

Having defined the named complex type globally, as a direct child of the schema element, we can use its name as the value of the type attribute in an element declaration, as follows:

```
<xs:element name="BillingAddress" type="AddressType" />
<xs:element name="ShippingAddress" type="AddressType" />
```

Here, we are indicating that the respective BillingAddress and ShippingAddress elements can only contain the markup defined by the AddressType complex type. Indeed, we could have any number of elements associated with this type.

> **Named complex types are very helpful for representing class-like information in data-orientated applications.**

3.4.1.2.1 You Cannot Validate a Fragment against a Complex Type (as you could with Globally Declared Elements)

We saw that one side effect of declaring an element globally is that it can be used as the root element of a document, and therefore, a fragment could be validated using the same schema.

When elements are declared inside a named complex type, they are not globally declared, so this is no longer an issue. However, we still have the benefit of being able to reuse the elements. (Another option we will look at in a moment is **named model groups**.)

3.4.1.2.2 Complex Types are Associated with Containing Elements

You will see a structural difference between creating named complex types to associate with element declarations, and using globally defined elements.

When you associate a named complex type with an element declaration, the content model defined by the complex type goes inside that element. For example, take the following snippet of a schema:

```
<xs:schema xmlns:xs="http://www.w3.org/2001/XMLSchema">
...
    <xs:complexType name="AddressType">
        <xs:sequence>
            <xs:element name="Address1" type="xs:string" />
            <xs:element name="Address2" type="xs:string" />
            <xs:element name="Town" type="xs:string" />
            <xs:element name="City" type="xs:string" />
            <xs:element name="State" type="xs:string" />
            <xs:element name="ZipCode" type="xs:string" />
        </xs:sequence>
    </xs:complexType>
...
    <xs:element name="BillingAddress" type="AddressType" />
    <xs:element name="ShippingAddress" type="AddressType" />
...
</xs:schema>
```

Here, the Address1, Address2, Town, City, State, and ZipCode elements will go inside the BillingAddress and ShippingAddress elements:

```
<BillingAddress>
    <Address1></Address1>
    <Address2></Address2>
    <Town></Town>
    <City></City>
    <State></State>
    <ZipCode></ZipCode>
</BillingAddress>
```

However, if we had declared an Address element globally, and then used it by reference, we would end up with a different structure. Here is the snippet of the schema with the Address element declared globally:

```
<xs:schema xmlns:xs="http://www.w3.org/2001/XMLSchema">
...
<xs:element name="AddressType">
    <xs:complexType>
        <xs:sequence>
            <xs:element name="Address1" type="xs:string" />
            <xs:element name="Address2" type="xs:string" />
            <xs:element name="Town" type="xs:string" />
            <xs:element name="City" type="xs:string" />
            <xs:element name="State" type="xs:string" />
            <xs:element name="ZipCode" type="xs:string" />
        </xs:sequence>
    </xs:complexType>
</xs:element>
...
<xs:element name="BillingAddress">
    <xs:complexType>
        <xs:sequence>
```

```
                 <xs:element ref="Address" />
            </xs:sequence>
         </xs:complexType>
   </xs:element>
   <xs:element name="ShippingAddress">
      <xs:complexType>
         <xs:sequence>
               <xs:element ref="Address" />
         </xs:sequence>
      </xs:complexType>
   </xs:element>
   . . .
   </xs:schema>
```

In this case, we would have all the address details contained inside an `Address`
element, which itself is inside the `BillingAddress` and `ShippingAddress` elements:

```
<BillingAddress>
   <Address>
      <Address1></Address1>
      <Address2></Address2>
      <Town></Town>
      <City></City>
      <State></State>
      <ZipCode></ZipCode>
   </Address>
</BillingAddress>
<ShippingAddress>
   <Address>
      . . .
   </Address>
</ShippingAddress>
```

Therefore, you should only declare an element globally when you want to reuse the
element *and* its content model (as we did in the earlier example of classified ads). If
you are representing class-like information, named complex types are ideal for
content models.

> *Although it is possible to derive new types from a named complex type by*
> *extending or restricting the named complex type, it should only be done if*
> *there is a real value in doing so – for example, when representing object-*
> *oriented concepts such as inheritance and polymorphism. Deriving new*
> *types by restrictions of a complex type, in particular, requires a thorough*
> *understanding of the topic. In most cases, the same results can be achieved*
> *using named model groups.*

There's an interesting aspect of XML Schema to be noted here; the ability to associate
the name of an element in its declaration with a type, whether named or anonymous,
means that two elements with the same name *can* have different content models
provided they are in different scopes (generally, this would be confusing for other
users and should be avoided).

3.4.1.3 Named Model Groups as Building Blocks for Content Models

The **named model group** is very useful as a building block for creating element content models that we want to reuse, because it allows us to group together a set of element declarations inside an element called group, whose name attribute gives the group its name. Having defined a group globally (which means it is a direct child of the schema element, just like when we created a named complex type) we can reuse it in other complex types within this (and any other) schema.

We create a reference to the group by using another group element, this time taking an attribute called ref, whose value is the name of the group (in the same way we created a reference to a global element declaration).

In the following example, we define an AddressGroup globally, and reuse it inside BillingAddress and ShippingAddress elements (eg3.xsd):

```
<?xml version="1.0" ?>
<xs:schema xmlns:xs="http://www.w3.org/2001/XMLSchema">

    <xs:group name="AddressGroup">
        <xs:sequence>
            <xs:element name="Address1" type="xs:string" />
            <xs:element name="Address2" type="xs:string" />
            <xs:element name="Town" type="xs:string" />
            <xs:element name="City" type="xs:string" />
            <xs:element name="State" type="xs:string" />
            <xs:element name="ZipCode" type="xs:string" />
        </xs:sequence>
    </xs:group>

    <xs:element name="Invoice">
        <xs:complexType>
            <xs:sequence>
                <xs:element name="CustomerName" type="xs:string" />
                <xs:element name="OrderID" type="xs:integer" />
                <xs:element name="InvoiceAmount" type="xs:decimal" />
                <xs:element name="BillingAddress">
                    <xs:complexType>
                        <xs:sequence>
                            <xs:group ref="AddressGroup"   />
                        </xs:sequence>
                    </xs:complexType>
                </xs:element>
                <xs:element name="ShippingAddress">
                    <xs:complexType>
                        <xs:sequence>
                            <xs:group ref="AddressGroup"   />
                        </xs:sequence>
                    </xs:complexType>
                </xs:element>
            </xs:sequence>
        </xs:complexType>
    </xs:element>

</xs:schema>
```

As you can see, having created the `AddressGroup` named model group globally, we reference it inside the `BillingAddress` and `ShippingAddress` elements.

3.4.1.3.1 You Cannot Validate a Fragment against a Named Model Group (as you could with Globally Declared Elements)

We saw that one side effect of declaring an element globally is that it can be used as the root element of a document, and therefore, a fragment could be validated using the same schema.

When elements are declared inside a named model group, they are not globally declared, so this is no longer an issue; however, we still have the benefit of being able to reuse the elements.

3.4.1.3.2 You can Create Repeating Groups with Named Model Groups

Note that named model groups can also take the occurrence constraints `minOccurs` and `maxOccurs`, which is very helpful when building repeating structures in particular when representing comma-delimited formats as XML.

3.4.1.3.3 Avoid Overuse of Named Complex Types

When you learn to write named complex types, it is very tempting to use them to declare content models for each element. However, referencing named model groups within anonymous complex types, as we did in the previous example, is usually a better option.

The syntax for using named model groups to represent element content models is slightly longer than when we just associate a named complex type with an element. However, there are good reasons for writing those extra lines:

❑ You can only associate one complex type with each element, whereas you can nest several model groups inside a complex type, which means that named model groups are more flexible as building blocks for content models.

❑ If several elements use the same named complex type and you just want to add to the content model for just one of these elements, you either have to create a new complex type for that element, or derive a complex type for that element using the complicated extension or restriction mechanisms. If you are using named model groups within an anonymous complex type, you can just add declarations to the anonymous complex type for that element.

❑ Using the extension method provided by XML Schema to extend complex types with new elements, you can only add new elements at the end of ones already in the complex type. For example, when representing names, you might have a FirstName and LastName element in a complex type called NameType. If you then want to add a Title element for Mr., Mrs., Miss, Dr., etc., before the FirstName element, you cannot use extensions, because this element would go after the LastName element; you have to create a new complex type. If you use named model groups as building blocks for complex types, you can add new element declarations before or at the end of the group that you reference.

❑ Using the restriction method provided by XML Schema to restrict complex types, not only do you have to learn another set of rules (rules we do not have space to go into in this chapter), but you also have to repeat all element declarations that make up the complex type in the first place. Therefore, it is not quicker than writing a new named model group.

Unless you are trying to represent object-oriented principles, such as inheritance and polymorphism, where you need to derive a new complex type that represents class-like data, then named model groups are a lot more flexible, extendable, and easier to learn than named complex types.

Having looked at the three main mechanisms for reuse of content models, we now turn our attention to namespace use in XML Schemas, as there are some obstacles just waiting to trip us up. Having looked at namespace complexities, we will be able to look at some of the common models for writing schemas, and issues we face with these models.

3.5 Namespaces

If you wanted to support namespaces with DTDs, it would involve complicated workarounds that would make the DTD very hard to read, and difficult for users to understand. XML Schema's flexible support for XML Namespaces is one of its great advantages over DTDs. However, it is also a minefield to those who are not prepared. Thus, it is important to carefully consider the key issues that we need to be aware of when working with namespaces in our schemas and instance documents.

This section assumes that you are familiar with XML Namespaces and the concept of scope in XML Namespaces.

3.5.1 The Three Uses of Namespace in XML Schemas

XML Schema uses namespaces in three areas:

1. Within the schemas we write, so as to distinguish between the elements, attributes, and types that we are creating, and the markup defined by the XML Recommendation, similar to that introduced when creating named complex types. We look at this point in detail in the next section.

2. The three namespaces that XML Schema defines for itself:

    ❑   http://www.w3.org/2001/XMLSchema, which identifies the markup of the XML Schema recommendation (such as element, attribute, complexType, group, sequence, choice, and all). This is the main namespace used in the root element of our schemas so far.

    ❑   http://www.w3.org/2001/XMLSchema-datatypes, which contains a copy of the built-in types that XML Schema defines. Since the built-in datatypes are present in the main namespace (http://www.w3.org/2001/XMLSchema) as well, we do not need to use this in the schemas that we write.

    ❑   http://www.w3.org/2001/XMLSchema-instance, the XML Schema for instances that namespaces used in the instance documents. In instance documents, we use four attributes from this namespace:

        •   xsi:schemaLocation to indicate where a processor might find a copy of the schema(s) used to author the document, and the vocabulary defined in the schema belongs to a namespace that the processor need not search for that particular schema

        •   xsi:noNamespaceSchemaLocation to indicate where a processor might find a copy of the schema used to author the document although the vocabulary defined in the schema does not belong to a namespace

        •   xsi:nil to indicate that an element has a nil value to distinguish between a zero-length string and no given entry for a field (which is important when we are using a datatype such as an integer, because the parse would treat an empty element as an empty string, which would not be a valid integer value)

        •   xsi:type for when we want to indicate that we are using a complex type derived from the one associated with the element name in the schema

3. So that we can validate an instance document against markup of a given namespace, or indeed a document that is marked up using elements and attributes from multiple namespaces.

It is this third use of namespaces that will take up most of this section, so that you can see how to create schemas and instance documents, whose markup belongs to a namespace. Before we do, let's take a look at *why* we have been qualifying elements and types from the XML Schema namespace.

87

3.5.2 Distinguish between your Elements, Attributes, and Types, and those of XML Schema

You might have been wondering why, in the examples so far, we prefixed the elements and types from the XML Schema namespace with xs:. Why didn't we just use the XML Schema namespace as the default namespace for the whole schema? If we had used a default namespace in that way, the schema might have looked like this:

```
<schema xmlns="http://www.w3.org/2001/XMLSchema">
...
    <complexType name="AddressType">
      <sequence>
        <element name="Address1" type="string" />
        <element name="Address2" type="string" />
        <element name="Town" type="string" />
        <element name="City" type="string" />
        <element name="State" type="string" />
        <element name="ZipCode" type="string" />
      </sequence>
    </complexType>
...
    <element name="BillingAddress" type="AddressType" />
    <element name="ShippingAddress" type="AddressType" />
...
</schema>
```

The problem with this is not obvious at first, but look at how we associate the BillingAddress and ShippingAddress elements with the AddressType. Because we have used the XML Schema namespace as the default namespace for this document, an XML Schema-aware processor will infer that the AddressType is in the XML Schema namespace. Obviously, there is no AddressType in the XML Schema namespace – we just defined that at the top of the schema – so this schema is not valid.

To distinguish between the elements, attributes, and types that we create, and those that belong to the XML Schema namespace, either all of our markup must be explicitly qualified, or the markup from the XML Schema namespace must be qualified, or indeed, both. In our examples, we have qualified the markup from the XML Schema namespace:

```
<xs:schema xmlns:xs="http://www.w3.org/2001/XMLSchema">
...
    <xs:complexType name="AddressType">
      <xs:sequence>
        <xs:element name="Address1" type="xs:string" />
        <xs:element name="Address2" type="xs:string" />
        <xs:element name="Town" type="xs:string" />
        <xs:element name="City" type="xs:string" />
        <xs:element name="State" type="xs:string" />
        <xs:element name="ZipCode" type="xs:string" />
      </xs:sequence>
    </xs:complexType>
...
    <xs:element name="BillingAddress" type="AddressType" />
```

```
        <xs:element name="ShippingAddress" type="AddressType" />
    ...
    </xs:schema>
```

As you can see, the XML Schema-aware processor will now know that the AddressType is not found in the `http://www.w3.org/2001/XMLSchema` namespace, and will not look for it there.

3.5.3 Introducing Namespaces into your Markup

When it comes to writing a schema whose markup should belong to a namespace, we can indicate whether an element or attribute should be qualified in an instance document – be this explicitly using a prefix, or implicitly by default. This is another great advantage of XML Schemas over DTDs, and is a mechanism that allows us to validate documents that contain markup belonging to more than one namespace.

When you write a schema, the elements, attributes, and types that you create either belong to a namespace, or have no namespace. In the schemas we have seen so far, the declarations and definitions have had no namespace (if you look back, none of the instance documents contain namespaces). So, what happens if we want our markup to belong to a namespace, and the instance documents to reflect this?

When it comes to checking that an instance document conforms to a schema, the schema processor needs to check the use of elements and attributes against the declarations that it finds in one or more schemas. This means that if an instance document contains markup declared in more than one schema, we will need to be able to distinguish the schema that the processor should use when checking elements and attributes in the instance document.

If a document indicates that the elements and attributes it contains belong to a specific namespace, the processor will try to check the document markup against the declarations and definitions that belong to that namespace. Therefore, if the schema does not inform the processor that the markup it defines belongs to the same namespace as that indicated in the instance document, the processor might not be able to validate the document. This is why, when our markup belongs to a namespace, it is important that both the schema and the document instances specify the namespaces to which the elements and attributes belong.

As we introduce namespaces, complexities regarding the structure of schemas and how elements and attributes need to be represented in the instance documents creep in, and *where* you declare an element in a schema will affect its representation in an instance document. So, let's start by looking at how we create a vocabulary that belongs to a namespace.

3.5.4 Creating Vocabularies that Belong to a Namespace

So far we have been using examples where neither the instance documents nor the schemas indicate that the markup we have been creating belongs to a particular namespace. To indicate that the elements, attributes, and types declared and defined in a schema belong to a namespace, we have to add an attribute called `targetNamespace` (whose value is the namespace that we want our markup to belong to) to the root `schema` element.

As soon as we declare a **target namespace**, something interesting happens. For the purposes of this example, we will work with a very simple schema for customer names. To illustrate the point in this example, the `LastName` element has been defined globally, and we use a reference to it as part of the content model for the `Customer` element:

```xml
<?xml version="1.0" ?>
<xs:schema xmlns:xs="http://www.w3.org/2001/XMLSchema"
              targetNamespace="http://www.example.org/Customers"
              xmlns="http://www.example.org/Customers">

    <xs:element name="Customer">
        <xs:complexType>
            <xs:sequence>
                <xs:element name="FirstName" />
                <xs:element name="MiddleInitial" />
                <xs:element ref="LastName" />
            </xs:sequence>
        <xs:complexType>
    </xs:element>

    <xs:element name="LastName" type="xs:string" />

</xs:schema>
```

On the root `schema` element, you can see we have added the `targetNamespace` attribute to indicate the namespace to which the markup we are creating belongs. Also, the value of the `xmlns` attribute is the same as the target namespace so that it becomes the default namespace for the document. By making the target namespace the default namespace, we do not have to qualify the elements, attributes, and types (the ones we have declared and defined in this document) when we want to reuse them.

Here is a conforming instance document; as you can see, the namespace is used in a rather interesting fashion:

```xml
<?xml version="1.0" ?>
<cust:Customer xmlns:cust="http://www.example.org/Customers"
         xmlns:xsi="http://www.w3.org/2001/XMLSchema-Instance"
         xsi:schemaLocation="Customers.xsd">
    <FirstName>Kevin</FirstName>
    <MiddleInitial>G</MiddleInitial>
    <cust:LastName>Williams</cust:LastName>
</cust:Customer>
```

90

As you can see, both the `Customer` and the `LastName` elements must be qualified as belonging to the `http://www.example.org/Customers` target namespace. The following example, where we make `http://www.example.org/Customers` the default namespace, would not be a valid instance document:

```xml
<?xml version="1.0" ?>
<Customer xmlns="http://www.example.org/Customers">
    <FirstName>Kevin</FirstName>
    <MiddleInitial>G</MiddleInitial>
    <LastName>Williams</LastName>
</Customer>
```

The second example is not valid. This is so because globally declared elements and attributes must be qualified, whereas locally declared elements and attributes need not always be qualified. Indeed, in this example, they must not be qualified (as we will soon see, you only qualify locally declared elements and attributes when you are specifically indicated to do so). If your definitions and declarations do not belong to a namespace, you can ignore this problem, but as soon as you introduce target namespaces to schemas, your instance documents will have to obey this requirement; therefore, it is something to be highly aware of.

The reason behind this is that globally declared elements, attributes, and types are added to the target namespace, while the locally declared elements and attributes belong in no namespace, and are interpreted according to their containing element. This schema indicates that the `Customer` element and the `LastName` element are to be added to the target namespace. Therefore, to associate the elements in the instance document with the information items in a schema, they need to be qualified. It is the target namespaces in the schema that control the validation of corresponding namespaces in the instance document.

3.5.5 Requiring all Elements and Attributes to be Qualified

There are two very helpful attributes we can add to the root `schema` element to indicate whether we want our elements and attributes to be qualified or not. These act as a global switch for the whole document, and indicate that all of the elements and attributes declared in the document (unless we specifically declare otherwise) should be qualified.

These two attributes are `elementFormDefault` and `attributeFormDefault`, and the default value for both is `unqualified`, which is why only globally declared elements and attributes need to be qualified in instance documents when the attributes are not added and given a value of `qualified`. Let's see what happens when we give these attributes a value of `qualified`.

Here, we revisit our simple Customer schema with `elementFormDefault` and `attributeFormDefault` set to qualified:

```xml
<?xml version="1.0" ?>
<schema xmlns="http://www.w3.org/2001/XMLSchema"
                targetNamespace="http://www.example.org/Customers"
                xmlns:cust="http://www.example.org/Customers"
                elementFormDefault="qualified"
                attributeFormDefault="qualified">

    <element name="Customer">
        <complexType>
            <sequence>
                <element name="FirstName" type="string" />
                <element name="MiddleInitial" type="string" />
                <element ref="cust:LastName" />
            </sequence>
            <attribute name="clubCardMember" type="boolean" />
            <attribute ref="cust:customerID" />
        </complexType>
    </element>

    <element name="LastName" type="string" />
    <attribute name="customerID" type="integer" />

</schema>
```

Now let's look at how a valid instance document might look. We could qualify each element and attribute individually, as follows:

```xml
<?xml version="1.0" ?>
<cust:Customer xmlns:cust="http://www.w3.org/2001/Customer"
                cust:clubCardMember="true"
                cust:customerID="12553">
    <cust:FirstName>Kevin</cust:FirstName>
    <cust:MiddleInitial>G</cust:MiddleInitial>
    <cust:LastName>Williams</cust:LastName>
</cust:Customer>
```

However, the following example, using a default namespace in the root `Customer` element, would *not* be valid, since unqualified attributes are in the null namespace rather than in the default namespace:

```xml
<?xml version="1.0" ?>
<Customer xmlns="http://www.w3.org/2001/Customer"
                clubCardMember="true"
                customerID="12553">
    <FirstName>Kevin</FirstName>
    <MiddleInitial>G</MiddleInitial>
    <LastName>Williams</LastName>
</Customer>
```

Therefore, we still need to explicitly qualify references to attributes on the root element as shown in the next example. Here, the default namespace works for elements, but we still need to qualify the attributes:

```
<?xml version="1.0" ?>
<Customer xmlns="http://www.w3.org/2001/Customer"
               xmlns:cust="http://www.w3.org/2001/Customer"
               cust:clubCardMember="true"
               cust:customerID="12553">
   <FirstName>Kevin</FirstName>
   <MiddleInitial>G</MiddleInitial>
   <LastName>Williams</LastName>
</Customer>
```

This still has the potential to confuse document authors, because it's unlikely that they would expect to have to qualify the attributes on the root element. So, let's see what happens if we give `elementFormDefault` a value of `qualified`, but leave off the `attributeFormDefault` or set it to have a value of `unqualified` (as follows):

```
<?xml version="1.0" ?>
<schema xmlns="http://www.w3.org/2001/XMLSchema"
            targetNamespace="http://www.example.org/Customers"
            xmlns:cust="http://www.example.org/Customers"
            elementFormDefault="qualified">

    <element name="Customer">
        <complexType>
            <sequence>
                <element name="FirstName" type="string" />
                <element name="MiddleInitial" type="string" />
                <element ref="cust:LastName" />
            </sequence>
            <attribute name="clubCardMember" type="boolean" />
            <attribute ref="cust:customerID" />
        </complexType>
    </element>

    <element name="LastName" type="string" />
    <attribute name="customerID" type="integer" />

</schema>
```

You might think we could leave off the `cust:` prefix for the attributes, but this is not the case. So, the following instance will still not be validated:

```
<?xml version="1.0" ?>
<Customer xmlns="http://www.w3.org/2001/Customer"
               clubCardMember="true"
               customerID="12553">
   <FirstName>Kevin</FirstName>
   <MiddleInitial>G</MiddleInitial>
   <LastName>Williams</LastName>
</Customer>
```

The instance above is not validated, because we are still expected to qualify the `customerID` attribute, as it was declared globally. So a valid instance document, when `attributeFormDefault` is left out or set to `unqualified`, might look like this:

```
<?xml version="1.0" ?>
<Customer xmlns="http://www.w3.org/2001/Customer"
                xmlns:cust="http://www.w3.org/2001/Customer"
                clubCardMember="true"
                cust:customerID="12553">
    <FirstName>Kevin</FirstName>
    <MiddleInitial>G</MiddleInitial>
    <LastName>Williams</LastName>
</Customer>
```

If you need to define attributes globally, you can avoid this complication by putting them in an attribute group. You thus do not have to qualify them in the instance document, because it is the `attributeGroup` that has been defined globally, and not the `attribute` declaration itself. Here is an example of the schema using an attribute group:

```
<?xml version="1.0" ?>
<schema xmlns="http://www.w3.org/2001/XMLSchema"
                targetNamespace="http://www.example.org/Customers"
                xmlns:cust="http://www.example.org/Customers"
                elementFormDefault="qualified">

    <element name="Customer">
        <complexType>
            <sequence>
                <element name="FirstName" type="string" />
                <element name="MiddleInitial" type="string" />
                <element ref="cust:LastName" />
            </sequence>
            <attributeGroup ref="cust:rootAttributes" />
        </complexType>
    </element>

    <element name="LastName" type="string" />

    <attributeGroup name="rootAttributes">
        <attribute name="customerID" type="integer" />
        <attribute name="clubCardMember" type="boolean" />
    </attributeGroup>

</schema>
```

With this solution, we can now have a valid instance document that will probably be nearer to what a document author would expect to write:

```
<?xml version="1.0" ?>
<Customer xmlns="http://www.w3.org/2001/Customer"
                clubCardMember="true"
                customerID="12553">
    <FirstName>Kevin</FirstName>
    <MiddleInitial>G</MiddleInitial>
    <LastName>Williams</LastName>
</Customer>
```

94

As we have seen, introducing namespaces brings a lot of complexity to instance documents. By giving `elementFormDefault` a value of `qualified` while leaving `attributeFormDefault` as unqualified, and by avoiding globally declared elements, we can make use of namespace defaulting, and create schemas for which it will be easier to author instance documents.

> **Unless you want to explicitly have to qualify attributes, do not declare them globally; you are better off creating an attribute group.**

Qualified attributes are typically used in a document that is not based on that namespace. For example, the use of the `xsi:type` and `xsi:nil` attributes from the XML Schema for Instances namespace. In such cases, you can either declare the attributes globally in the schema, or say that they are qualified, using the `attributeFormDefault` switch or the form attribute on the individual attribute declarations.

We should just look at one final point before we move on. If we only allow the root element to be declared globally, put the attribute declarations in an attribute group, and remove the `elementFormDefault` attribute from the root element of the schema, we will end up with a schema that looks like this:

```
<?xml version="1.0" ?>
<schema xmlns="http://www.w3.org/2001/XMLSchema"
            targetNamespace="http://www.example.org/Customers"
            xmlns:cust="http://www.example.org/Customers">

    <element name="Customer">
        <complexType>
            <sequence>
                <element name="FirstName" type="string" />
                <element name="MiddleInitial" type="string" />
                <element name="LastName" type="string" />
            </sequence>
        </complexType>
    </element>

</schema>
```

With the following schema, you might expect the following example to be valid. However, it is not. Look closely and see if you can spot the reason:

```
<?xml version="1.0" ?>
<Customer xmlns="http://www.example.org/Customers">
    <FirstName>Kevin</FirstName>
    <MiddleInitial>G</MiddleInitial>
    <LastName>Williams</LastName>
</Customer>
```

The problem is that we are expected to qualify globally declared elements and attributes, and *only* globally declared elements and attributes. Therefore, having removed the `elementFormDefault` attribute from the schema, the proper way of showing an instance document would be as follows:

```
<?xml version="1.0" ?>
<cust:Customer xmlns:cust="http://www.example.org/Customers">
   <FirstName>Kevin></FirstName>
   <MiddleInitial>G</MiddleInitial>
   <LastName>Williams</LastName>
</cust:Customer>
```

Complicated, isn't it? Well, here is a summary of some points to help you remember how to deal with namespaces:

❑   When `elementFormDefault` has a value of `unqualified` – be careful because locally declared elements must not be qualified.

❑   When `elementFormDefault` has a value of `qualified` – you can use namespace defaulting on elements.

❑   When `attributeFormDefault` has a value of `qualified` – you have to explicitly qualify all attributes because they do not inherit the default namespace.

❑   When `attributeFormDefault` has a value of `unqualified` – you have to explicitly qualify all globally declared attributes. If you do not want to qualify any attributes, define global attribute groups and create references to them.

❑   When namespaces are required, XML schema authors often use the settings: `elementFormDefault="qualified"` `attributeFormDefault="unqualified"` (attributeFormDefault can be left off as it this is the default value).

For finer-grained control over whether individual elements and attributes need to be qualified, you can use the `form` attribute on individual element and attribute declarations – this again takes the values `qualified` and `unqualified`.

3.6 Models and Issues for Local Versus Global Declarations

Having seen the possibilities for reuse, you might be tempted to declare all elements that you are likely to reuse globally. As we have just seen, however, there are pitfalls regarding namespaces. Therefore, we need to think a bit more carefully, since these pitfalls can complicate the creation of instance documents that require namespace qualifications, and allow document fragments to be validated against the same schema, which we might not want to permit. So, let's look at different ways of creating element content models. In practice, you will probably use a mixture of the techniques described in this section to get the best design for your particular requirements.

A lot of discussion regarding schema design took place on the XML-Dev list, and this has been written up by one of the main contributors to the discussions, Roger Costello, who maintains an excellent schema resource at http://www.xfront.com/bestpractices.html. Here is a summary of the three models these discussions resulted in:

- ❑ Russian Doll Design

- ❑ Salami Slice Design

- ❑ Venetian Blind Model

We'll start by introducing the Russian Doll Design (which we briefly met at the beginning of this chapter) and Salami Slice Design, which are almost opposite approaches, and then evaluating each in turn. After having looked at both these designs, we will then come back to look at the Venetian Blind Model, which is a compromise between the two. Throughout these examples, we will start by looking at XML Schemas that have the following settings on the root schema element:

```
elementFormDefault = "qualified"
attributeFormDefault = "unqualified"
```

However, we will also examine what an instance documents might look like if we had the settings elementFormDefault = "unqualified" and attributeFormDefault = "unqualified".

3.6.1 Russian Doll Design

As we saw earlier in this chapter with the **Russian Doll Design**, the schema mirrors the structure of the instance document (for example, if we had the following document):

```
<?xml version="1.0" ?>
<Customer xmlns="http://www.example.org/Customers"
          customerID = "12557"
          clubCardMember = "true">
   <FirstName>Kevin</FirstName>
   <MiddleInitial>G</MiddleInitial>
   <LastName>Williams</LastName>
</Customer>
```

In the schema, each element is declared inside its parent element in the same way that it would appear in the instance document:

```
<?xml version="1.0" ?>
<schema xmlns="http://www.w3.org/2001/XMLSchema"
        targetNamespace="http://www.example.org/Customers"
        xmlns:cust="http://www.example.org/Customers"
        elementFormDefault="qualified"
        attributeFormDefault="unqualified">

   <element name="Customer">
```

97

```
        <complexType>
            <sequence>
                <element name="FirstName" type="string" />
                <element name="MiddleInitial" type="string"
                            minOccurs="0" maxOccurs="1" />
                <element name="LastName" type="string" />
            </sequence>
            <attribute name="customerID" use="required" type="integer" />
            <attribute name="clubCardMember" type="boolean" />
        </complexType>
    </element>

</schema>
```

The schema bundles the declarations together, in the same way that the document bundles all of its components . The child element declarations sit inside the containing element declaration like Russian Dolls inside a parent container. Because all of the elements are declared within the parent container, there are no `ref` attributes used. So, you might have to declare an element several times. There is no reuse.

If we had given `elementFormDefault` a value of `unqualified` in the schema, a valid instance document would look like the following:

```
<?xml version="1.0" ?>
<cust:Customer xmlns:cust="http://www.example.org/Customers"
            customerID = "12557"
            clubCardMember = "true">
    <FirstName>Kevin</FirstName>
    <MiddleInitial>G</MiddleInitial>
    <LastName>Williams</LastName>
</cust:Customer>
```

Here, the `cust:` namespace prefix is used to qualify the globally declared `Customer` element, which is the only one that needs to be qualified, while the other elements must not be qualified.

3.6.2 Salami Slice Design

The **Salami Slice Design** takes the opposite approach. Sometimes, this is also known as the **Flat Catalog Design**. Here, each element and attribute is declared globally, and content models are then created by adding references to the global element and attribute declarations inside the declaration of the parent.

This time, references to all of the elements that the `Customer` element can contain and the attributes that it can carry are added to the anonymous complex type definition in the `Customer` element's declaration. If we were dealing with the same document, the schema using the Salami Slice Design would look like this:

```
<?xml version="1.0" ?>
<schema xmlns="http://www.w3.org/2001/XMLSchema"
        targetNamespace="http://www.example.org/Customers"
```

98

```
                xmlns:cust="http://www.example.org/Customers"
                elementFormDefault="qualified"
                attributeFormDefault="unqualified">

    <element name="FirstName" type="string" />
    <element name="MiddleInitial" type="string" />
    <element name="LastName" type="string" />
    <attribute name="customerID" type="integer" />
    <attribute name="clubCardMember" type="boolean" />

    <element name="Customer">
        <complexType>
            <sequence>
                <element ref="cust:FirstName" />
                <element ref="cust:MiddleInitial"
                        minOccurs="0" maxOccurs="1" />
                <element ref="cust:LastName" />
            </sequence>
            <attribute ref="cust:customerID" use="required" />
            <attribute ref="cust:clubCardMember" />
        </complexType>
    </element>

</schema>
```

Note that the occurrence constraints for attributes and elements *cannot* be placed upon the global declarations. Rather, they appear in the references to the globally declared elements and attributes.

The schema here is longer than the one using the Russian Doll Design, but the declarations are no longer bundled together. Therefore, any of the elements or attributes can be reused in other content models, just as they have been used in the Customer element. Here, we are taking the individual slices required to make a content model, and piecing them together as required. An instance document would look like the following:

```
<?xml version="1.0" ?>
<cust:Customer xmlns:cust="http://www.example.org/Customers"
        cust:customerID = "12557"
        cust:clubCardMember = "true">
    <cust:FirstName>Kevin</cust:FirstName>
    <cust:MiddleInitial>G</cust:MiddleInitial>
    <cust:LastName>Williams</cust:LastName>
</cust:Customer>
```

If elementFormDefault had a value of unqualified, the resulting document would still look the same, as we would have to qualify all globally declared elements.

Having introduced the two designs, let's compare their characteristics.

3.6.3 *Comparing the Russian Doll and Salami Slice Designs*

The Russian Doll and Salami Slice Designs differ in several important ways. Let's consider them.

3.6.3.1 The Salami Slice Design Facilitates Individual Component Reuse; the Russian Doll Design does not

In the Salami Slice Design, the elements and attributes appearing in the content model for the `Customer` element can be used by other elements and complex types, because they are declared globally. In this sense, they are considered **transparent** because other schema components can reuse them.

In the Russian Doll Design, however, the child elements and attributes are declared locally, and are thus considered **opaque**. They are given this name because other schema components, and indeed other schemas, cannot see them to reuse them.

3.6.3.2 Components of the Russian Doll Design have Localized Scope; Components of the Salami Slice Design have Global Scope

Components of the Russian Doll Design have **localized scope**, which means that we could use a second `FirstName` element in the same document, and let it have a different content model as long as it was used outside the scope of the `Customer` element.

Because each element and attribute is declared globally, each has a **global scope**, which means that we cannot have another element with the same name and a different content model, and we cannot have an attribute with a different simple type.

3.6.3.3 Components of the Russian Doll Design are Decoupled; Components of the Salami Slice Design are Coupled

Changes made to the component elements of the Russian Doll Design will not have any effect outside their containing element, because elements and attributes are declared locally. The child declarations are therefore considered to be **decoupled**, as they do not interact with each other.

In the Salami Slice Design, the declarations are considered **coupled**, because if a change is made to any of the global elements, it will affect any content model that uses them by reference.

3.6.3.4 The Russian Doll Design Allows only One Document Element to be used; Salami Slice Design offers all Globally Defined Elements

The Russian Doll Design allows only one document element to be used, whereas the Salami Slice Design allows any globally defined element to be used as the document element of a conforming document. This means that different fragments of a document, as well as the documents that use the intended document element, can be validated against the same schema.

3.6.3.5 The Salami Slice Design Facilitates Hiding of Namespace Complexities; the Russian Doll Design does not

With the Russian Doll design, bearing in mind that all global elements need to be namespace qualified, if the schema declares elementFormDefault to be unqualified (the default), then only the Customer element should be qualified. This requirement would mean that document authors have to know which elements and attributes to qualify. Furthermore, if we are using XSLT, we have to process ancestor elements so that we can determine which vocabulary they belong to, and if we are using SAX to process the document, we have to record the context of the element or attribute in order to check which vocabulary it belongs to.

This approach also means that we cannot use namespace defaulting if we do not set elementFormDefault to qualified.

In the Salami Slice Design, the elementFormDefault and attributeFormDefault settings have no effect because all elements and attributes are global, and these settings only affect local declarations.

Note that this also means that we can use namespace defaulting on elements even when elementFormDefault has a value of unqualified (which we could not do with the Russian Doll Design), although we still have to qualify attributes, as follows:

```
<?xml version="1.0" ?>
<Customer xmlns="http://www.example.org/Customers"
          xmlns:cust="http://www.example.org/Customers"
          cust:customerID = "12557"
          cust:clubCardMember = "true">
   <FirstName>Kevin</FirstName>
   <MiddleInitial>G</MiddleInitial>
   <LastName>Williams</LastName>
</Customer>
```

From a processing point of view, whether validating an instance document or the schema itself, the Salami Slice Design introduces more work for the processing application that has to deal with the overhead of all of the references.

3.6.3.6 The Salami Slice Approach is more Similar (than the Russian Doll Design) to DTDs

The approach of the Salami Slice design is more like that used with DTDs, where each element or attribute has to be declared before it can be used in a content model. This approach has also been compared to that of cloning an object; having defined the element or attribute, it can be used by reference, in which case two elements are clearly instances of the same class.

The way in which Russian Doll Design schemas are constructed is very different than the way in which a DTD declares elements and attributes, which means that it can be difficult to programmatically transform DTDs into schemas, or for humans to follow the patterns in each design. Furthermore, you cannot use the same design guidelines for both technologies.

3.6.3.7 On Balance

The Russian Doll Design is ideal for constraining small documents with a rigid structure (which will often mean small data-oriented documents, because related declarations are bundled together (and not spread out), making it more compact and easier to read than the Salami Slice Design.

For larger documents, and when flexibility is introduced, however, you end up with one very long element declaration for the root element, with everything else nested inside. In particular, when you introduce choices that have to be modeled (such as a choice of elements with different content models), the declaration can become very hard to follow. Furthermore, there are no benefits of reusing structures.

In the Salami Slice Design, you get benefits of reuse, as all element and attribute declarations are global. However, this means that schemas can end up being quite verbose in comparison to the Russian Doll Design, unless you have complex elements appearing in multiple content models, in which case Salami Slice is shorter because you don't have so much repetition. In practice, you will probably want something a little less severe than this design, somewhere in between the two. While globally declaring some elements allows fragments of documents to be processed by the same schema as a whole document instance (for example, in a schema for books, you might want to be able to validate just one Chapter element and its content, rather than a whole Book element with every chapter), you will rarely want to globally declare every element.

The third approach we mentioned is the Venetian Blind Model, which creates a middle ground that hides namespace complexities, while still allowing a degree of reuse.

3.6.4 The Venetian Blind Model

The Venetian Blind Model encourages the use of complex type definitions rather than just the declaration of elements. In this approach, we will define a named complex type for elements that hold details about a person's name.

3.6.4.1 Venetian Blind Model Allows Reuse of Content Models without Globally Defining Each Element

Even though we may rarely want to globally define each element, we'd still want the benefits of reuse in our schemas. By creating a named complex type, which we will call `NameType`, we will be able to associate the same complex type with both the `Customer` element and any other element, such as an `Employee` element, that wishes to share the same content model. Let's define the `NameType` named complex type to use in the `Customer` element as below:

```
<?xml version="1.0" ?>
<xs:schema xmlns:xs="http://www.w3.org/2001/XMLSchema"
     targetNamespace="http://www.example.org/Customers"
     xmlns="http://www.example.org/Customers"
     elementFormDefault="qualified"
     attributeFormDefault="unqualified">

  <xs:complexType name="NameType">
    <xs:sequence>
       <xs:element name="FirstName" type="xs:string" />
       <xs:element name="MiddleInitial" type="xs:string"
                   minOccurs="0" maxOccurs="1" />
       <xs:element name="LastName" type="xs:string" />
    </xs:sequence>
    <xs:attribute name="customerID" type="xs:integer"
                  use="required" />
    <xs:attribute name="clubCardMember" type="xs:boolean" />
  </xs:complexType>

  <xs:element name="Customer" type="NameType" />

</xs:schema>
```

Having abstractly defined the `NameType`, we can use it to define the allowable content of any element. So, we could declare an `Employee` element in the schema to have the same type, as follows:

```
<xs:element name="employee" type="NameType" />
```

Here is an example of a conforming document instance:

```
<?xml version="1.0" ?>
<Customer xmlns="http://www.example.org/Customers"
     customerID="12557"
     clubCardMember="true">
  <FirstName>Kevin</FirstName>
  <MiddleInitial>G</MiddleInitial>
  <LastName>Williams</LastName>
</Customer>
```

Here, we are reusing the content model defined by the complex type, without having each element and attribute declared globally as we did in the Salami Slice Design.

103

3.6.4.2 Venetian Blind Model Keeps Related Information Together without the Deeply Nested Complex Structures of the Russian Doll Design

This approach is particularly useful when working with large complex schemas. Rather than having one big declaration containing all other declarations and definitions as in the Russian Doll Design, we keep the related components' declarations together in named complex types, and then create more complex structures using these groups of elements.

3.6.4.3 Venetian Blind Model Hides Namespace Complexities, as Child Elements are Declared Locally

By setting elementFormDefault to a value of qualified, and attributeFormDefault to unqualified, we have hidden namespace complexities. The attributes are declared locally, and therefore do not need to be qualified in the instance document, while the elements can use the default namespace in the root element.

This approach also minimizes the namespace complexities of having to declare a child element's namespaces in an instance document when elementFormDefault is set to unqualified, because the child declarations are not global. However, the author still needs to qualify the root element, as shown here:

```
<?xml version="1.0" ?>
<cust:Customer xmlns:cust="http://www.example.org/Customers"
    customerID="12557"
    clubCardMember="true">
  <FirstName>Kevin</FirstName>
  <MiddleInitial>G</MiddleInitial>
  <LastName>Williams</LastName>
</cust:Customer>
```

This contrasts with the Salami Slice Design, where authors have to expose all the elements' namespaces. In this design, you can remove the need to qualify local elements by simply changing the value of elementFormDefault so that it acts as a global **switch** over the whole document, unlike a schema written using the Salami Slice Design, which would need to be completely rewritten to remove the need for qualifying every element.

3.6.4.4 Venetian Blind Model Allows for More Compact Schemas

If we want to add a containing element for customer name details, without changing any other element that uses this type (such as an Employee element which is associated with the NameType), we create a new type that uses the existing one:

```
<xs:complexType name="CustomerType">
  <xs:sequence>
    <xs:element name="Name" type="NameType" />
```

```
      </xs:sequence>
    </xs:complexType>

    <xs:element name="Customer" type="CustomerType" />
```

This design thus maximizes the reuse of child elements, and can lead to more compact schemas. Then we assemble the complex types into the larger structure. The idea behind complex types and the Venetian Blind model is analogous to the notion of defining a class and using the class to create an object.

This approach is typically used in data-oriented applications, where the representation of class-like information is important. For example, each row of a database table can be modeled in a complex type, and each class of information, in an object-oriented application. This approach is also particularly useful when you have choices regarding the elements that a document author can use, and each choice has a different content model, such as being able to include a paragraph, table, or image in a book or paper. Rather than repeating the content model for each choice, we just indicate that the element can appear, and then associate it with the relevant type.

3.6.5 Avoid Overuse of Named Complex Types in the Venetian Blind Model

While named complex types seem like a great solution, as we mentioned earlier when looking at reuse mechanisms, you are often better off using named model groups than complex types to create flexible content models. Let's look at some more reasons for this.

3.6.5.1 Model Complex Types on Real World Entities

The main concern with complex types is that you have to be very careful about what you put in a named complex type definition. If the information that you put in is inadequate or in excess, and then if, at a later date, you want to remove or add an element or attribute for just one element that uses this type definition (while the other elements associated with that type stay the same), you would have to create a new complex type.

If you plan to use type definitions, they should (because of the reasons above), only model one real world entity. For example, if you are working on a contact information schema, you should define separate named complex types for each class of information, such as name, address, and telephone numbers. This way, each type can be changed individually.

So, when defining named complex types, you have to make sure that they associate everything that you need to put within an element representing an entity, while at the same time making it general enough for reuse. If you are trying to represent a person in a named complex type, stick to elements that represent the person only, and add other items outside that complex type definition, or use named model groups.

While you *can* extend and restrict existing named complex types, this has issues.

3.6.5.2 Problems with Extending and Restricting Named Complex Types

You can only extend a named complex type with new child elements that follow those in the existing named complex type; new elements cannot come before or in the middle of the elements that have already been defined in the named complex type associated with the parent element. This is done to ease the implementation of parsers and processors that are XML Schema-aware. If we wanted to add a `Title` element to the beginning of the `NameType` we saw earlier (to contain title information such as Mr., Mrs., Miss, Dr., etc.), and we wanted to make the change for just one element associated with it, while other elements associated with the type remained the same, we would have to create a whole new named complex type. We cannot do this by extension of the existing one.

When you restrict a named complex type, apart from having to learn new rules (which we won't cover in this chapter), you will also need to repeat all of the declarations in the new complex type. Thus, it may not offer the economy you might expect.

3.6.5.3 You can Associate only One Element with One Type Definition

You are also limited in that you can associate only one element with one type definition, as we mentioned earlier. Therefore, if you wanted to associate more than one named complex type with the same element (for example, one named complex type representing a person's name and another representing his/her address details, within the same parent containing element) you would have to add containing elements to the structure. Named model groups are a better alternative as building blocks for content models, since they can be combined within the same containing element.

3.6.6 The Alternative: Venetian Blind and Named Model Groups

As we have already mentioned, named model groups often make better building blocks for content models, and now we have seen some more reasons why. Named model groups:

❑ can be combined with other named model groups in complex type definitions

❑ offer more flexibility, especially in the way we can alter and extend our content models, as they can nest inside another complex type or model group and thus extend the model with a new element at the beginning or the end of the model group

In a data-orientated application, complex types are often ideal. However, when you might need flexibility in the future, named model groups are particularly helpful for creating building blocks that can be used in complex types.

The only disadvantages with using named model groups over named complex types is that we cannot reuse the element declarations that are inside the group by reference, and that it does not mirror the approach used by DTDs. If you were using XQuery and XSLT, it is also worth noting that the model group is not exposed in the PSVI, whereas complex types are.

In summary, the advantages of using named model groups in the Venetian Blind technique are:

❑   Named model groups allow us to reuse content models within and across schemas

❑   They allow us to add elements to the beginning and end of the content model

❑   They hide namespace complexities because the child element declarations are not made globally

❑   They allow control over whether elements require namespaces using elementFormDefault as a switch for the whole document

❑   They allow us to apply minOccurs and maxOccurs attributes to the element declarations that affect their use throughout the schema, because the element declarations are not global

Therefore, it is best to use named model groups to define reusable structures for content models, and to use named complex types for defining class-like information.

3.7 Tightening u p your Schemas

Any application that processes an XML document should be able to cope with all possible structures that a document can contain, and should raise an error if the document does not match one of the allowed structures. Because XML Schema offers more powerful validation features than DTDs (such as allowing more flexible structures, support for data types and value constraints), not only can you control the possible structures, but you can also control potential values that a document can contain.

A key advantage of tightening up your schema is that you can let the parser do more of the validation work than was traditionally performed by the application. The more business requirements in the schema, and the tighter its restrictions, the less validation code you have to write. Tightening the schema also makes it easier to write applications to create documents that can be validated against the schema.

In this final section, we will look at ways in which you can tighten up your schema so that the possible structures and values are limited to those that you want to accept. We will cover:

❑ Occurrence and value constraints

❑ Providing null values

❑ Creating your own simple data types

3.7.1 Adding Constraints

There are two key types of constraints that help us write tighter schemas:

❑ Occurrence constraints – allow us to give minimum and maximum numbers of times an element can appear, and whether attributes are optional or required

❑ Value constraints – allow us to provide default values and fixed values for element and attribute content

3.7.1.1 Use Occurrence Constraints to Indicate the Number of Times an Element may Appear

When an element is declared, it should by default appear once, and once only, in instance documents. When we want to make an element's appearance in a document optional, or allow it to repeat, we can use the minOccurs and maxOccurs attributes on the element declaration. These attributes can only be added to local element declarations, not to global ones. The values of these attributes are the number of times an element can appear, and are therefore much easier to use than the cardinality operators in DTDs (namely ?, *, and +). The maxOccurs attribute can also take a value of unbounded, which means there is no maximum number of times that an element can appear.

The following table shows the mapping of DTD cardinality operators to the equivalent values of minOccurs and maxOccurs:

Cardinality Operator	minOccurs value	maxOccurs value	Number of child element(s)
[none]	1	1	1 and only 1
?	0	1	0 or more
*	0	unbounded	0 or more
+	1	unbounded	1 or more

Because an attribute can only appear once on the same element, there is no need for minOccurs and maxOccurs attributes. However, we might want to specify that an attribute must appear, or explicitly state that it is optional. We can do this with the use attribute on any local attribute declaration, which can take the following values:

❑ Required, when indicating that an attribute must appear

❑ Optional, when it can either appear once or not at all (the default value)

❑ Prohibited, to exclude an attribute from being inherited during derivation by restriction

3.7.1.2 Use Value Constraints for Default or Fixed Values

With DTDs, it was possible to supply a default attribute value for an attribute that was left empty in an instance document, but there was no equivalent for elements. With XML Schema, we can supply a default value for text-only element content *as well as* attribute values by using the default attribute on an element declaration. A schema-aware processor will treat the document as if the document had the default value when parsing it. For example, consider the following fragment of an instance document:

```
<MailOut>
    <Subscribe></Subscribe>
</MailOut>
```

We want the default content of the Subscribe element to be no if we receive the document with an empty Subscribe element, so we add the default attribute to the element declaration, whose value is simple element content we want:

```
<element name="Subscribe" type="string" default="no" />
```

Meanwhile, the fixed attribute is used on an element whose content must either be empty or must match the value of the fixed attribute. If the document carries any value other than that expressed by the fixed attribute, it would not be valid.

Note that you cannot give the use attribute, a value of required *and* give it a default value.

3.7.2 Avoid Over-dependence on Built-in Datatypes

When developers work on an XML Schema, they often take the path of least resistance to get the schema working properly. This may mean using built-in XML Schema datatypes for values in an XML Schema, rather than creating their own datatypes. If you review the examples in this chapter so far, you'll see that I've been guilty of this myself.

Consider the following example:

```
<xs:schema xmlns:xs="http://www.w3.org/2001/XMLSchema">
  <xs:element name="Invoice">
    <xs:complexType>
      <xs:sequence>
        <xs:element name="CustomerName" type="xs:string" />
        <xs:element name="Address" type="xs:string" />
        <xs:element name="City" type="xs:string" />
        <xs:element name="State" type="xs:string" />
        <xs:element name="Zip" type="xs:string" />
        <xs:element name="Item" maxOccurs="unbounded">
          <xs:complexType>
            <xs:sequence>
              <xs:element name="ID" type="xs:string" />
              <xs:element name="Description" type="xs:string" />
              <xs:element name="Count" type="xs:integer" />
              <xs:element name="TotalCost" type="xs:decimal" />
            </xs:sequence>
          </xs:complexType>
        </xs:element>
      </xs:sequence>
    </xs:complexType>
  </xs:element>
</xs:schema>
```

The following is a perfectly valid instance of the Invoice document:

```
<Invoice>
  <CustomerName>asdflkjdsgin</CustomerName>
  <Address></Address>
  <City>KJKJKJ</City>
  <State>This is the value for the state that I have entered</State>
  <Zip>X81276346SDh2823476</Zip>
  <Item>
    <ID>This is not a valid ID.</ID>
    <Description>83475634536456345364536456</Description>
    <Count>0</Count>
    <TotalCost>-282456345346.7834345636456</TotalCost>
  </Item>
</Invoice>
```

You can see the problems here. Values like State that we know should be constrained to a particular domain are not; numeric values like Count and TotalCost are not properly restricted (Count should be positive). To ensure that documents conforming to our schema don't contain any surprises, we need to add restrictions to our simple types.

Of course, there is a balance between imposing controls and allowing flexibility. If you make your datatypes too rigid, you can create new problems too. Dealing with existing records is a common example where you might need to capture and communicate information that obviously appears wrong. For example, in a legacy system, we could have a date field that contains something like "10(?) March 1985", and accepting the date will give us an idea that the person entering the data was not sure exactly of the date, but it was around the 10th March 1985 – this might actually make your system more useful if you allow the value.

3.7.2.1 How to Add Restrictions to Simple Types

Restrictions may be added to simple types by declaring them inside an anonymous simple type declaration where they appear in the document, or, if the restriction applies to more than one text-only element or attribute value, in globally declared named simple types. Restrictions serve to reduce the set of allowable values for a particular simple type. For example, restrictions may be used to force a value to come from an allowable list, or to force a value to be within a certain range. Again, try to compare the pros and cons of implementing restrictions.

Let's look at an example. Here's our earlier invoice schema, now with restrictions added:

```
<xs:schema xmlns:xs="http://www.w3.org/2001/XMLSchema">
  <xs:element name="Invoice">
    <xs:complexType>
      <xs:sequence>
        <xs:element name="CustomerName">
          <xs:simpleType>
            <xs:restriction base="xs:string">
              <xs:minLength value="1" />
              <xs:maxLength value="50" />
            </xs:restriction>
          </xs:simpleType>
        </xs:element>
        <xs:element name="Address">
          <xs:simpleType>
            <xs:restriction base="xs:string">
              <xs:minLength value="1" />
              <xs:maxLength value="50" />
            </xs:restriction>
          </xs:simpleType>
        </xs:element>
        <xs:element name="City">
          <xs:simpleType>
            <xs:restriction base="xs:string">
              <xs:minLength value="1" />
              <xs:maxLength value="50" />
            </xs:restriction>
          </xs:simpleType>
        </xs:element>
        <xs:element name="State">
          <xs:simpleType>
            <xs:restriction base="xs:string">
              <xs:enumeration value="AK" />
              <xs:enumeration value="AL" />
              <xs:enumeration value="AR" />
                   ...
            </xs:restriction>
          </xs:simpleType>
        </xs:element>
        <xs:element name="Zip">
          <xs:simpleType>
            <xs:restriction base="xs:string">
              <xs:minLength value="5" />
              <xs:maxLength value="10" />
            </xs:restriction>
          </xs:simpleType>
        </xs:element>
```

111

```
          <xs:element name="Item" maxOccurs="unbounded">
            <xs:complexType>
              <xs:sequence>
                <xs:element name="ID">
                  <xs:simpleType>
                    <xs:restriction base="xs:string">
                      <xs:pattern value="[0-9]{2}-[0-9]{5}" />
                    </xs:restriction>
                  </xs:simpleType>
                </xs:element>
                <xs:element name="Description">
                  <xs:simpleType>
                    <xs:restriction base="xs:string">
                      <xs:maxLength value="200" />
                    </xs:restriction>
                  </xs:simpleType>
                </xs:element>
                <xs:element name="Count">
                  <xs:simpleType>
                    <xs:restriction base="xs:unsignedShort">
                      <xs:minInclusive value="1" />
                    </xs:restriction>
                  </xs:simpleType>
                </xs:element>
                <xs:element name="TotalCost">
                  <xs:simpleType>
                    <xs:restriction base="xs:decimal">
                      <xs:minExclusive value="0" />
                    </xs:restriction>
                  </xs:simpleType>
                </xs:element>
              </xs:sequence>
            </xs:complexType>
          </xs:element>
        </xs:sequence>
      </xs:complexType>
    </xs:element>
  </xs:schema>
```

The schema is much larger than the version with no restrictions, but this version does a good job of constraining what values may appear for each text-only element. We see several different examples of this at work.

3.7.2.2 Limit Allowable Lengths for Fields that use Strings

For string values, we restrict the allowable lengths. The use of the minLength attribute with a value of 1 ensures that the field is not empty, as we did with City:

```
        <xs:element name="City">
          <xs:simpleType>
            <xs:restriction base="xs:string">
              <xs:minLength value="1" />
              <xs:maxLength value="50" />
            </xs:restriction>
          </xs:simpleType>
        </xs:element>
```

The use of the maxLenth attribute can be controversial in text fields. These constraints are usually added because you are working with an existing database that has a maximum field length, or because you want to create a database with a maximum field length to keep size down.

Some people will argue that this restriction doesn't sound like one that exists in the real world, and that it's really bad to impose it just because you think there ought to be a limit; after all, there may be real world violations. The same issue arises with the CustomerNames, which could conceivably exceed 50 characters.

3.7.2.3 Consider Limiting the Range of Allowable Values in Numeric Fields

We also use restrictions to govern the allowable values for our numeric fields; for example, the number of items ordered must be greater than zero, as must the total cost for the items:

```
<xs:element name="TotalCost">
  <xs:simpleType>
    <xs:restriction base="xs:decimal">
      <xs:minExclusive value="0" />
    </xs:restriction>
  </xs:simpleType>
</xs:element>
```

It is important to be mindful of all possible scenarios regarding these constraints. For example, if we were able to order a catalog for free from the web site, we might end up with a total cost for the items that is in fact 0.

3.7.2.4 Restrict Integer rather than Platform-Programming-Oriented Types when Working with Numbers

When we created a restriction for the Count element, we derived our new type from the unsignedShort type, which is a built-in derived type, derived from an integer to be a non-negative integer whose value is between 0 and 65535:

```
<xs:element name="Count">
  <xs:simpleType>
    <xs:restriction base="xs:unsignedShort">
      <xs:minInclusive value="1" />
    </xs:restriction>
  </xs:simpleType>
</xs:element>
```

These hardware-oriented types, such as xs:unsignedShort, use numbers that do not occur naturally in the real world. Therefore, sometimes it is better to restrict an integer and choose an upper bound for the allowed values that will make sense to people rather than computers. In terms of helping people understand the count, we might therefore have been better off restricting the integer datatype:

```
<xs:element name="Count">
  <xs:simpleType>
    <xs:restriction base="xs:integer">
      <xs:minInclusive value="1" />
      <xs:maxInclusive value="5000" />
    </xs:restriction>
  </xs:simpleType>
</xs:element>
```

3.7.2.5 Provide Enumerated Values for a Fixed Set of Options

When the document must contain one value from a set of possible values, we can provide a list of enumerated values. We did this with the State element, since it should only contain a two-letter abbreviation for the state. This prevents users from entering the whole state name, or indeed an incorrect abbreviation:

```
<xs:element name="State">
  <xs:simpleType>
    <xs:restriction base="xs:string">
      <xs:enumeration value="AK" />
      <xs:enumeration value="AL" />
      <xs:enumeration value="AR" />
        ...
    </xs:restriction>
  </xs:simpleType>
</xs:element>
```

3.7.2.6 Use Regular Expressions to Control Allowable Values that have Patterns

The ability to match values against regular expression patterns is powerful. It is particularly useful to check things like credit card numbers, phone numbers, and identifiers. In our example, we use regular expressions for controlling the allowable values of the ID for Item elements so that it is two digits, a dash, followed by five digits:

```
<xs:element name="ID">
  <xs:simpleType>
    <xs:restriction base="xs:string">
      <xs:pattern value="[0-9]{2}-[0-9]{5}" />
    </xs:restriction>
  </xs:simpleType>
</xs:element>
```

If you need to get helpful whitespace normalization (in particular, when dealing with regular expressions), you can restrict the xs:token simple type, which represents tokenized strings without any line feeds, carriage returns, tab characters, and no leading or trailing spaces.

While these examples are relatively simple, they provide some insight into the level of control over values provided by the XML Schema language.

3.7.3 Representing Null Values in XML Instance Documents

The representation of null values has always presented a challenge for data designers. Null values are important for fields that do not contain any information for whatever reason (such as the second line of an address which is not populated for many residential addresses). However, there can be some confusion in the mind of data designers concerning whether such a value should be represented as a null or as a simple empty string.

There are several ways of representing a null value using XML Schema; you can:

❑ use an empty element in the instance document if the null value is within an element (for example <null />)

❑ allow users to omit the element or attribute, although the structure of the document is more rigid if you indicate a null value rather than just omit it

❑ use the built-in xsi:nil attribute from the XML Schema for the Instances namespace in the instance document

❑ use your own custom attribute with more descriptive values such as unknown, not provided, invalid, and unreadable, which distinguish among the reasons why a value is missing

In this section, we will look at the last two options. First let's look at why explicitly stating that a value has not been provided can save you time and effort in the long run.

3.7.3.1 The Difference Between a Null and an Empty Value

When is a null value preferable to a simple empty value? It depends on the meaning of the data. Normally, a null value means "unknown" or "not provided". For example, let's say we were gathering information in an Internet survey. One of the questions asked, which the respondent could optionally answer, is to give his or her age. If the respondent chooses not to answer the question, what gets stored in the Age field (which is constrained to be an integer between 0 and 200)? One option would be to simply store a zero, but this can lead to problems. For example, what happens when you run a stored procedure that calculates the average age of the respondents? Unless you specifically exclude the value zero from the average calculation, your answer will be significantly less than it should be.

Furthermore, if the element has an integer datatype, and the instance document contained an empty element, the processor might not validate the instance document because an empty string is not a valid integer. The problem is less pronounced for string values, but imagine a next-of-kin field on an insurance application – if this field is left blank, does it mean that the person has no next of kin? Or did the person forget to enter a name in this field? From the perspective of the insurance company, this can be a very important distinction. Naturally, the problem of nulls needs to be addressed on a case-by-case basis. If you decide you *do* need to indicate that a field can allow null values in an XML Schema specification, how do you go about it?

3.7.3.2 Solving the Problem by Using xsi:nil

The XML Schema specification provides a mechanism for indicating that an element may contain a null value. While this is permitted for both complex type elements and simple type elements, it is the use of this mechanism for simple type elements that interests us here. Let's take a look at an example. Say we had the following document that we were in the process of designing:

```
<Survey>
   <ResponseDate>2002-11-17T09:12:34</ResponseDate>
   <Age>33</Age>
   <PreferredFood>Nachos</PreferredFood>
   <FavoriteElement>Molybdenum</FavoriteElement>
   <SodasPerDay>17</SodasPerDay>
</Survey>
```

We'd like to indicate that the Age element is allowed to take a null value in an instance document. To do so, we need to set the nillable attribute on the declaration of the Age element:

```
<xs:schema xmlns:xs="http://www.w3.org/2001/XMLSchema">

   <xs:element name="Survey" type="SurveyType" />

   <xs:complexType name="SurveyType">
     <xs:sequence>
       <xs:element name="ResponseDate" type="xs:dateTime" />
       <xs:element name="Age" type="xs:integer"
                   nillable="true" />
       <xs:element name="PreferredFood" type="xs:string" />
       <xs:element name="FavoriteElement" type="xs:string" />
       <xs:element name="SodasPerDay" type="xs:integer" />
     </xs:sequence>
   </xs:complexType>

</xs:schema>
```

To represent the null value in an instance document, we need to introduce a namespace to the instance document that corresponds to XML Schema instances mentioned in the namespaces section of this chapter. The namespace is `http://www.w3.org/2001/XMLSchema-instance`, and usually takes the prefix `xsi:` by convention. After we declare this namespace in our instance document, we can indicate that the `Age` element is null by setting the `xsi:nil` attribute to `true` for the element:

```
<Survey xmlns:xsi="http://www.w3.org/2001/XMLSchema-instance">
  <ResponseDate>2002-11-17T09:12:34</ResponseDate>
  <Age xsi:nil="true" />
  <PreferredFood>Nachos</PreferredFood>
  <FavoriteElement>Molybdenum</FavoriteElement>
  <SodasPerDay>17</SodasPerDay>
</Survey>
```

When an element has the `xsi:nil` attribute with a value of `true`, it must be empty; if it contains any content at all, it will generate an error. Here, a processor could check to see if the `xsi:nil` attribute was set to `true`, and if so, it could insert a null into a database for the age value.

The advantage in using this technique, rather than simply omitting the element in question, is that your schema can be used to validate the instance documents that require the `Age` element in their structure even when no value is given. Therefore, when writing code to process the document, you would not have to deal with an element that may or may not be present. You will always have an `Age` element, and if it carries the `xsi:nil` attribute, you know you have to add a null value to the database.

Unfortunately, this approach only works on documents that use elements to represent element information items. How can we approach the representation of null values for attribute datapoints? We could simply make the attribute optional. However, to make processing simpler, we might want to "expect" the attribute, and then deal with the null value.

3.7.3.3 Using xsd:union to Create Null Values for Attributes

In an XML Schema declaration, it is possible to create a datatype that combines allowable values from more than one value space by using the `union` element. When this element is used in a type declaration, it indicates that the allowable values for the element may come from any of the simple type declarations inside the `union` element. Let's see an example. Say we had our earlier survey information document, but that it was structured as attribute data:

```
<xs:schema xmlns:xs="http://www.w3.org/2001/XMLSchema">

  <xs:element name="Survey" type="SurveyType" />

  <xs:complexType name="SurveyType">
    <xs:attribute name="responseDate" type="xs:dateTime" />
```

```
      <xs:attribute name="age" type="xs:unsignedShort" />
      <xs:attribute name="preferredFood" type="xs:string" />
      <xs:attribute name="favoriteElement" type="xs:string" />
      <xs:attribute name="sodasPerDay" type="xs:unsignedShort" />
    </xs:complexType>

  </xs:schema>
```

We can use union to enable the age attribute to contain a special value that would translate to a null when the document was parsed. For example, we might want the field to contain either a numeric value for the age, or the value unknown if the age was not provided. The following declaration accomplishes this:

```
<xs:schema xmlns:xs="http://www.w3.org/2001/XMLSchema">

  <xs:element name="Survey" type="surveyType" />

  <xs:complexType name="SurveyType">
    <xs:attribute name="responseDate" type="xs:dateTime" />
    <xs:attribute name="age" type="AgeType" />
    <xs:attribute name="preferredFood" type="xs:string" />
    <xs:attribute name="favoriteElement" type="xs:string" />
    <xs:attribute name="sodasPerDay" type="xs:integer" />
  </xs:complexType>

  <xs:simpleType name="AgeType">
    <xs:union>
      <xs:simpleType>
        <xs:restriction base="xs:integer">
          <xs:minInclusive value="0" />
          <xs:maxInclusive value="130" />
        </xs:restriction>
      </xs:simpleType>
      <xs:simpleType>
        <xs:restriction base="xs:string">
          <xs:enumeration value="unknown" />
        </xs:restriction>
      </xs:simpleType>
    </xs:union>
  </xs:simpleType>

</xs:schema>
```

If the age is not provided, we can create the following valid document:

```
<Survey
  responseDate="2002-11-17T09:12:34"
  age="unknown"
  preferredFood="Nachos"
  favoriteElement="Molybdenum"
  sodasPerDay="17" />
```

This technique allows us to indicate that an attribute has a null value in a generated document. Note that there still needs to be a specialized processor that "knows" that the value unknown actually translates to a null in the database.

3.7.3.4 Saying Why There is No Value with Custom Attributes

While the ability to make an element's content nillable is useful, especially for those dealing with relational databases, now that we have seen the previous technique that uses the `union` element, we can adding custom attributes into instance documents that offer more explanation as to why the information is missing. After all, if there is no value, it is often helpful to know why, because a value that is unknown is sometimes different than a value that is missing, or even unreadable.

By creating our own custom attributes, we can offer more details as to why the data is missing. Here, we create a simple type called `AgeType` again, this time allowing different values if the user does not provide an `Age`:

```
<xs:simpleType name="AgeType">
   <xs:union>
     <xs:simpleType>
       <xs:restriction base="xs:integer">
         <xs:minInclusive value="0" />
         <xs:maxInclusive value="130" />
       </xs:restriction>
     </xs:simpleType>
     <xs:simpleType>
       <xs:restriction base="xs:string">
         <xs:enumeration value="unknown" />
         <xs:enumeration value="notProvided" />
         <xs:enumeration value="unreadable" />
       </xs:restriction>
     </xs:simpleType>
   </xs:union>
 </xs:simpleType>
```

Our look at how to represent null values (which are particularly important when working with databases) brings us to the end of this chapter. If you were working a lot with data that is stored in relational databases, you would also benefit from looking at the `key` and `keyref` mechanisms in XML Schema, which allow you to model relationships between elements and attributes, as well as the `unique` identity constraint.

3.8 Summary

In this chapter, we've seen some of the most common issues developers encounter as they start to create XML Schema documents. XML Schemas are very powerful as a way of constraining both allowable structure and content of a document instance. The power, however, comes at the price of complexity.

We started off looking at some general issues, such as when to validate documents, naming conventions, and the consistency, order, and structure of schemas. Then we went on to look at how we can reuse structures and content models with global declarations, named complex types, and named model groups. Next, we tried to avoid some expected pitfalls while introducing namespaces. In particular, we saw how global declarations had to be qualified, and the effects of the `elementFormDefault` and `attributeFormDefault` attributes as global switches for qualification of elements and attributes in instance documents.

We looked at some schema design models, starting with the extremes of the Russian Doll and Salami Slice designs, before finding a middle ground with the Venetian Blind Model which permits reuse and helps avoid namespace complexities. We finished off by looking at tightening up our schemas using occurrence and value constraints, creating our own simple data types, and how to represent null values in schemas.

Using the techniques shown in this chapter, you should be able to write more effective schemas, and create vocabularies that ideally have a longer life and will be easier for others to work with.

XML Design

Handbook

4

Parsing Strategies

In the last two chapters, we've given you a solid basis to help you design your documents and define schemas for those documents. The next step is to figure out how, based on the structure of the document and the requirements of the application, best to parse the document. The design of the document and your parsing strategy can greatly affect the performance characteristics of your application. Thus, carefully choosing your parsing strategy is as critical as carefully designing your document structure. When you have no control over the document design, the parsing strategy is even more critical, as it is unlikely that the document designer keeps your application's requirements in mind when designing.

As with many of the other topics presented in this book, there is no "silver bullet" when choosing how to parse documents with a given structure. When parsing, the requirements of the application will likely shape the parsing strategy that you choose. With that in mind, this chapter is organized so as to help you make the right decisions based on common constraints of real-world applications.

The chapter breaks down into three basic sections:

❑   **What you need to know before you start planning your parsing strategy**: It's vital to have a good understanding of the technologies available to you, so we'll briefly discuss the basic concepts behind:

- The **Document Object Model (DOM)** API – the most popular all-in-memory parser

- The **Simple API for XML (SAX)** API – the standard streaming push parser

We'll also briefly touch on pull parsers, but since there is no widely accepted standard API for pull parsers as of now, it is not a major focus of this chapter. (For the sake of reference, "pull" parsers are so called because their APIs give the developer control over the loop that actually pulls XML tokens from the document; "push" parsers, on the other hand, hide the interaction with the actual document and simply "push" the tokens to the user through callback methods.)

❑ **Design points to help you decide which technology to use based on the constraints of your application**: Here, we'll look at the most common constraints and requirements that XML-enabled applications encounter, and their expected effect on your parsing strategy.

❑ **Implementation patterns**: While most of the rest of the chapter deals with rather high-level concepts, this section is devoted explicitly to patterns that you can use while implementing parsing strategies specifically using DOM or SAX. These patterns will help you to write clean, robust, manageable parsing code.

The examples presented in this chapter will largely be in Java, but there are also a couple of C# examples. The entire example source is available for download at www.wrox.com. To run the Java-based examples, you'll need a few things:

❑ **JDK 1.4** or greater. You can download the latest JDK from http://java.sun.com.

❑ A **SAX2- and DOM2-compliant JAXP implementation**, such as Apache's Crimson, which comes with the JDK 1.4. The examples were tested against Crimson, Apache's Xerces, and GNU's Ælfred. You can find Xerces at http://xml.apache.org/xerces2-j/index.html and Ælfred at http://www.gnu.org/software/classpathx/jaxp/jaxp.html.

To run the C#-based examples, you'll need to download and install **Microsoft's .NET Framework**, which is available at http://msdn.microsoft.com/downloads/default.asp?url=/downloads/sample.asp?url=/msdn-files/027/001/829/msdncompositedoc.xml.

In addition, timing results for many of the examples in this chapter using each of the three parsers mentioned above are available in *Appendix A*.

The examples that are presented in this chapter will be complete, robust, and designed with the rigor that you'd expect from a real-world professional software application. This will make the example code a little bit more verbose, but it will be more robust.

4.1 Before You Start

Here, we'll cover a couple of very important issues that need to be addressed before you start planning your parsing strategy.

4.1.1 In General, the Intended use of the Document Should Drive your Parsing Strategy

This point should be familiar from just about every other aspect of software engineering that you've encountered: **it is practically impossible to build an adequate software solution to a problem if you don't understand how that software will be used**. This is as true with XML documents and parsing strategies as with anything else; just as you wouldn't design a class library or an algorithm without understanding how it would be used, you wouldn't want to design a parsing strategy without understanding the intended use of the document.

Keep in mind that you should resist the temptation of taking the simplest approach from a coding standpoint. As we'll see throughout this chapter, naive parsing strategies can cripple an XML-enabled application's performance faster than any other single factor (except for poor document design). At the most basic level, you can always parse an XML document in one line of code using DOM. However, this is rarely the most ideal strategy for a whole host of reasons that we'll be exploring in this chapter. In the same vein, you can always sort an array using bubble sort, but in most cases it will yield undesirable performance results in comparison to less naive algorithms like quicksort (bubble sort is always $O(n^2)$, while quicksort is usually $O(n \log n)$).

Similarly, simply using the document's structure to define the parsing strategy is rarely enough. This is not to suggest that you ignore the document structure when deciding on a parsing strategy. On the contrary, the document structure *is* a very important constraint. However, simply knowing the structure, in the absence of any usage information, can yield poor results. Let's look at a small example that illustrates this point.

Let's say that we have an XML document that represents the configuration information for an application. Let's also say that our application has many different modules, each of which requires its own configuration. However, we want to store all of those configurations in *one* place. Each configuration must be able to store name-value property pairs, and contain sub-configurations. An example document might look something like this:

```
<configurationContainer>
  <!-- The database configuration -->
  <configuration name="databaseConfig">
    <property name="driverClassName"
      value="jdbc:postgres:template"/>
    <property name="serverName"
      value="db01.somecompany.com"/>

    <subconfiguration name="connectionPoolConfig">
      <property name="poolName" value="appPool"/>
      <property name="maxConnections" value="5"/>
    </subconfiguration>
```

```
    </configuration>

    <!-- The web server configuration -->
    <configuration name="webServerConfig">
      <property name="maxConnections" value="50"/>
      <property name="maxThreads" value="10"/>
    </configuration>
  </configurationContainer>
```

> *This is a trivial example, but it is based in reality; a large number of
> applications now use XML as a means to store their configuration
> information. Unlike the example above, there may exist applications with
> very large and complicated configuration files.*

Now, based on the document structure described above, how would you go about
parsing this document? I hope your first thought was, "I don't have enough information
to decide yet". There are a lot of factors that should play a part in making the decision
on how to parse a document. Here are a few of the questions that you should be able
to answer before settling on a parsing strategy for your documents (we'll spend the
next section discussing exactly these kinds of questions, and what their answers mean
for your parsing strategy, so don't worry if we breeze over some of them here):

- ❏ How big is the document likely to be?
- ❏ Is the document going to be manipulated, or is it effectively read-only?
- ❏ How often will the document need to be parsed, and by how many threads simultaneously?
- ❏ Is the document data-oriented or is it a narrative (we have discussed these styles and their uses in *Chapter 2: Basic Document Design*)?
- ❏ Is the data going to be accessed purely sequentially, or is there a need/advantage to having random-access to the data?

Suppose I told you that the document would hold on an average 10 configurations,
and would never exceed 200 kilobytes in size, that it was read-only, and parsed only
once at the application's startup. Based on this information, you could conclude that it's
perfectly acceptable to use *any* of the technologies that I've described earlier.

The file is small, so the memory overhead of DOM won't be an issue (a little later we'll
see some actual numbers for both memory usage and processing time). It is read-only,
so the fact that streaming parsers don't give you a built-in mechanism for manipulation
doesn't matter. Also, since the document is going to be parsed only once at application
startup, parsing speed isn't really an issue. In this instance, you are free to use
whatever technology you see fit.

What if the circumstances were different? Suppose I told you that the document would be large, approximately 5 megabytes of text or more. On top of that, let's say that the application, for which you're devising a parsing strategy, is a management application that manages many of these large configuration documents, allowing many simultaneous users to read, manipulate, and persist them. In this situation, the memory requirements and parsing performance issues associated with DOM will probably cause you to rule it out. You'll most likely want to use a streaming parser and define your own in-memory representation of the configurations so that you'll have greater control over the memory usage of the application. Thus, the usage of the document needs to be considered very carefully when designing your parsing strategy.

4.1.2 Learn and Understand the Standard Parsing APIs: DOM and SAX

This point may seem self-evident, but it's very important and worthy of a brief discussion here. To make good decisions about devising the parsing strategy for your application, you must understand the libraries available to you, including the functionality each library provides as well as the resource requirements and performance characteristics associated with that functionality.

While it's true that both DOM and SAX provide similar functionality (they allow you to read in XML documents), there are times when you'd need to use one over the other. Knowing the differences between the functionalities of each of the technologies is analogous to knowing the differences between a hammer and a sledgehammer. Sure, you could use a sledgehammer to drive in a half-inch nail, or a hammer to knock down a wall, but you won't get the performance or results that you're looking for. Each of these technologies is just another tool in your tool belt, and what we need to do is make good decisions on when to use each tool.

Since the content of the rest of the chapter relies on them heavily, I'll present a brief overview of each of the major parsing APIs and technologies. The following explanations are not meant to be complete, so if you're not familiar with these APIs or would like a refresher, I'd suggest picking up a copy of *Beginning XML, 2nd Edition* from *Wrox Press (ISBN- 1-86100-559-8)*. You can also learn more about SAX from http://www.saxproject.org, and DOM from http://www.w3.org/DOM.

Parsing technologies fall broadly into two main categories: all-in-memory parsers, and streaming parsers. Beyond that, the streaming parsers category is broken down into two subdivisions, namely push parsers (sometimes known as event-driven parsers), and pull parsers. The following diagram demonstrates the relationship among these different parsing technologies:

Figure 1

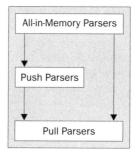

In general, pull parsers are at the lowest level, with push parsers being built on top of (in some form or other) a pull parser. All-in-memory parsers are generally built on top of either a pull parser or a push parser.

All-in-memory parsers load the entire XML document into memory and provide you with a tree-like view of the document. As a result, the entire document must be processed before you can access any piece of the document at all. Streaming parsers provide forward-only access to the document, allowing the programmer to process each element as it is parsed in. Push and pull parsers only differ in how you gain access to that data. With push parsers, the parser reads the XML stream, and when it encounters an element (or entity, etc.), it generates an event. It is up to the application to handle those events, usually via a callback or an event handler class. With pull parsers, the application developer is responsible for the parsing loop, pulling elements (or entities, etc.) out of the XML stream explicitly.

Since the functionality they provide is rather hierarchical, you may draw the conclusion that most all-in-memory parsers are implemented on top of a streaming parser, and that push parsers are implemented on top of a pull parser. While this is becoming increasingly true, it isn't always the case.

> *The most popular all-in-memory API, DOM (which we'll explore in a moment), actually preceded SAX, the first and still the most popular streaming API. In addition, SAX preceded a widely-adopted pull parsing API (more on this in a moment as well).*

The DOM API is associated with all-in-memory parsers. The SAX API is associated with push parsers. There is no widely accepted standard API for pull parsers as of now, but both C# and Java have their own implementations. Microsoft's .NET Framework SDK's System.XML.XmlReader class provides an abstract class for pull parsing. As for Java, at the time of this writing, a **Java Specification Request (JSR)** for a pull parser (JSR 173, "StAX: Streaming API for XML") has been accepted for development. You can find more information about the JSR at http://www.jcp.org/jsr/detail/173.jsp. Let's take a quick look at the major features and differences between these parsing technologies.

4.1.2.1 DOM

DOM is the oldest of all the parsing technologies that we'll cover here. It was actually created by Netscape, and appeared as early as version 2.0 of the Navigator browser. It was designed as a means to provide JavaScript with an object-oriented view of an HTML document.

DOM is much more than just a parsing technology; it is a generic document object model, as its name suggests. DOM, whose development is overseen by the W3C, can read in an XML stream, can optionally validate it against a schema or DTD, and when it's done parsing, it provides you with a nice tree view of the document. In DOM, each element corresponds to a node in the tree and using DOM, you can manipulate the document in any number of ways, including addition, modification, and removal of nodes and text content (text is also represented as a node in the tree). You can prune entire subtrees by simply deleting the root of the tree, and similarly you can move subtrees around by removing them from one place in the tree and adding them somewhere else. A DOM instance can also be serialized to an XML stream. These features make DOM a very powerful tool at your disposal.

There are, of course, downsides to using DOM, namely resource requirements and parsing performance. There is a great deal of overhead to using DOM, and for very large documents that can be a big problem. For each element, there must be a corresponding node instance in memory, as well as a collection to hold any attributes that the node may contain. DOM stores everything, including attribute values, as a string. Thus, if you have Boolean or numerical attributes, DOM wastes space storing them as strings. All of these factors, plus others, make DOM quite a memory hog.

As for parsing performance, DOM will almost certainly be outperformed by a streaming parser for a couple of reasons. First off, most DOM implementations are now built on top of a streaming parser, so it clearly can't be faster than the streaming parser it is built upon. If we assume that the DOM implementers chose a good streaming parser to build upon, we can generalize that even the best DOM implementation is at best going to be on par with a good streaming parser. (Of course, the actual implementation does matter. Most DOM and SAX implementations have been through many revisions at this point, so most are fairly efficient, but it is prudent to understand the performance characteristics and limitations of the current generations of parsers. *Appendix A* shows how the more popular Java-based implementations fared when running the examples from this chapter.)

The last major performance issue is the overhead of creating and maintaining the tree structure that makes DOM so useful in the first place. For example, when DOM reads in an element from the XML stream, it has to not only create an object to represent that element, but it needs to create and initialize a node to house that element, add that node to the proper place in the tree, and perhaps perform other housekeeping work, depending on the implementation.

4.1.2.2 SAX

The XML-DEV community originally defined SAX version 1.0 in late 1997 as a mechanism for providing forward-only, event-based XML processing. SAX allows you to define a set of handler objects through which it notifies you when interesting events occur during the sequential parsing of a document. In SAX version 2.0, which we will be discussing in this book, there are four interesting handler interfaces based on the types of information encountered during the parsing process (in Java, each is in the org.xml.sax package):

Handler Interface	Description
ContentHandler	Used by SAX to report content-related events, such as the start or end of the document, the start or end of an element, text content, and prefix to URI namespace mapping. This interface replaces the deprecated DocumentHandler interface from SAX 1.0.
DTDHandler	SAX uses this interface to report DTD-related events, such as entity declarations.
EntityResolver	SAX uses this interface to give the application control over how entities are resolved.
ErrorHandler	SAX uses this interface to report any errors or warnings that occur during parsing.

There is a convenient class (org.xml.sax.helpers.DefaultHandler) that implements all of these interfaces that your parser class can extend.

As with just about any technology, there are positives and negatives associated with using SAX. On the positive side, since it is forward-only, SAX is not particularly resource-intensive. In addition, since it basically just reads XML content from a stream and then passes that content on to the application through the event handler interfaces, SAX implementations generally have very little overhead, which in turn usually leads to good parsing performance.

On the negative side, if it is not implemented properly, the event-handling code for dealing with complex or deeply nested documents can become very convoluted and difficult to read and maintain. Also, since SAX doesn't define an object model of its own (which, coincidentally, is one of the main reasons it performs so well), in most cases you as the application developer will have to define data structures to store your data (you may view this as a negative or a positive, depending on the circumstances). Finally, once the SAX implementation has commenced the parsing process, the only way to terminate the process is to throw an exception, which is less than ideal, since there are certainly conceivable non-exceptional circumstances that may cause the application to want to stop processing a document before it is completed.

Pull parsers are the last parsing technology that we're going to cover here. At the time of this writing, as there didn't exist a widely-adopted standard API for pull parsing, so what we'll cover here will have to be fairly generic. Pull parsing is another streaming parsing technology that sits at a slightly lower level (as we saw in the diagram earlier) than SAX. Based on what we've discussed about these APIs so far and what we saw in the diagram earlier, you can imagine that SAX could be implemented in terms of a pull parser, and in turn DOM could be implemented in terms of SAX or in terms of a pull parser.

Like SAX, pull parsing is also a forward-only, streaming technology. The major difference between pull parsing and push parsing is that the application developer, not the parser implementation, is in control of the loop that processes the XML stream. This is a small but important distinction, as it allows pull parsers to give the application developer more fine-grained control over the actual parsing process, which in turn can lead to better performance in certain situations.

For example, if you are processing a very large document but are only interested in a handful of the elements, using a pull parser instead of SAX saves the overhead of two function calls (for the start and end element events) for each of the elements that you don't care about. In addition, because you have control over the parsing loop, you can terminate the process whenever you see fit without incurring the overhead of throwing an exception.

As pull parsers and SAX are functionally similar, they can often be used interchangeably. This naturally leads to the question of when you might choose one over the other. We'll cover this in more detail later in the chapter, but I'll give you a brief overview now. The major advantage of pull parsing, as we discussed a moment ago, is the more fine-grained control that it gives you over the parsing loop. So the question to ask when you're trying to figure out if you should use SAX or a pull parser is "Would my application benefit from more fine-grained control during parsing?"

In a lot of cases, such as when you have documents that your application will always parse in their entirety, there isn't any tangible benefit to having that extra control. If you choose to use a pull parser in a situation like that, then you're basically rewriting a bunch of code that already lives inside your favorite SAX implementation. However, if you know beforehand that you will be doing a lot of conditional parsing or will have to ignore a lot of elements in large documents, you may want to consider using a pull parser instead.

This section should give you a little bit of background on the various parsing technologies that we'll be discussing for the rest of the chapter and the rest of the book. Remember that parsers are just tools in your arsenal, and it's up to you to pick the right tool for the right job.

4.2 Choosing between DOM and SAX: Which and When?

In the previous section, we talked about the prerequisites that need to be satisfied before you can start making informed decisions about your parsing strategy. In this section, we'll explore which technologies make sense given a set of common constraints.

One note as you read this section: in the majority of the subsections that follow, we'll be discussing DOM versus SAX and neglecting pull parsers. There are a couple of reasons for this.

First off, SAX and DOM are standardized APIs that have achieved widespread adoption, while pull parsing has no standardized API. So for the purposes of building the examples, I chose SAX explicitly because, like DOM, the API is consistent across platforms and implementations.

Secondly, since SAX is just a streaming push parser, and since push and pull parsers share a great deal of the same performance characteristics (particularly in comparison to DOM), you can assume that the arguments that apply to SAX also apply to pull parsers. Towards the end of the section I've devoted a subsection to discussing when you might choose to use a pull parser instead of SAX.

4.2.1 Avoid DOM when the XML is just a Storage or Encoding Mechanism

Applications are increasingly looking to XML as an external storage or encoding mechanism. Many applications, including several that have come out of the Apache Software Foundation, such as Log4J or the Tomcat Application Server, now use XML to store all of their configuration data. Major software systems, such as SQL Server 2000 from Microsoft and FileMaker Pro from FileMaker, Inc., now allow you to import and export data in XML. Other utilities, like the Ant build system from Apache, use XML files to describe a process (in Ant's case, a build process).

In each of these cases, the content that lives in the document is likely to have some other kind of representation that is native to the application, making the XML just a convenient, platform-agnostic encoding mechanism. Often the encoded data is read-only, like import or export files or Ant build files. When the encoded data is modifiable, it usually isn't modified in its document form; the internal representation is modified, and the XML is regenerated when the data needs to be persisted.

At parse time, the data is usually read in piece-by-piece out of a stream and transformed into whatever form the application uses internally. The **pseudocode** for this operation usually looks something like this:

```
open XML stream
loop until stream dries up
    read unit of data from stream
    transform data/act on data
end loop
close XML stream
```

That usage pattern looks a lot like a loop that you'd see in an application using a streaming parser, and for good reason. Streaming parsers are generally a much better fit for these kinds of applications than DOM for a variety of reasons, which we can crystallize in an example.

Let's say that you're working on an order fulfillment system that works in concert with a corresponding order entry system. The order entry system allows end users to create orders by using a web application and also allows call center representatives to enter orders taken in over the phone.

The order entry system takes the orders that it receives and publishes them to XML so that they can be processed by the order management system. The order entry system experiences a very high load, so rather than creating dozens of smaller XML documents every minute, it catalogs all of the orders received over a half-hour period and publishes them all in a single XML document You have been tasked with writing the code that reads in those XML documents and creates the corresponding orders in the order fulfillment system.

The document you'll be parsing contains a digest of orders. An order contains some customer information relating to the order such as shipping and billing address (you can assume that a separate customer management application contains the rest of the customer information so all you need is an ID), as well as the actual items that were ordered. The ordered items contain a **Stock Keeping Unit (SKU)** product identifier, quantity, and unit price. Here's what an example document with just one order would look like:

```
<orderDigest>
  <order id="31459" shippingType="Ground">
    <customer id="tx78734">
      <address type="billing">
        <name>Scott Bonneau</name>
        <street>123 Outatha Way</street>
        <city>Austin</city>
        <state>TX</state>
        <zip>78701-1234</zip>
      </address>

      <address type="shipping">
        <name>Rich Bonneau</name>
        <street>321 Youreinmy Way</street>
        <city>Boston</city>
        <state>MA</state>
        <zip>02210-4321</zip>
      </address>
```

```
      </customer>

      <item sku="TK-421">
        <quantity>1</quantity>
        <unitPrice>$39.95</unitPrice>
      </item>

      <item sku="SB-007">
        <quantity>4</quantity>
        <unitPrice>$1.00</unitPrice>
      </item>
    </order>
  </orderDigest>
```

It's your task to build a system that takes documents like this one and gets them into
your order entry system. I've suggested that a DOM-based solution is not the best
approach to take in this case, but I haven't given you any proof yet. First let me show
you what a DOM-based implementation would look like and then we'll talk about
what characteristics would make it inappropriate in this context. We'll walk through the
important parts of this implementation here, but you can find the full listing for this
and all of the other examples at www.wrox.com. Let's look at processOrderDigest(),
the central public method of our OrderDigestSAX class:

```
public void processOrderDigest(InputSource is)
{
  try {
    // Parse the InputSource into a Document using a DocumentBuilder
    Document orderDigestDocument =
      DocumentBuilderFactory.newInstance()
      .newDocumentBuilder().parse(is);

    // Get the root element of the document, in this case the
    // <orderDigest> element that encloses all of the order elements
    Element rootElement = orderDigestDocument.getDocumentElement();

    // All of the element node-type children of the root element are
    // order elements.
    // Loop over all of these nodes and process each order
    // individually.
    NodeList orderNodeList = rootElement.getChildNodes();
    for (int x = 0, size = orderNodeList.getLength(); x < size; ++x)
    {
      // Get the next node in the loop and process it if it's an
      // element node.
      Node orderNode = orderNodeList.item(x);
      if (orderNode.getNodeType() == Node.ELEMENT_NODE)
      {
        Element orderElement - (Element)orderNode;
        Order order = parseOrder(orderElement);

        // This is where we would insert the order into the
        // system, but for this example we'll just keep track of how
        // many we've processed.
        m_count++;
      }
    }
  } catch (Exception e) {
    System.err.println("An exception occurred during processing.");
```

```
        e.printStackTrace(System.err);
    }
}
```

This method first uses DOM to parse the given `InputSource` into a DOM `Document` instance. Once it has that `Document` instance, it finds all of the children of the root element (the `<orderDigest>` element), which represent the orders, and it passes each of these `<order>` elements on to a private helper function called `parseOrder()`, which parses that element and its sub-elements into our in-memory `Order` instance. As the comment in the code suggests, after retrieving that in-memory `Order` instance, a real-world application would insert the order into the system, but the example just increments a counter.

Let's take a look at the `parseOrder()` method, since it does most of the interesting work in the example:

```
private Order parseOrder(Element orderElement)
{
    // Get the id and shipping type attributes
    String id = orderElement.getAttribute("id");
    String shippingType = orderElement.getAttribute("shippingType");

    // Construct the order and set the shipping type.
    Order order = new Order(id);
    order.setShippingType(shippingType);

    // Get the customer element.  There should be only one.
    NodeList customerNodeList =
        orderElement.getElementsByTagName("customer");
    Element customerElement = (Element)customerNodeList.item(0);

    // Parse the customer out of the customer element and set the
    // customer on the order instance.
    CustomerInfo customer = parseCustomer(customerElement);
    order.setCustomer(customer);

    // Parse out the individual order items and add them to the order
    // instance.
    NodeList orderNodeList =
        orderElement.getElementsByTagName("item");
    for (int x = 0, size = orderNodeList.getLength(); x < size; ++x)
    {
        Element itemElement = (Element)orderNodeList.item(x);
        Item item = parseItem(itemElement);
        order.addItem(item);
    }

    return order;
}
```

This method pulls the id and shippingType attributes off the <order> element and uses those to construct a new in-memory Order instance. It then finds the <customer> element and uses another private helper function, parseCustomer(), to parse that element into an in-memory CustomerInfo instance. Then it iterates over all of the <item> elements that make up the actual items of the order and it uses yet another private helper method, parseItem(), to parse these elements into in-memory Item instances. For the sake of brevity, I'm not including listings for parseCustomer() or parseItem(), but it's sufficient to say that they perform very similar tasks in terms of converting the appropriate DOM elements into their respective in-memory representations.

The major problem with this implementation is this: when we have the in-memory order instance, we no longer need the DOM node that represents that same order data, but are rather stuck with it. Sure, we could delete the node from the DOM document when we're done with it to release the memory that we no longer need, but by the time that we have access to the document the damage has already been done.

The code as it's presented, even though it is structured very cleanly and implemented with rigor, simply doesn't scale because the underlying technology doesn't scale. The practical limit for this code on my machine (an IBM ThinkPad Pentium III 450 with 384MB RAM) is somewhere between 30K and 60K orders in a single document (60K orders is roughly 44MB of text). Anything in the 30K+ range causes memory usage to spiral out of control, which in turn causes parsing time to grow radically as well (for a complete timing and memory usage benchmark of this example and the others from this chapter, see *Appendix A*). In fact, even after allocating as much as 512MB of virtual memory to the VM, this code never successfully processed the 60K document; it always eventually exited with an out-of-memory error.

It's not that every program will need to parse 44MB documents, but these limitations don't occur only with large documents; they also crop up when you're dealing with multiple smaller documents simultaneously. It's not uncommon for certain applications to have ten 1MB documents or fifty 200KB documents open simultaneously, and DOM will exhibit similar practical limitations in these situations as well.

Now that we've seen a solution that doesn't scale, let's take a look at one that does. Here is a piece of code very similar to what I've just presented, but instead of using DOM as the underlying parsing technology it uses SAX. The code is functionally identical to the DOM example, and I've tried to keep it as structurally similar as possible given the limitation that SAX and DOM are architecturally distinct. The OrderDigestSAX class extends the DefaultHandler SAX class, which is just a default no-op implementer of all of the SAX handler interfaces. Let's take a look at the main() method, since it's more integral to the example for SAX than for DOM:

```
public static void main(String[] args) throws Exception
{
    if (args.length < 1)
    {
```

```
        System.err.println("Must specify filename on the commandline.");
        return;
    }

    // Collect the current time so that we can time the entire process
    long start = System.currentTimeMillis();

    // Create the handler instance (our class)
    OrderDigestSAX ods = new OrderDigestSAX();

    // Create a SAX XMLReader instance and set our handler instance as
    // the content handler.  Note that here we could set our handler
    // instance as any of the other handler types as well, since it
    // extends DefaultHandler.  However, since our example only deals
    // with content and we've only implemented ContentHandler methods,
    // we'll only set the reader's content handler here.
    XMLReader reader = XMLReaderFactory.createXMLReader();
    reader.setContentHandler(ods);

    // Tell the reader to parse the document in the filename that was
    // specified on the commandline.
    reader.parse(new InputSource(new FileReader(args[0])));

    // Collect the current time and calculate the total time in
    // seconds.
    long end = System.currentTimeMillis();
    double seconds = (double)(end - start)/1000.0;

    // Print out the number of orders processed and the timing
    // information.
    System.out.println();
    System.out.println("Parsed " + ods.m_count + " orders in "
      + seconds + " seconds.");
}
```

The `main()` method instantiates an `OrderDigestSAX` instance and an `XMLReader` instance, and sets the `OrderDigestSAX` instance as the content handler on the reader. It then tells the reader to parse, which is where the fun begins. Our class implements three of the `ContentHandler` methods: `startElement()`, `endElement()`, and `characters()`. Let's take a look at each of these, starting with **startElement()**:

```
public void startElement(String uri, String localName, String qName,
                    Attributes attributes) throws SAXException
{
    // Switch on each of the element names that we expect and then
    // take the appropriate action.  In some cases, there's nothing
    // we need to do, so we just return from the method.  For the
    // elements we do care about, we delegate to a function to take
    // care of the specific element.

    if ("orderDigest".equals(qName))
        return;

    if ("order".equals(qName))
    {
        parseOrder(attributes);
        return;
    }
```

```
if ("customer".equals(qName))
{
  parseCustomer(attributes);
  return;
}

if ("address".equals(qName))
{
  parseAddress(attributes);
  return;
}

if ("item".equals(qName))
{
  parseItem(attributes);
  return;
}

// For each of these elements, the only data we care about is the
// character data that is a child of the element. The characters()
// method only records the data if m_currentCharacterData is
// non-null, so we assign m_currentCharacterData here.
if ("quantity".equals(qName) || "unitPrice".equals(qName)
    || "name".equals(qName) || "street".equals(qName)
    || "city".equals(qName) || "state".equals(qName)
    || "zip".equals(qName))
{
  m_currentCharacterData = new StringBuffer(100);
  return;
}

throw new RuntimeException("Unrecognized element: " + qName);
}
```

The startElement() method basically switches on the element name and calls into an appropriate private helper function to process the element successfully. These helper functions, parseOrder(), parseCustomer(), etc., are very similar in functionality to their counterparts in our DOM example, the main difference being that instead of using a DOM element for their state, these helper functions rely on some member variables and SAX attributes for their state.

The OrderDigestSAX class defines four member variables that keep around the currently processing order, address, and item objects, as well as the current character data for the elements that don't use attributes for their content (address, street, city, etc). These variables are assigned to a new StringBuffer instance in the code that handles the start element and assigned to null in the code that handles the end element. This is actually a rather naïve state-maintenance mechanism that can lead to highly non-maintainable code, since it requires adding additional member variables to store parsing state as the complexity of the document increases. We'll cover a more robust mechanism a little later in the chapter in *Section 4.3.1: With Sax, use a Context Stack when Parsing Deeply Nested Documents*.

The private helper methods rely on these member variables in order to keep their context straight. For example, the parseOrder() method creates a new Order instance and assigns it to m_currentOrder so that subsequent elements can have a reference to the Order instance that contains them. Here's what the **parseOrder()** method looks like:

```
private void parseOrder(Attributes attributes)
{
    // Pull out the id and shippingType attributes
    String id = attributes.getValue("id");
    String shippingType = attributes.getValue("shippingType");

    // Create a new order instance and assign it to m_currentOrder
    m_currentOrder = new Order(id);
    m_currentOrder.setShippingType(shippingType);
}
```

Now let's take a look at **endElement()**:

```
public void endElement(String uri, String localName, String qName)
    throws SAXException
{
    if ("orderDigest".equals(qName))
        return;

    if ("order".equals(qName))
    {
        // This is where we would insert the order into the system, but
        // for this example we'll just keep track of how many we've
        // processed.
        m_count++;
        m_currentOrder = null;
        return;
    }

    if ("customer".equals(qName))
        return;

    if ("address".equals(qName))
    {
        m_currentAddress = null;
        return;
    }

    if ("item".equals(qName))
    {
        m_currentItem = null;
        return;
    }

    if ("quantity".equals(qName))
    {
        try {
            String qtyString = m_currentCharacterData.toString();
            m_currentItem.setQuantity(Integer.parseInt(qtyString));
```

```
      m_currentCharacterData = null;
    } catch (NumberFormatException nfe) {
      throw new RuntimeException("Quantity was not an integer.");
    }
    return;
  }

  if ("unitPrice".equals(qName))
  {
    try {
      String priceString = m_currentCharacterData.toString();
      Number priceNumber = m_currencyFormat.parse(priceString);
      m_currentItem.setUnitPrice(priceNumber.doubleValue());
      m_currentCharacterData = null;
    } catch (ParseException pe) {
      throw new RuntimeException("Price not formatted properly.");
    }
    return;
  }

  if ("name".equals(qName))
  {
    m_currentAddress.setName(m_currentCharacterData.toString());
    m_currentCharacterData = null;
    return;
  }

  if ("street".equals(qName))
  {
    m_currentAddress.setStreet(m_currentCharacterData.toString());
    m_currentCharacterData = null;
    return;
  }

  if ("city".equals(qName))
  {
    m_currentAddress.setCity(m_currentCharacterData.toString());
    m_currentCharacterData = null;
    return;
  }

  if ("state".equals(qName))
  {
    m_currentAddress.setState(m_currentCharacterData.toString());
    m_currentCharacterData = null;
    return;
  }

  if ("zip".equals(qName))
  {
    m_currentAddress.setZip(m_currentCharacterData.toString());
    m_currentCharacterData = null;
    return;
  }
}
```

A call to endElement() indicates the closing of an element's context, which in turn is when we usually want to process that data related to that element. Thus, it makes sense that a significant chunk of work is done by endElement(). In this case, we use endElement() to reset our temporary state member variables for the currently processing order, address, and item, and to assign the character data we accumulated from calls to the characters() method to the correct place. In a real-world application, when we see the end of the <order> element, we'd turn and pass our in-memory Order instance (from m_currentOrder) into our system; once again, for the example, we just increment a counter.

Let's take a quick look at the **characters()** method to demonstrate how our fourth temporary state member variable is used:

```
public void characters(char ch[], int start, int length)
    throws SAXException
{
    // There are only a few cases where we care about the character
    // data, specifically when we're in the context of the address
    // sub-elements (name, street, city, state, and zip) or in the
    // context of the item sub-elements (quantity and unitPrice).
    // In the startElement() method for those elements we assign
    // m_currentCharacterData to a new StringBuffer instance so that
    // in this method we'll have somewhere to put the new character
    // data.
    if (m_currentCharacterData != null)
      m_currentCharacterData.append(ch, start, length);
}
```

You can see that we just *append* the character data to our StringBuffer member variable, m_currentCharacterData, whenever it is non-null. If you look back at the bottom of the startElement() method, you can see *where* we assign a new StringBuffer instance to m_currentCharacterData; if you look at the end of endElement() you can see *where* we handle assigning that character data and setting m_currentCharacterData to null.

Procedurally, this code follows fairly closely the pseudocode that we discussed at the start of *Section 4.2.1: Avoid DOM when the XML is just a Storage or Encoding Mechanism*. It reads from the stream, processing each element in useful units (in this case, orders). At the point when endElement() is processing the end of an <order> element, we have what we were interested in; namely, a native order instance. The difference between this solution and the DOM solution is that at this point we haven't parsed anything that wasn't directly related to the current order, and once we submit the order into the system, we simply free that memory by assigning null to m_currentOrder, and the garbage collector takes care of cleaning up for us.

The practical limit for this solution is more than that of the DOM solution. On my machine, this solution handles 60K orders in about 35 seconds, and it never uses more than about 7MB of RAM.

When your application's constraints and requirements don't preclude one technology or the other, I would strongly encourage you to consider using SAX even in situations where your documents are relatively small and resource requirements aren't an issue, since there is hardly ever a good reason for having two in-memory representations of the same data simultaneously. The code complexity of these two approaches (notwithstanding the naïve state management code, which we'll remedy a little later) is roughly equal in this case, despite the fact that DOM allows you to parse the entire document in just one call.

Ultimately, the code ends up not being all that different in a lot of cases; it's just a matter of *where* the complexity lies. With SAX, it lies in the actual parsing of the document, whereas in DOM it lies in mapping the DOM's object model onto your native object model. As a result, in a lot of cases there's no real gain to using DOM from a brevity of code standpoint either. SAX is usually a better fit here on all fronts.

4.2.2 Favor DOM when the XML is the Primary Representation of the Document

Data oriented documents model data. Whether that data explicitly maps on to data structures that exist within the context of an application, is a function of the requirements and implementation of the application. In many cases, however, the data has some kind of representation native to the application. Thus, the structure of the document generally has little value; the data could just as easily have been encoded using some other mechanism, like the purchase order example from *Section 4.2.1*. In other cases, the actual structure of the data is of critical importance; these are usually cases when the data being represented is hierarchical in nature. For example, you could imagine representing an arithmetic expression as an XML document:

```
<!-- Arithmetic expression using prefix notation -->
<expression>
  <plus>
    <times>
     <literal value="6"/>
     <literal value="3"/>
    </times>
    <minus>
      <times>
        <literal value="2"/>
        <literal value="8"/>
      </times>
      <literal value="9"/>
    </minus>
  </plus>
</expression>
```

You may think this is a rather trite example; when would you need to encode an arithmetic expression in XML? The reason I chose this example is twofold: it is easy to understand, and it is representative of a larger class of more compelling but much more complex examples. For instance, an abstract syntax tree generated by a compiler would have very similar characteristics to this example if encoded in XML.

Narrative-style documents also tend to model some kind of data, but in general they don't map as cleanly on to application-specific data structures. For most narrative-style documents, the document content *is* the text, and the markup is simply a convenient mechanism for augmenting the text with some more data. The most obvious example of this is HTML (ignoring for the moment that HTML and XML are distinct, though related, technologies). HTML is, if you'll allow me to slightly oversimplify, simply a way of displaying text. The HTML markup tags give document authors an easy way to influence how their text is presented to the user. In such cases, the document is really the most convenient representation of the data.

DOM can provide a good deal of value in cases where there isn't a clean mapping from document data into an application's data structures, and in cases where the structure of the data is of keen importance. Keep in mind that DOM is more than just a simple parser; DOM's generic hierarchical object model offers a nice, clean solution to precisely these kinds of problems. You should consider using DOM in these cases when resource requirements permit.

To understand why this is the case, let's take a look at the functionality that DOM provides. Beyond the basic parsing functionality, you've got a generic n-ary tree implementation, complete with fully functional (and tested!) manipulation methods allowing you to add, change, or delete nodes in the tree, navigate the tree, search the tree, and so forth. If the data that you're trying to represent is hierarchical in nature, this is exactly the kind of data structure that you're likely to need. There will, of course, always be situations when you may want to implement your own hierarchical data structure or use a different existing tree structure (like Swing's JTree class), but you can often save yourself time and bugs by using DOM.

Let's consider the arithmetic expression example for a moment. Implementing a solution to evaluate expressions of this form is a much simpler and cleaner task in DOM than it is in SAX. Let's take a look at a DOM implementation:

```java
public double evaluate(Element element)
{
  String elementName = element.getNodeName();

  // Make sure the element is one we recognize.
  if (!elementName.equals("plus") && !elementName.equals("minus")
      && !elementName.equals("times") && !elementName.equals("divide")
      && !elementName.equals("mod") && !elementName.equals("literal"))
    throw new RuntimeException("Got unrecognized element: " +
                               elementName);

  // If the element is a literal, simply return the value of the
  // "value" attribute.
  if ("literal".equals(elementName))
  {
    try {
      return Double.parseDouble(element.getAttribute("value"));
    } catch (NumberFormatException nfe) {
      throw new RuntimeException("Literal value not formatted " +
        "properly.");
```

```
        }
      }

      // For all of the other elements, evaluate each of the child
      // nodes, put them in a list, and perform the operator on each
      // element in the list.
      List values = new ArrayList();
      NodeList childNodes = element.getChildNodes();
      for (int x = 0, count = childNodes.getLength(); x < count; ++x)
      {
        Node childNode = childNodes.item(x);
        if (childNode.getNodeType() == Node.ELEMENT_NODE)
          values.add(new Double(evaluate((Element)childNode)));
      }

      if ("plus".equals(elementName))
        return addList(values);

      if ("minus".equals(elementName))
        return subtractList(values);

      if ("times".equals(elementName))
        return multiplyList(values);

      if ("divide".equals(elementName))
        return divideList(values);

      if ("mod".equals(elementName))
        return modList(values);

      throw new RuntimeException("Unexpected element: " + elementName);
    }
```

As you can see from the code snippet, the evaluation process is a very simple recursive procedure. In the base case (a literal element), we simply return the literal's value. In an operation element, we iterate over the child elements and recursively call evaluate() on them. We queue up the results of those calls to evaluate() (allowing the function to handle any number of arguments), and then we perform the specified operator on the list. The xxxList() methods simply perform the operator on the list (say value1 op value2 op value3), and in the case of a null or empty list, they return 0.

Implementing this same solution in SAX is a more daunting task, primarily because we're responsible for parsing the document and managing the data ourselves. A tree structure is the most elegant solution to the problem, but if we end up using a tree structure in the SAX implementation we're effectively re-implementing DOM. In this situation, it makes sense just to use DOM in the first place.

DOM is often a good solution for parsing narrative-style documents. This is unsurprising, given its origins. DOM was designed specifically to represent these kinds of documents, and although its original use was HTML documents, its usefulness is not limited to presentation-oriented documents.

144

DOM's effectiveness in dealing with narrative documents is a result of its hierarchical structure and how it deals with text data. Text data is just another node in the document, and can thus be a child of another node, which is precisely what you want when you're working with narrative documents. You want to be able to associate text with some state, and you want that state to be hierarchical in nature. Since you're probably familiar with HTML, let's look at a quick example. Here's a small HTML snippet:

```
<html>
  <body>
    This is some text that should be rendered, since it lives inside
    the body tag.  <font face="arial">This is some text that
    should be rendered <b>(in bold)</b> in Arial.</font>
  </body>
</html>
```

The state that is encoded in these tags is hierarchical in nature: the fact that the *text* is inside the <body> tag means that it should be rendered; that it is inside the <font> tag means it should be rendered in a given font; and that it is inside the <b> tag means that it should be rendered in the given font and in bold.

DOM's view of this document looks like this:

```
html
    #text
    body
        #text
        font
            #text
            b
                #text
            end b
            #text
        end font
        #text
    end body
    #text
end html
```

The root element (the <html> element) has one child node, namely the <body> element (ignoring the two text elements wrapping the body tag that occur only because of the indentation of the <body> element). The <body> element has three child nodes: a text node (everything up to the <font> tag), the font element, and then another text node (the text after the <font> tag). The <font> element also has three children: a text node (everything up to the <b> tag), the bold element, and another text node (the text after the <b> tag). The <b> element has just one child, a text node.

You could easily parse this kind of document with SAX or a pull parser, but how would you store the data? If you were trying to build a data structure to represent these documents, there's a good chance it would come out looking a lot like DOM. In these situations, take advantage of the generic document model available in DOM.

145

4.2.3 Avoid DOM when You're Only Interested in Parts of the Document

Suppose you don't need the entire contents of a given document. It could either be that you're only interested in certain elements in the document so you want to just ignore the others, or that you only want to process the document up to a certain point. Also, as more and more data ends up in XML documents, it is more likely to be the case that the same basic document may be passed amongst different processing agents, all of whom only need a (sometimes very small) subset of the data contained within the entire document.

In these situations, it's generally a good idea to avoid using DOM because of the lack of control over the parsing process it gives you. Let's see why DOM is wasteful here:

❑ **DOM forces you to read and parse the entire stream**. That's clearly less than ideal, and depending on the size of the document, the performance costs can be extremely high.

❑ **DOM will need to create a node for every XML token** (entities, entity references, comments, etc.) in the document, even those you don't care about. All of this adds up to a substantial memory requirement, and much of it will never be accessed.

❑ After DOM reads in the stream, you're still going to have to traverse at least some of the Document instance yourself to do whatever processing you need to do. This means that **every element that you are interested in must be visited twice**, which can be very costly if you're interested in most of the document or if the document is very large.

Streaming parsers don't experience these kinds of problems: they give you precisely the kind of control that you need in these situations. Pull parsers are actually a little bit more flexible than SAX in this regard for a couple of reasons:

❑ SAX doesn't provide a mechanism for gracefully stopping the parsing process; you must throw an exception to stop parsing. Since pull parsers give you complete control over the parsing loop, you can simply choose to exit the loop whenever it is appropriate.

❑ SAX will always make calls to its callback functions (startElement(), endElement(), etc.), even if you're not interested in those particular elements or character data. With a pull parser, you can truly process only those XML tokens that you are interested in, without even the overhead of an unnecessary function call.

In general, it makes sense to use a streaming parser for documents that you intend to parse conditionally. Despite the two disadvantages SAX has in comparison to pull parsers, it is still a much better choice than DOM in most situations.

You may be wondering what happens when, for instance, you have a narrative document that you want to use DOM to represent, but you're only interested in parts of that document. A little later in the chapter, we'll cover a hybrid technique that will let you get the best of both worlds, so to speak.

4.2.4 Choose your Parsing Strategy Carefully when Dealing with Pointer-heavy Documents

In *Chapter 2*, we talked about pointer-heavy document structures and why you should try to avoid them where possible. Of course, in practice, pointer-heavy document structures *do* occur. Let's discuss an approach for parsing them.

The major problem with pointer-heavy documents is, unsurprisingly, pointer resolution. The major problem with pointer resolution, in turn, is that it requires that you maintain enough state in memory throughout the parsing process to do the resolution. Depending on the situation, this might not be a big deal or it might significantly affect how you choose to parse the document.

It's important that you understand that there is no magic involved in either DOM or SAX with respect to dealing with pointers. In the end, the application code is going to be responsible for doing the actual resolution. The difference lies in who is responsible for maintaining the state necessary to do the resolution. Since DOM reads the entire document into memory before giving you access to any part of it, it does the state maintenance for you. SAX on the other hand is a forward-only process and thus doesn't read the entire document into memory, so the responsibility for maintaining the state falls to you as the application developer.

Since state maintenance is really the central issue you need to consider here, if you were going to use DOM, based on the other characteristics of the document and its usage, then the fact that it also uses pointers probably shouldn't have any effect on your decision. You'll still have to do all of the pointer resolution on your own, but using DOM saves you the trouble of writing any of the state maintenance code yourself. This means that the focus of our discussion needs to be on SAX and how to use it to process pointer-heavy documents.

Maintaining state during the SAX-based parsing process is not, in and of itself, a particularly daunting task; in fact, only the most trivial of documents can be parsed without maintaining at least some kind of state. Of course, for most parsing tasks the goal is to keep the scope of the state to a minimum; you don't want to have state kicking around any longer than is absolutely necessary because that state is consuming a most precious resource, namely memory. As we saw in *Section 4.2.1*, keeping around unnecessary state can destroy your parsing application's performance. On top of that, the more complicated the state, the more complicated the state maintenance code is likely to be, and statistically speaking that usually leads to more error prone code.

The problem with using SAX in pointer-heavy documents is that if you want to perform the parsing step in just one pass through the document, you may need to keep almost the *entire* document in memory at the same time. Consider a document in which all the pointer references come before any of the referencing data in the document. You'll need to store all of the data related to *those* pointer references, until you come across the corresponding referencing data, because you can process all of the data related to the pointer only after you've found the referencing data. Thus, you'll need to store a large amount of data in memory, in a large document of this type. This is a worst-case scenario, of course, and you should avoid this type of document structure at all costs because of its implications on parsing performance.

If a document is structured this way, you're left with one of two often unappealing choices: either deal with storing the majority of the data in memory at once, or parse the document in two passes, with the first pass bypassing the referenced data and retrieving and storing only the referencing data (which should hopefully be relatively small), and the second pass dealing with just the referenced data.

The pathological case of having all the referenced data appear in the document before any of the referencing data shouldn't occur too often, but examining it is useful as it introduces and exaggerates the problems you're likely to encounter when dealing with documents that are similar but less extreme. If your document is structured in this manner, and is small enough to allow you to parse it all in one pass, you may want to consider using DOM even if the other characteristics of the document might suggest SAX. If you have to keep most of the document in memory anyway, it may make sense to save yourself the trouble of writing and maintaining any state maintenance code.

4.2.5 When to Favor a Pull Parser

Up to now, we've discussed the tradeoffs of DOM and SAX without any substantive discussion of where pull parsers fit in the mix. Specifically, both SAX and pull parsers are streaming parsers, and since all of the comparisons so far in this chapter have been based on the distinction between streaming parsers and all-in-memory parsers, there's been no real need to cover pull parsers specifically. All of the arguments contrasting DOM and SAX also apply when contrasting DOM and a pull parser. The goal of this section is to familiarize you with the differences between SAX and pull parsers, and to discuss the circumstances under which you might choose one over the other.

The major difference between SAX and pull parsers is that pull parsers give you control over the actual parsing loop, whereas SAX controls the parsing loop and forwards the "events" on to the application via its callback methods. Thus, pull parsers give you a slightly greater degree of control over the processing of the document. You need to decide whether or not that extra amount of control is important for your application.

To give you a good foundation for comparing SAX and pull parsers, let's walk through an example using a pull parser. We don't have a standard for a Java-based pull parser yet (but there will be soon, with JSR 173, "StAX: Streaming API for XML" currently in development). However, I'd like to keep the language I use for the examples consistent, so for the examples in this chapter I've chosen to write them in Java using the **XML Pull Parser (XPP3)** library, which implements the Common API for XML Pull Parsing (for C# users, there is a corresponding example using the .NET XmlTextReader class available on the web site for the book). The reason I've chosen this particular API is because the designer of the Common API for XML Pull Parsing, Aleksander Slominski, is in the expert group for the StAX JSR, so StAX is likely to bear some resemblance to this API. You can find out more about the Common API for XML Pull Parsing at http://www.xmlpull.org.

The example that we're using here will help you to understand the relationship between push parsers (like SAX) and pull parsers. We're going to walk through using a pull parser to implement a subset of SAX. Building a full implementer of SAX based on a pull parser is a valuable exercise, but it's beyond the scope of this book. For this example, we'll just implement a subset of the XMLReader interface that interacts with the ContentHandler interface. This is what the parse(InputSource) method for our XMLReader implementer looks like, minus the code that actually calls into the content handler:

```
public void parse(InputSource input)
   throws IOException, SAXException
{
   // A real SAX implementation wouldn't do this, but for our case
   // we only care about when we have a content handler, so we'll
   // throw an exception if it's not set.
   if (m_contentHandler == null)
     throw new RuntimeException("No content handler set!");

   try {
     // Instantiate the pull parser from its factory and set the
     // input on the parser.
     XmlPullParserFactory factory = XmlPullParserFactory.newInstance();
     XmlPullParser parser = factory.newPullParser();
     parser.setInput(input.getCharacterStream());

     // This method returns the type of the event, such as
     // START_ELEMENT, TEXT, END_DOCUMENT, etc.
     int eventType = parser.getEventType();

     // Loop until we see the end of the document.
     Boolean done = false;
     while (!done)
     {
       // Here is where we would call into the content handler
       // depending on the event type.  We'll expand this ellipsis
       // in a moment.
       ...

       // If we're not done, get the next event.
       if (!done)
         eventType = parser.next();
```

```
        }
    } catch (XmlPullParserException xppe) {
        // Wrap an XmlPullParserException in a SAXException
        throw new SAXException(xppe);
    }
}
```

This method creates a pull parser from a factory, opens up the input stream, and then loops over the input stream using the parser until we see the end of document tag. With a pull parser, you tell the parser to read the next token out of the stream. That token stays "in scope" until you tell the parser to get the next token. In XPP3, we start the process by calling `parser.getEventType()`, which reads the first token in from the stream and returns the event type for that token. We process that event in a loop, and then call `parser.next()`, which causes the parser to read in the next token, and so on until the end document tag has been read.

The "interesting" code, namely the code that actually deals with the contents of the XML stream, has been omitted in this listing, but the ellipsis indicates where it would go. The parsing loop for most pull parser-based applications will most likely have a very similar structure to this, so I wanted to show it to you minus the application-specific code. Now that we've got the structure covered, let's move on and take a look at the code that calls into our content handler (this code expands on the ellipsis in the previous code block):

```
// Set some local variables so we can pass them on to
// the content handler methods.
String namespaceURI = parser.getNamespace();
String localName = parser.getName();
String qName = localName;
if (parser.getPrefix() != null &&
    parser.getPrefix().length() > 0)
    qName = parser.getPrefix() + ":" + localName;

// Switch on the event type so we can call the correct
// content handler method.
switch (eventType)
{
    case XmlPullParser.START_DOCUMENT:
        m_contentHandler.startDocument();
        break;

    case XmlPullParser.END_DOCUMENT:
        m_contentHandler.endDocument();
        done = true;
        break;

    case XmlPullParser.START_TAG:
        // 'MyAttributes' is a local private implementer of the
        // SAX Attributes interface.
        Attributes attributes = new MyAttributes(parser);
        m_contentHandler.startElement(namespaceURI, localName,
            qName, attributes);
        break;

    case XmlPullParser.END_TAG:
```

150

```
            m_contentHandler.endElement(namespaceURI, localName, qName);
            break;

        case XmlPullParser.TEXT:
            // 'sAndL' holds the start index and length of the run in
            // the char[] that holds the data we care about.
            int[] sAndL = new int[2];
            char[] characters = parser.getTextCharacters(sAndL);
            m_contentHandler.characters(characters, sAndL[0], sAndL[1]);
            break;
    }
```

This code just switches on the event type for the current event, transforms the data from the pull parser's format into the SAX parser's format, and then passes that data on to the content handler. (The m_contentHandler member variable is of ContentHandler type and gets set by our XMLReader's implementation of the setContentHandler() method.)

To test this code, I took the order digest processing example code from *Section 4.2.1*, and changed the line that instantiates the XMLReader instance in the main() method. Instead of getting the XMLReader instance from the XMLReaderFactory.createInstance() method, I simply created a new instance of my PullParserXMLReader class, from which the above code is taken. Since the order digest code only uses a content handler and it only uses the start and end element events, using the pull parser-based XMLReader works just fine.

I ran the same set of large documents through the modified order digest example, and for the document containing 60K orders, which took about 35 seconds using Xerces' SAX parser, this new pull parser-based XMLReader took just 24 seconds. This gives us a concrete example where using a pull parser can have a fairly dramatic effect on performance. You can't say precisely *what* causes the performance increase, without profiling the Xerces SAX parser code. It is fair to assume that some of it may be due to Xerces' less efficient pull parser implementation under the covers. It is also fair to assume, however, that some of it is due to the overhead of having to support the full set of SAX features, even though not all of them will be used in every application.

For instance, say you have a document that is full of comments and entities and other XML tokens that your application does not care about. SAX parsers are forced to deal with those tokens through callbacks to the various handler interfaces, and the time spent processing those tokens eats away at performance even though they have no effect on the application whatsoever. With a pull parser, you can simply ignore those other tokens, as I have in the example code, and you don't even waste as much time as a method call to a no-op method implementation. For large documents where you only care about a fraction of the content, this can add up to a significant cost savings.

So it's clear that using a pull parser and tailoring your parsing code can yield substantial gains under the right circumstances. The specific "right circumstances" will vary from implementation to implementation, but speaking in general terms, there are a few guidelines that should be broadly applicable:

❑   You're only interested in part of the document, particularly if you don't intend to parse the document through to its end. Earlier in the chapter we discussed why DOM was a bad idea if you're only interested in part of the document. Here we complete that discussion by saying that pull parsers can be a good idea in this situation. The reason is clear: since you've got complete control over the entire parsing loop, you can filter out the tokens that you don't care about without any of the overhead imposed by SAX (like a call to `startElement()` and `endElement()` for element tokens that you're not interested in).

❑   Your parsing code only relies on a small subset of SAX's available functionality. In these situations, the overhead of having to support the entire SAX 2.0 specification can cause performance issues that you can avoid by having that extra degree of control that pull parsers provide.

The major downside to using a pull parser is that for complicated document structures or parsing processes you can end up having to write and maintain more code than you would if you used SAX. For instance, if your application processes every single token that exists in your document (and a lot, if not most, applications will do this), then there's little value in a using a pull parser, because not only do you need to maintain all of the code to handle the tokens (which you'd also have to do using SAX), but you need to maintain the parsing loop as well. In addition, as the complexity level of your application grows and you start dealing with things like resolving entities and handling DTDs, you end up effectively implementing more and more of the same code that SAX gives you for free.

With the advent of JSR 173, there should be a standard in the near future, which will help with interoperability and will allow the same degree of freedom that exists right now with SAX to write code against a standard interface and swap out implementations at runtime.

> **Pull parsers are a great alternative to SAX when your application could benefit from cutting some corners off the complete SAX parsing process. However, for complicated document structures, if your application processes every token in the document, pull parsers should be avoided.**

4.2.6 Consider using a Hybrid Approach when neither SAX nor DOM Provides the Necessary Functionality

So far we've covered a variety of the characteristics of a document and its usage patterns that will help you make good decisions when choosing a parsing strategy. I've presented these issues in the straightest possible manner in order to get the concepts across. Of course, in practice, things are rarely so clear-cut, and there will always be situations where some characteristics of a document suggest that you use DOM while others suggest you use SAX; for example, when some documents have a mixture of both narrative and structured data, or where some of the data maps well onto existing data structures and some data is well represented by DOM's hierarchical structure.

In these situations, you can take advantage of DOM being more than just a parsing technology. DOM allows you to build up a tree programmatically as well as through an XML stream, and that fact gives you some interesting options when dealing with these kinds of document structures; it allows you to take a hybrid approach that draws on the strengths of both DOM and SAX and avoids many of their respective weaknesses.

Let's look at an example document structure that contains a mix of narrative data and structured data. In this example, we'll look at a document that could be used to represent the contents of a message in an instant messaging system. There is some structured data that represents header and delivery information to make sure that the message is routed and received properly, and then there is the text content of the message itself, which we'll say allows the author of the message to include some markup to affect the presentation of the message. Here's a sample document:

```
<message id="1001290192" sentDate="10.31.2002 3:13:33PM GMT">
  <sender address="SomeScreenName" ip="10.0.0.10"/>
  <recipientList>
    <recipient address="SomeOtherScreenName" ip="10.0.0.1"/>
    <recipient address="YetAnotherScreenName" ip="10.0.0.2"/>
  </recipientList>

  <header>
    <property name="priority" value="normal"/>
    <property name="sensitivity" value="normal"/>
    <property name="sendingClient" value="Some Instant Messanger"/>
    <property name="sendingClientVersion" value="1.0"/>
  </header>

  <content>
    Hey there, this is some <b>bold</b> text.  This is some
    <i>italicized</i> text.
    <br/>
    This is some text after a break.
  </content>
</message>
```

You can see from the example that the document is comprised of four main pieces of data: the sender, a list of recipients, a list of header properties, and the actual message content. The first three pieces of data are all well-structured, and could conceivably map directly to an existing data structure within our instant messaging application. The message content, however, is unstructured, narrative data. Ultimately, we want to take that content and pass it to an XHTML renderer to draw the message content on the screen; it doesn't have a specific data structure to represent it in our system.

In addition to being able to represent just a single message, our messaging system catalogs a history of all the messages sent to, or received from, our messaging client. Those message histories can be imported from and exported to, unsurprisingly, XML. The import/export file is comprised of a list of messages in the format shown above, wrapped in a <messageHistory> tag. A sample message history document would look like this:

```
<messageHistory>
   <message id="1001290192" sentDate="10.31.2002 3:13:33PM GMT">
      ...
   </message>
   <message id="2592839102" sentDate="10.31.2002 3:22:40PM GMT">
      ...
   </message>
   <message id="8372204105" sentDate="10.31.2002 3:47:28PM GMT">
      ...
   </message>
</messageHistory>
```

Given these requirements, we can rule out using DOM as the parser, as DOM's memory footprint when parsing in a large import file would be huge. At the same time, while SAX would be the best choice for the majority of the data, we clearly want to use DOM to represent the actual message content. This conundrum can be solved by using a hybrid approach.

The basic outline for the hybrid approach is fairly simple. We use SAX to parse the entire document, but when we're processing the markup related to the message content (everything within the <content> tag), we simply use that data to construct a DOM instance that just holds the content of the current message that we're processing. This accomplishes several important goals:

❑ We avoid absorbing the overhead of DOM for the structured data by using SAX to parse the entire document.

❑ We get the benefit of using DOM exclusively for the content that requires it.

❑ The solution will scale well even with large import/export files.

The only minor caveat here is that it requires the developer to understand both SAX and DOM.

This solution is actually not very difficult from a coding standpoint, either. In the interest of reusability, we've encapsulated all of the code required to build a DOM `Document` instance out of SAX events into a class called `DOMAdapter`. The `DOMAdapter` class has three methods on it that each correspond to a method from the SAX interface `ContentHandler`: `startElement()`, `endElement()`, and `characters()`.

In an application's actual SAX parsing code, when you're processing the elements that you want encoded in a DOM document, you simply call into your `DOMAdapter` instance's method corresponding to the event that you're currently handling (start element, end element, or characters). When you're done processing the last tag for the DOM content, you can get access to the newly-constructed `Document` instance by calling `DOMAdapter`'s `getDocument()` method.

Now that I've given you a quick run-down of the structure of the code, it's time to walk through the implementation. First we'll look at the structure of the code:

```
public class DOMAdapter
{
  /**
   * We make the document builder static since there's no need for
   * each DOMAdapter instance to have its own.
   */
  private static final DocumentBuilder s_builder;
  static {
    DocumentBuilderFactory factory =
      DocumentBuilderFactory.newInstance();
    try {
      s_builder = factory.newDocumentBuilder();
    } catch (Exception e) {
      throw new RuntimeException("Error creating document", e);
    }
  }

  /**
   * This is the document instance that we'll be building up.
   */
  private Document m_document = s_builder.newDocument();

  /**
   * This variable keeps track of how deeply nested the current
   * element is.
   */
  private int m_depth = 0;

  /**
   * Get the DOM Document instance for this DOMAdapater.
   * @return The Document instance.
   */
  public Document getDocument()
  {
    return m_document;
  }

  public void startElement(String namespaceURI, String localName,
                           String qName, Attributes atts)
```

```
            throws SAXException
    {
        ...
    }

    public void endElement(String namespaceURI, String localName,
                            String qName)
        throws SAXException
    {
        ...
    }

    public void characters (char ch[], int start, int length)
        throws SAXException
    {
        ...
    }
}
```

The structure is pretty straightforward. The first thing to notice is the static `DocumentBuilder` member, which we'll use to construct the initial, empty `Document` instance, which in turn is stored in the member variable m_document. The other member variable, m_depth, is used to keep track of how many calls to `startElement()` have occurred that haven't been offset by a call to `endElement()`. This is important for keeping track of where to create the new element and text nodes as we read them. Beyond that, there are the three methods from the `ContentHandler` interface, plus the accessor for the `Document` instance. We'll be adding a private helper method shortly; it's not a part of the public interface, so I've omitted it here.

Now that we've got the structure covered, let's take a look at the implementations for the three `ContentHandler` methods, starting with the **startElement()** method:

```
    public void startElement(String namespaceURI, String localName,
                            String qName, Attributes atts)
        throws SAXException
    {
        // Create the element to add
        Element newElement = m_document.createElementNS(namespaceURI,
            qName);

        // Copy the attributes into the element
        for (int x = 0, count = atts.getLength(); x < count; ++x)
        {
            String attrNamespaceURI = atts.getURI(x);
            String attrQName = atts.getQName(x);
            String attrValue = atts.getValue(x);
            newElement.setAttributeNS(attrNamespaceURI,
                attrQName, attrValue);
        }

        // Find the parent node and append the element to that node.
        Node parent = findParentNode();
        parent.appendChild(newElement);

        // Finally, increment the current depth.
        ++m_depth;
    }
```

The startElement() first creates a DOM Element instance from the SAX data it receives as arguments, and then it copies all of the attributes into that Element instance. At this point, we have our new Element, so all we have to do is figure out where to add it into our document. This is where the private helper method findParentNode() comes in. The findParentNode() method uses the current depth to find the Element instance that should be the parent of any new Element instances. Here is what the implementation looks like:

```
private Node findParentNode()
{
  // Get the document element, and if it is null return the
  // document itself as the parent node.
  Node parent = m_document.getDocumentElement();
  if (parent == null)
    return m_document;

  // This loop finds the last Element node at the current depth.
  // Note that the loop runs until m_depth - 1, since m_depth
  // reflects the depth of the element we're adding, which means
  // that the parent element lives at m_depth - 1.
  for (int x = 0; x < m_depth - 1; ++x)
  {
    // Find the last child of the parent element.
    Node node = parent.getLastChild();

    // We loop here to find the last child node that is also
    // an element node.
    while (node != null)
    {
      // Make sure that the node is of type Element
      if (node.getNodeType() == Node.ELEMENT_NODE)
      {
        parent = node;
        break;
      }

      // If the node is not of type Element, move to the previous
      // sibling (since we're starting from the last child)
      // and try again.
      node = node.getPreviousSibling();
    }

    // This should never happen since we're controlling the creation
    // of the document, but let's handle it gracefully anyway.
    if (node == null)
      throw new RuntimeException("Something went horribly wrong");
  }

  return parent;
}
```

The method first checks to see if the document element of our document is `null`; if so, it returns the document instance itself as the parent. This code path will occur only on the first call to `startElement()`. If the document element is not `null`, the method needs to find the right parent from somewhere in the document. The right parent will always be the last `Node` of type `Element` at one less than the current depth. We know it will be the last `Node` of type `Element`, because we're building the document up from beginning to end, and we know that the depth must be one less than the current depth because the current depth refers to the element that we're adding, so the parent of that element must lie at the previous depth.

The final two methods, `endElement()` and `characters()`, are both very simple. Let's see their implementations:

```
public void endElement(String namespaceURI, String localName,
                       String qName)
   throws SAXException
{
   // For an end element, all we need to do is decrease the
   // current depth.
   --m_depth;
}

public void characters(char ch[], int start, int length)
   throws SAXException
{
   // For a text node, we simply need find the correct parent,
   // create the text node, and add the text node to the parent.
   Node parent = findParentNode();
   Node textNode =
     m_document.createTextNode(new String(ch, start, length));
   parent.appendChild(textNode);
}
```

The `endElement()` method simply needs to decrease the current depth, and `characters()` just needs to create a text node from the character data it receives as arguments and add that text node to the appropriate parent, which it finds using the `findParentNode()` helper method.

So, how would this look if we applied it to our instant messaging document example? I've built an example class called `MessageHistoryHybrid` to demonstrate how to apply this approach. The class extends `org.xml.sax.helpers.DefaultHandler` and overrides the methods `startElement()`, `endElement()`, and `characters()`. It's a pretty straightforward class, so for the sake of brevity I'll only include the interesting bits here, starting with the `startElement()` method. I've omitted some of the code in these methods, so the code listed here won't quite match up with the example code available on the Wrox web site:

```
public void startElement(String uri, String localName,
                         String qName, Attributes attributes)
   throws SAXException
{
   // Create the message and store it in m_currentMessage
```

```
    if ("message".equals(qName))
    {
      String id = attributes.getValue("id");
      String sentDateString = attributes.getValue("sentDate");
      try {
        Date sentDate = m_dateFormat.parse(sentDateString);
        m_currentMessage = new Message(id, sentDate);
        return;
      } catch (ParseException e) {
        throw new SAXException(e);
      }
    }

    // Create the sender and set it on the current message
    if ("sender".equals(qName))
    {
      String address = attributes.getValue("address");
      String ip = attributes.getValue("ip");
      m_currentMessage.setSender(new MessageAddress(address, ip));
      return;
    }

    // Create a recipient and add it to the current message
    if ("recipient".equals(qName))
    {
      String address = attributes.getValue("address");
      String ip = attributes.getValue("ip");
      m_currentMessage.addRecipient(new MessageAddress(address, ip));
      return;
    }

    // Set a header property on the current message
    if ("property".equals(qName))
    {
      String name = attributes.getValue("name");
      String value = attributes.getValue("value");
      m_currentMessage.addHeaderProperty(name, value);
      return;
    }

    // Note that we don't "return" here because we want to pass
    // the <content> tag on to the adapter.
    if ("content".equals(qName))
      m_adapter = new DOMAdapter();

    // If we get here, we're either at or inside the <content> tag,
    // so pass the data to the DOMAdapter.
    m_adapter.startElement(uri, localName, qName, attributes);
}
```

This looks like a very straightforward SAX `startElement()` method. You can see where we parse in all of the sender, recipient, and header data at the beginning of the method. The only really interesting bit here is the last three non-commented lines. When we see the <content> tag, we instantiate a new `DOMAdapter` and store it in the member variable `m_adapter`. Then, at the end of the function, which will only ever be reached if we're inside the <content> tag, we turn around and call `startElement()` on the `DOMAdapter` instance. As we saw before, this will end up creating a new DOM element and inserting it at the right place in the document. Now let's look at `endElement()`:

```
public void endElement(String uri, String localName, String qName)
   throws SAXException
{
   if ("message".equals(qName))
   {
      // We've finished with this message, so if we were building this
      // for real, we'd want to do something with the message here.
      // But for now, we'll just set the current message to null and
      // return;
      m_currentMessage = null;
      return;
   }

   // We're done with the content.  Pass the final end element on to
   // the adapter, set the content on the current message to be the
   // document instance from the adapter, and set the adapter to
   // null.
   if ("content".equals(qName))
   {
      m_adapter.endElement(uri, localName, qName);
      m_currentMessage.setContent(m_adapter.getDocument());
      m_adapter = null;
      return;
   }

   // If we get here we're inside the content tag, so pass the
   // end element on to the adapter.
   if (m_adapter != null)
      m_adapter.endElement(uri, localName, qName);
}
```

This code is also very straightforward, and again the only interesting bit is in dealing with the <content> tag. Here, when we see the end of the <content> tag, we make the final endElement() call on the adapter, retrieve the Document instance from the adapter to set on the current message, and then set the adapter to null. The last line of the method ensures that endElement() is called on the adapter for any elements that are inside the <content> tag.

The characters() method is trivial; it simply calls through to the adapter when the adapter is not null:

```
public void characters(char ch[], int start, int length)
   throws SAXException
{
   if (m_adapter != null)
      m_adapter.characters(ch, start, length);
}
```

There you have it. When this parsing code is run, you get messages that are processed individually (there are never two Message instances in memory at once), and you have a DOM document that only represents the content of the message. This demonstrates a very effective way to use a hybrid approach when dealing with documents that don't fit an exclusively SAX or exclusively DOM approach.

4.3 Implementation Patterns

So far, we've covered several important issues to help you understand how to create a proper parsing strategy based on the requirements of your application and the constraints implied by the structure of the document. These issues are largely conceptual, which in turn forces their discussion to be somewhat abstract so as to get those concepts across.

Of course, in practice these abstract concepts need to be applied in code. In the examples corresponding to each concept, I've tried to present elegant implementations for the given concept; each example implementation has been necessarily rather narrow in scope. In this section, we'll cover a variety of broader implementation patterns that you can use in a wide variety of situations to help you write clean, maintainable parsing code.

4.3.1 With SAX, use a Context Stack when Parsing Deeply Nested Documents

Earlier we covered the fact that SAX is a forward-only, streaming parser technology, and we talked about the effects that its characteristics have on your parsing strategy. Building your implementation using SAX can present some challenges that perhaps aren't obvious when you're choosing your parsing strategy. Probably the most frustrating thing about working with SAX is that since SAX is forward-only, it is effectively stateless; thus, when you receive a SAX event, SAX doesn't give you any information about the context in which that event occurred. Let's look at a quick example to make this point clear:

```
<book>
    <name>Catcher in the Rye</name>
    <author>
        <name>J.D Salinger</name>
    </author>
</book>
```

This simple document presents an interesting parsing challenge because it has elements that have the same name in different contexts; there is the `<name>` element in the context of the `<book>` element as well as in the context of the `<author>` element. (Note that these issues can largely be resolved by the intelligent use of namespaces, but since documents don't always make good use of namespaces, this discussion is important.) Since SAX is stateless, the two events for the `<name>` elements that get generated when parsing this document are indistinguishable from one another unless you keep track of the context yourself.

There are many ways of keeping track of the context. A naïve way to do this would be to use Boolean flags to keep track of your context. You create a member variable to represent a flag for each element whose context you need to keep track of, which, in this case, is just the <author> element, since it is nested within the <book> element. When you receive the start element event for a given element, you set its flag to true, and when you receive the end element event, you set the flag to false. In the meantime, when you receive the start element for the context-dependent element, you check the flag to see how you should proceed with processing that element. Here is a code snippet that indicates how you might use this technique to parse the above document:

```java
private StringBuffer m_characterData = null;
private Boolean m_inAuthor = false;

public void startElement(String uri, String localName,
                         String qName, Attributes attributes)
  throws SAXException
{
  if ("author".equals(qName))
    m_inAuthor = true;

  if ("name".equals(qName))
    m_characterData = new StringBuffer();
}

public void endElement(String uri, String localName, String qName)
  throws SAXException
{
  if ("author".equals(qName))
    m_inAuthor = false;

  if ("name".equals(qName))
  {
    String name = m_characterData.toString();
    m_characterData = null;
    if (m_inAuthor)
    {
      // Set the name on the author object
    }
    else
    {
      // Set the name on the book object
    }
  }
}

public void characters(char ch[], int start, int length)
  throws SAXException
{
  if (m_characterData != null)
    m_characterData.append(ch, start, length);
}
```

This code has two member variables used during parsing: m_inAuthor and m_characterData. The variable, m_inAuthor, is a Boolean flag, the value of which indicates whether the parser is currently in the context of the <author> element. The variable, m_characterData, is used to represent the character data received by the characters() method when in the context of the <name> element.

In startElement(), when we see the <author> tag, we set m_inAuthor to true, and when we see the <name> tag, we create a new StringBuffer instance and assign it to m_characterData.

In endElement(), when we see the <author> tag, we set m_inAuthor to false, and when we see the <name> tag, we check to see if m_inAuthor is true, so as to determine what to do with the name that we have. In characters(), we simply append the character data to m_characterData if it is not null, which is only the case when we're in the context of the <name> tag.

Thus, this code will effectively process the given document, but the mechanism that it uses for maintaining context is very brittle and doesn't scale well. For instance, suppose the document looked like this:

```
<book>
    <name>Catcher in the Rye</name>
    <author>
        <name>J.D Salinger</name>
    </author>
    <publisher>
        <name>Some publishing house</name>
    </publisher>
    <distributor>
        <name>Some distributor</name>
    </distributor>
</book>
```

There are four different contexts in which the <name> tag can appear, which would mean we'd need flags for each of those contexts, which means a new member variable for each flag. This doesn't lead to particularly clean or maintainable code, since you're going to be constantly keeping track of which flags are true and which are false.

The problem is only compounded the more complicated the nesting of the document gets, since you can simultaneously be in multiple contexts at once. For example, the <author> tag's <name> tag is also in the context of the <book> tag's <name> tag, since <author> is a child of <book>. Thus, if we had a flag to indicate that we were inside the <book> tag, it wouldn't suffice to just check that flag; we'd also have to check the <author> tag's flag, and any other tag that was nested at any depth inside the <book> tag. Clearly, writing code to handle this becomes untenable very quickly.

It's easy to imagine how a document could become even more context-dependent. For instance, each of the elements (except for the <book> element) could have an associated <address> element, which itself could be complex, containing sub-elements for street, city, state, etc. Using flags to keep track of all of this information won't scale well on any axis.

163

A better solution would be to maintain a stack to keep track of the context, with the object that is currently in scope on the top of the stack. When you encounter a context-dependent element, you simply check the object on the top of the stack and set the value on *that* object. This approach scales much better, and results in more maintainable code, because it doesn't require a whole bunch of state variables, just the context stack itself. On top of that, implementing this approach is very straightforward as well. Let's look at how we would revise the code from the naive approach to use a context stack.

First, we get rid of the `m_inAuthor` member variable and replace it with a variable of `Stack` type. We keep the `m_characterData` variable for keeping track of the character data, so our member variable declarations look like this:

```
private Stack m_context = new Stack();
private StringBuffer m_characterData = null;
```

Next, we modify the `startElement()` method to use the stack to store the currently processing object:

```
public void startElement(String uri, String localName,
                         String qName, Attributes attributes)
    throws SAXException
{
  if ("book".equals(qName))
    m_context.push(new Book());

  if ("author".equals(qName))
    m_context.push(new Author());

  if ("publisher".equals(qName))
    m_context.push(new Publisher());

  if ("distributor".equals(qName))
    m_context.push(new Distributor());

  if ("name".equals(qName))
    m_characterData = new StringBuffer();
}
```

This code is very straightforward. For each <book>, <author>, <publisher>, or <distributor> tag we encounter, we simply push a new object instance of the type indicated by the element name onto the context stack. For the <name> tag, we don't need to do anything differently from the previous example; we still just create a `StringBuffer` instance and assign it to `m_characterData`.

There are no changes to the `characters()` method. The `endElement()` method is where the significant changes occur. Let's take a look:

```
public void endElement(String uri, String localName, String qName)
    throws SAXException
{
  if ("book".equals(qName) || "author".equals(qName)
```

```
        || "publisher".equals(qName) || "distributor".equals(qName))
    {
      m_context.pop();
    }

    if ("name".equals(qName))
    {
      Object top = m_context.peek();
      String name = m_characterData.toString();
      m_characterData = null;

      if (top instanceof Book)
        ((Book)top).setName(name);
      else if (top instanceof Author)
        ((Author)top).setName(name);
      else if (top instanceof Publisher)
        ((Publisher)top).setName(name);
      else if (top instanceof Distributor)
        ((Distributor)top).setName(name);
    }
  }
```

Here, if we encounter a <book>, <author>, <publisher>, or <distributor> tag, we simply pop the top object off the stack, since it is no longer in scope. In a real-world application, you would actually take some kind of action in here, but as we want to only demonstrate the parsing, we just pop the stack to keep the context accurate. The context stack really comes into play when we encounter the <name> tag.

The first thing we do is peek at the object on the top of the stack. Next, we get the contents of the m_characterData member variable and store them in a local variable called name. Then, we assign m_characterData to null so that the characters() method doesn't unnecessarily keep track of character data. What follows is the truly interesting code. We effectively switch on the type of the top object, and based on the type of the object, we cast it to the appropriate type and call the setName() method and the right variable is updated.

In the setName() methods for the various classes, I've included code to print out the name of the method and the value of the parameter. Running this code demonstrates that the result is correct:

```
Book.setName was called with Catcher in the Rye
Author.setName was called with J.D Salinger
Publisher.setName was called with Some publishing house
Distributor.setName was called with Some distributor
```

You can see that as opposed to the naive solution, if we were to add another element with the <name> sub-element to this document, we don't need to add a new member variable. We just need to add another "else if" to this part of the endElement() method. Furthermore, if your application could stand for performance to suffer slightly, you could avoid the "if else" structure entirely, and use the Reflection API to invoke the setName() method on the object without respect to its type. If you were to do this, adding a new element to the document with a <name> sub-element requires no additional code at all.

This technique can also work if you don't have separate objects for each of the context-dependent elements. For instance, you could apply a variation on this technique if there weren't separate `Author`, `Publisher`, and `Distributor` objects, and instead, there were just author name, publisher name, and distributor name properties on the `Book` object. In this situation, instead of pushing objects of type `Author`, etc., onto the stack, you can just push a `String` (likely the element name) onto the stack. In this case, the `startElement()` method would look something like this:

```java
public void startElement(String uri, String localName,
                         String qName, Attributes attributes)
    throws SAXException
{
    if ("book".equals(qName))
        m_context.push(new Book());

    // If we see an author, publisher, or distributor tag, push the
    // tag's name onto the stack.
    if ("author".equals(qName) || "publisher".equals(qName)
        || "distributor".equals(qName))
        m_context.push(qName);

    if ("name".equals(qName))
        m_characterData = new StringBuffer();
}
```

The corresponding `endElement()` method would then use the name on the top of the stack to determine the correct property set method to call.

> **From a code maintenance standpoint, it's really very easy for parsing code to get out of control very quickly. Using context stacks to keep track of the current context is one good way to keep code maintenance down and to improve the readability and extensibility of your parsing code.**

4.3.2 When using SAX in Java, Consider using an Inner Class to do the Parsing for an XML-deserializable Class

To use SAX as a parsing mechanism, a class must implement, either directly or indirectly, SAX's `ContentHandler` interface. This is not a problem if you have a class whose sole purpose is to do parsing, but if you have a class that has other uses besides being able to be deserialized from XML, things can get a little messy.

It is possible to actually hijack the Java Serialization API to serialize the object to XML rather than the normal binary byte stream. However, it is relatively complex to make this happen, and it is beyond the scope of this book to explain how to do it, so for the purposes of this example, we're not going to have our class implement `java.io.Serializable`.

It can be argued that the SAX methods that a class implements, shouldn't really be a part of the public interface for the class if its primary job isn't to do parsing (of course, the opposite can also be argued, and I'll cover that point shortly). Beyond that, your parsing code will almost invariably require some state that you'll need to represent in terms of member variables. These member variables only have meaning during the parsing process. As a result, they don't really fit the mold of a member variable, and they especially don't make sense beside the other "real" member variables in the class.

On the other hand, you could argue that the SAX methods should be a part of the public interface for a class, in the same way that the `compareTo()` method from the `java.lang.Comparable` interface is a part of the public interface for a class. Those methods may not describe the primary function of the class, but they do describe an adjunct function of the class. This is a perfectly valid argument, and that argument actually fits in quite well with this point. To explain why, first let me walk you through the outline of the solution.

An elegant way to handle using SAX to deserialize a class is to use a private inner class to implement the SAX methods, rather than implementing them on the outer class. There are several advantages to this approach:

❑ **Transient parsing state member variables are contained within the inner class**. This is desirable because that state is really not a part of the outer class, and therefore shouldn't be grouped in with the other member variables (which represent the actual state of the class) for *that* class.

❑ **You can hide the fact that the class is SAX-deserializable**, as the outer class doesn't have to implement the SAX interfaces. This is advantageous if the details of the serialization shouldn't be available outside the class.

❑ **If you do want the SAX interfaces to be a part of the outer class' public interface**, using an inner class is still an elegant solution because it acts as a container for the parsing state member variables, which you still don't want mixed with the outer class' member variables. The outer class can still implement the necessary interfaces and simply delegate to the inner class; you thus get the best of both worlds.

Since inner classes have access to private members of the containing class, you can do anything with them that you could do in the outer class. You can use either a static or an automatic (non-static) inner class for these purposes; it's a rather stylistic decision, the differences between static and automatic inner classes notwithstanding.

Let's take a look at the structure of a class that doesn't expose the SAX interfaces on its public interface:

```
public class InnerClassExample
{
    // This static method takes an input source and returns an
    // instance of our class.
```

```
public static InnerClassExample fromXML(InputSource is)
  throws SAXException, IOException
{
  XMLReader reader = XMLReaderFactory.createXMLReader();
  InnerClassExample instance = new InnerClassExample();
  ParserHelper ph = new ParserHelper(instance);
  reader.setContentHandler(ph);
  reader.parse(is);
  return instance;
}

public InnerClassExample()
{
  // Normal constructor code goes here
}

///////////////////////////////////////
// Class's fields and methods go here

// ....

// End fields and methods.
///////////////////////////////////////

// Here's our parser helper class that actually implements
// the SAX interfaces via extending DefaultHandler
private static class ParserHelper extends DefaultHandler
{
  private InnerClassExample m_instance;

  public ParserHelper(InnerClassExample instance)
  {
    m_instance = instance;
  }

  // Override whatever SAX methods are necessary here.
}
```

The class looks just like any other class with two exceptions. First, it has a private static inner class called `ParserHelper` that extends `org.xml.sax.helpers.DefaultHandler` and will be responsible for all of the parsing code. Since the `ParserHelper` class is static, it needs an instance to store the data represented in the XML, so its constructor takes an instance of our class's type, `InnerClassExample`.

Second, there is a public static method called `fromXML()` that takes an `InputSource` instance and returns an instance of `InnerClassExample`. This method creates an `XMLReader`, an `InnerClassExample`, and a `ParserHelper`, and uses those instances to parse the given `InputSource`. After parsing is done, it returns the now fully-populated `InnerClassExample` instance to the caller.

It would be fairly easy to modify this example to have our class implement `ContentHandler` and other SAX interfaces. We would only need to add a member variable of type `ParserHelper` to our class, and then delegate the SAX methods to that interface.

All in all, using private inner classes to handle SAX parsing duties is an elegant solution for containing the functionality and state necessary to XML deserialization but otherwise not necessary for the class to function.

4.3.3 In C#, Consider using the XmlSerializer Class and XML Serialization Attributes for Simple Serialization

Microsoft's C# language is a great language to use for XML programming because it was designed specifically with XML in mind, since XML is a key piece of Microsoft's .NET product strategy. One of the many XML-related classes that they have in their common library is the `System.Xml.Serialization.XmlSerializer` class, which uses the .NET Reflection API to serialize and deserialize classes to and from XML.

You can use an `XmlSerializer` instance to serialize any public class that has a default constructor. Its usage looks like this:

```
XmlSerializer serializer = new XmlSerializer(typeof(User));
serializer.Serialize(Console.Out, userInstance);
userInstance = (User)serializer.Deserialize(xmlReaderInstance);
```

When you construct an `XmlSerializer` instance, you must give it the `System.Type` instance that corresponds to the object that you're going to try to serialize. To serialize an object to XML, you call the `Serialize()` method which has a handful of signatures, but each signature basically takes a stream of some sort to write to and an object to serialize. To deserialize an XML stream into an object, you call the `Deserialize()` method, which has three signatures: one that takes an `XmlReader`, one that takes a `TextReader`, and one that takes a `StreamReader`. Each signature returns an `object` instance that represents your deserialized object.

`XmlSerializer` will serialize any non-null public field and public smart property with both get and set methods defined. By default, it will use the name of the field or property as the element name, but you can customize this behavior by using XML serialization attributes. There are a whole host of attributes that you can use to control the manner in which a particular field or property gets serialized. An in-depth discussion of each of these attributes is beyond the scope of this book, so we'll just be discussing the simple `XmlElement` attribute, which controls the name, type, and namespace of a given field or property.

For more complete information about how to control serialization using XML serialization attributes, you can point your browser at MSDN at http://msdn.microsoft.com/library/default.asp?url=/library/en-us/cpguide/html/cpconcontrollingserializationbyxmlserializerwithattributes.asp.

To give you a hint of what the `XmlSerializer` and XML serialization attributes will let you do in C#, let's take a look at a small example that focuses just on the `XmlElement` attribute (note that `XmlSerializer` is a part of the .NET common library, so it's available to all .NET languages including VB.NET). Let's take a look at a simple class that might be used to represent a customer:

```
public class Customer
{
    private string name;
    private string phoneNumber;
    private string street;
    private string city;
    private string state;
    private string zip;

    public Customer()
    {
    }

    public string Name
    {
      get {return name;}
      set {name = value;}
    }

    public string PhoneNumber
    {
      get {return phoneNumber;}
      set {phoneNumber = value;}
    }

    public string Street
    {
      get {return street;}
      set {street = value;}
    }

    public string City
    {
      get {return city;}
      set {city = value;}
    }

    public string State
    {
      get {return state;}
      set {state = value;}
    }

    public String Zip
    {
      get {return zip;}
      set {zip = value;}
    }
}
```

This class simply has some private fields and corresponding public properties. You can see that the class is public, and has a public default constructor; both conditions are necessary for use with the `XmlSerializer` class. The code to serialize an instance of this class to the console looks like this:

```
Customer customer = new Customer();
customer.Name = "John Doe";
customer.PhoneNumber = "(123)555-1212";
customer.Street = "12345 Main Street";
customer.City = "Any Town";
customer.State = "TX";
customer.Zip = "12345";
XmlSerializer serializer = new XmlSerializer(typeof(Customer));
serializer.Serialize(Console.Out, customer);
```

The output of this code looks like this:

```
<?xml version="1.0" encoding="IBM437"?>
<Customer xmlns:xsd="http://www.w3.org/2001/XMLSchema"
    xmlns:xsi="http://www.w3.org/2001/XMLSchema-instance">
  <Name>John Doe</Name>
  <PhoneNumber>(123)555-1212</PhoneNumber>
  <Street>12345 Main Street</Street>
  <City>Any Town</City>
  <State>TX</State>
  <Zip>12345</Zip>
</Customer>
```

You can see that the names of the elements are based on the name of the class and then the names of the properties. This isn't always the behavior that you want, and that is where the `XmlElement` serialization attribute comes in. The `XmlElement` attribute allows you to specify the name of the element and the type of object being serialized. The type is important for when you have a field or property that may contain instances of a derived class. From the MSDN online documentation for `XmlElement`:

> Use the type parameter to specify a type that is derived from a base class. For example, suppose a property named MyAnimal returns an Animal object. You want to enhance the object, so you create a new class named Mammal that inherits from the Animal class. To instruct the XmlSerializer to accept the Mammal class when it serializes the MyAnimal property, pass the Type of the Mammal class to the constructor.

For our example, since all of our properties are strings, we'll just use the `XmlElement` attribute to change the name of the element. To do that, we simply place the attribute declaration directly before the property declaration. The affected code from our example looks like this with the attributes applied:

```
[XmlElement("CustomerName")]
public string Name
{
  get {return name;}
  set {name = value;}
}

[XmlElement("CustomerPhone")]
```

```
public string PhoneNumber
{
  get {return phoneNumber;}
  set {phoneNumber = value;}
}

[XmlElement("CustomerStreet")]
public string Street
{
  get {return street;}
  set {street = value;}
}

[XmlElement("CustomerCity")]
public string City
{
  get {return city;}
  set {city = value;}
}

[XmlElement("CustomerState")]
public string State
{
  get {return state;}
  set {state = value;}
}

[XmlElement("CustomerZip")]
public String Zip
{
  get {return zip;}
  set {zip = value;}
}
```

Now when we run the same serialization code from above, you can see how the element names have changed according to what we've specified in our attributes:

```
<?xml version="1.0" encoding="IBM437"?>
<Customer xmlns:xsd="http://www.w3.org/2001/XMLSchema"
    xmlns:xsi="http://www.w3.org/2001/XMLSchema-instance">
  <CustomerName>John Doe</CustomerName>
  <CustomerPhone>(123)555-1212</CustomerPhone>
  <CustomerStreet>12345 Main Street</CustomerStreet>
  <CustomerCity>Any Town</CustomerCity>
  <CustomerState>TX</CustomerState>
  <CustomerZip>12345</CustomerZip>
</Customer>
```

In addition to the XmlElement attribute, there are several others that you can use to control just about every other aspect of serialization that you could want. There are attributes for dealing with serializing array instances, for ignoring attributes that you don't want to have serialized, and several others. Refer to the URL provided above for a more thorough discussion of these attributes and how to apply them.

172

Even though using `XmlSerializer` clearly isn't the solution to every serialization/deserialization problem that you're likely to encounter in C#, it does provide useful functionality for when you want to do direct persistence of a class. The XML serialization attributes give you a very high degree of control over how the serialization occurs. Using the `XmlSerializer` in consort with these attributes can save you a good deal of time both coding and debugging, when your XML data maps very cleanly onto your class.

4.3.4 When using DOM as the Primary Representation of a Document, Consider Wrapping it for Type-safety

We've seen how DOM's usefulness is not limited to its ability to parse XML; it can be a powerful tool for representing hierarchical structured data, as well as narrative text-oriented data. The major problem with using the DOM as the primary representation of data is that because it is so generic, it's not particularly well suited to being the public API for an application. For instance, in most cases you don't want your API's users to have to deal with DOM `Node` instances to get at the data that you're using DOM to represent. Beyond that, DOM only represents data as strings, which is inadequate for the majority of applications.

If your application uses DOM to represent structured data, like our arithmetic expression example from *Section 4.2.2*, and it exposes DOM as the public representation of that data, you are inviting misuse. Since DOM is not type-safe (all data is represented as strings), there is nothing to stop users of your API from inserting data of the wrong type or in the wrong place. This could cause exceptions when your application is run. To prevent these exceptions from happening, you need to check the data every time you want to do something with it. That can be quite a bit of code and if you miss even one place, those exceptions can still crop up.

Because of these limitations with DOM, it often makes sense to use the DOM to represent your data internally, but have a class (or classes) that provides a wrapper around the DOM. Using a wrapper class allows you control how users of your API access the data represented in the DOM. Since you're in control of how your users access the DOM, you don't need to check the validity of the data before using it; the data is guaranteed to be of the right type since your wrapper methods are type-safe.

For example, let's say that you have a document that represents a file system structure. The document consists of directory elements that can contain other directory elements or file elements. This type of document is a good candidate for using the DOM, as it's just an n-ary tree. A sample document would look something like this:

```
<directory name="root">
  <directory name="temp">
    <file name="afile.txt"/>
```

```
    </directory>
    <directory name="bin">
      <file name="ls"/>
      <file name="cat"/>
    </directory>
    <directory name="usr">
      <directory name="home">
        <directory name="sbonneau">
          <file name=".plan"/>
        </directory>
      </directory>
      <directory name="bin">
        <file name="gcc"/>
      </directory>
    </directory>
  </directory>
</directory>
```

The application that we have to build on top of this document structure is similar to a simple file system manager; it has to be able to list the contents of a directory, add a file or directory, and delete a file or directory. You could clearly do all of these operations explicitly by exposing the DOM instance and letting the users do it for themselves, but a better approach would be to hide the fact that DOM is involved at all and provide a simple wrapper (that provides type-safe methods) around the DOM.

Let's take a look at how we might do this in code. Before we look at the innards of the class, let's look at its interface:

```java
public class FileSystemDOM
{
    // Initialize a FileSystemDOM instance with the file system data
    // from the InputSource.
    public FileSystemDOM(InputSource is) throws Exception
    {
    }

    // Print out the contents of the director
    public void listDirectory()
    {
    }

    // Add a file or directory in the given root dir with the given name
    public void addFile(String rootDir, String fileName, Boolean isDir)
    {
    }
    // Remove the given file or directory
    public void removeFile(String fileName)
    {
    }
}
```

You can see that we've got a constructor that takes in an `InputSource` that it will use to define the directory structure, along with methods for listing the directory, adding and removing files. Let's look at the constructor code, which is the code that actually deals with reading in the document that describes the file system:

```
public FileSystemDOM(InputSource is) throws Exception
{
  DocumentBuilderFactory factory =
    DocumentBuilderFactory.newInstance();
  DocumentBuilder builder = factory.newDocumentBuilder();
  m_document = builder.parse(is);
}
```

This code is very straightforward. It just uses a document builder to create the Document instance, and then stores the instance in a member variable called m_document. Since we're using DOM as the primary representation of our data, we don't need any other state besides that Document instance; all of the other methods simply act on m_document. Let's look at listDirectory() and its helper function, listElement():

```
// Print out the contents of the directory
public void listDirectory()
{
  listElement(m_document.getDocumentElement(), "");
}

private void listElement(Element element, String indent)
{
  // The name of this node is its type, directory or file.
  String type = element.getNodeName();

  // Get the file name of file represented by this element.
  String fileName = element.getAttribute("name");
  if ("directory".equals(type))
  {
    // If the element is a directory, print out the directory
    // name and then recursively call listElement on any
    // child elements
    System.out.println(indent + "[dir] " + fileName);
    NodeList children = element.getChildNodes();
    for (int x = 0; x < children.getLength(); ++x)
    {
      Node child = children.item(x);
      if (child.getNodeType() == Node.ELEMENT_NODE)
        listElement((Element)child, "  " + indent);
    }
  }
  else
  {
    // If the element is a file, just print out its name.
    System.out.println(indent + "[file] " + fileName);
  }
}
```

The listDirectory() method simply calls into the listElement() method with the root element of the m_document variable and no indentation. The listElement() method in turn prints out the name of the current element, its type (directory or file), and then, if the type is a directory, it recursively calls itself on all of its child elements. Calling listDirectory() on the file system represented by the example file listed above yields the following result:

```
[dir] root
  [dir] temp
    [file] afile.txt
  [dir] bin
    [file] ls
    [file] cat
  [dir] usr
    [dir] home
      [dir] sbonneau
        [file] .plan
    [dir] bin
      [file] gcc
```

Both the addFile() and removeFile() methods use a private helper method called
findElement() to do the majority of their work. The findElement() method takes
in a filename and returns the Element instance in m_document that corresponds to
that filename, or null if no such element exists. To accomplish this, findElement()
breaks the filename into its constituent parts (all of the elements of the path), and
walks up the directory tree starting with the root of the directory. Here's what the code
looks like:

```java
private Element findElement(String fileName)
{
    // Get the document element, which represents the root of our
    // file system.
    Element element = m_document.getDocumentElement();

    // Split the filename up by the directory separator character '/'
    // and loop to match elements in our Document with the path to the
    // file.
    StringTokenizer tok = new StringTokenizer(fileName, "/");
    while (tok.hasMoreTokens())
    {
        Boolean foundElement = false;

        // This is the directory/file name
        String name = tok.nextToken();

        // Iterate over the children of the element to see if one
        // matches the current path name.
        NodeList children = element.getChildNodes();
        for (int x = 0; x < children.getLength(); ++x)
        {
            Node child = children.item(x);
            if (child.getNodeType() == Node.ELEMENT_NODE)
            {
                String childName = ((Element)child).getAttribute("name");
                if (childName.equals(name))
                {
                    // If we get here we have a match, so set element to this
                    // child and break out of the loop
                    element = (Element)child;
                    foundElement = true;
                    break;
                }
            }
        }
    }
```

```
         // If we've found an element, continue on to the next token in
         // the filename.
         if (foundElement)
           continue;

         // If we got here, we didn't have a match, so return null.
         return null;
       }

     return element;
   }
```

Using this function, the addFile() and removeFile() methods are fairly straightforward:

```
public void addFile(String rootDir, String fileName, Boolean isDir)
{
  Element rootElement = findElement(rootDir);
  if (rootElement == null)
    System.out.println("No such directory: " + rootDir);
  else
  {
    Element newElement = null;

    // Create the new element with the appropriate node name
    if (isDir)
      newElement = m_document.createElement("directory");
    else
      newElement = m_document.createElement("file");

    // Append the new element to the root element.
    newElement.setAttribute("name", fileName);
    rootElement.appendChild(newElement);
    System.out.println("Successfully added " + fileName + " to " +
      "directory " + rootDir);
  }
}


// Remove the given file or directory
public void removeFile(String fileName)
{
  Element element = findElement(fileName);
  if (element == null)
    System.out.println("No such file: " + fileName);
  else
  {
    Node parent = element.getParentNode();
    parent.removeChild(element);
    System.out.println("Successfully removed file " + fileName);
  }
}
```

Let's look at a small example program that uses this API and see what the results are. The program will create a file system based on the sample document from above, list the contents of the directory, add a directory and a file in that directory, and then remove a different directory before listing the contents again. Here's what the code looks like:

```
public static void main(String[] args) throws Exception
{
  if (args.length < 0)
  {
    System.err.println("Must specify a file on the commandline");
    return;
  }

  FileSystemDOM fsd = new FileSystemDOM(new InputSource(args[0]));
  fsd.listDirectory();
  System.out.println("");
  fsd.addFile("usr/home", "joeschmoe", true);
  fsd.addFile("usr/home/joeschmoe", ".plan", false);
  fsd.removeFile("usr/bin");
  System.out.println("");
  fsd.listDirectory();
}
```

The output from running this code is just what you'd expect:

```
[dir] root
  [dir] temp
    [file] afile.txt
  [dir] bin
    [file] ls
    [file] cat
  [dir] usr
    [dir] home
      [dir] sbonneau
        [file] .plan
    [dir] bin
      [file] gcc

Successfully added joeschmoe to directory usr/home
Successfully added .plan to directory usr/home/joeschmoe
Successfully removed file usr/bin

[dir] root
  [dir] temp
    [file] afile.txt
  [dir] bin
    [file] ls
    [file] cat
  [dir] usr
    [dir] home
      [dir] sbonneau
        [file] .plan
      [dir] joeschmoe
        [file] .plan
```

That's really all there is to it; this class uses a DOM document as its only information store, but hides that fact nicely from the user by putting a type-safe wrapper around the document. By using this technique, you leverage the powerful data model that the DOM provides, but at the same time, avoid the pitfalls of exposing its generic API to your users.

4.4 Conclusion

That concludes our discussion of document parsing strategies. We've covered a lot of ground, starting with all of the things that you need to consider before you sit down to build your parsing strategy, the fundamental characteristics of the major standard parsing APIs, and which APIs are best suited to which tasks. Finally, we covered some concrete strategies that you can employ to help you build clean, robust parsing solutions for your applications. This material should give you a very strong foundation on which to build when implementing the parsing code for your own applications.

XML Design

Handbook

5

5

XSLT Strategies

Parsing and accessing information from XML documents through a DOM tree or a SAX stream can be hard work; there aren't many shortcuts that you can use to access the information you're interested in; also constructing documents can involve the usage of too much code. **Extensible Stylesheet Language Transformations (XSLT)** provide a higher-level language for accessing and manipulating XML structures.

As you can see, in the template the code is a lot simpler to read. It clearly shows the structure of the HTML that is being created, – the `<address>` and `<br>` elements are created literally with other information added using XSLT instructions – and the syntax for selecting nodes (XPath) is much shorter and easier to understand than the DOM method which do is the same thing.

In this chapter, we look at some tips and techniques for getting the best out of XSLT. It's assumed that you are familiar with the basics of how to use XSLT. If you do not already have experience with XSLT, *Beginning XSLT* from *Wrox Press (ISBN: 1-861005-94-6)* would be a good place to start.

This chapter is divided into four main sections:

- ❏ The first section, we review the **current state of XSLT standards**
- ❏ In the second section, we'll look at how to **work with the XSLT processing model**, which can take getting used to, if you're used to coding with procedural languages. We will look at some of the common temptations that you should watch out for
- ❏ In the third section, we'll turn our attention to **creating efficient stylesheets**
- ❏ In the final section we will look at the issues surrounding the **creation of modular and reusable transformations**

At the end of this chapter, you'll find a list of references to more information about XSLT, including a list of XSLT processors that you can use.

5.1 A Quick XSLT Example

In the last chapter, we reviewed the use of DOM and SAX to access information from an order digest of the form:

```
<orderDigest>
   <order id="31459" shippingType="Ground">
      <customer id="tx78734">
         <address type="billing">
            <name>Scott Bonneau</name>
            <street>123 Outatha Way</street>
            <city>Austin</city>
            <state>TX</state>
            <zip>78701-1234</zip>
         </address>

         <address type="shipping">
            <name>Rich Bonneau</name>
            <street>321 Youreinmy Way</street>
            <city>Boston</city>
            <state>MA</state>
            <zip>02210-4321</zip>
         </address>
      </customer>

      <item sku="TK-421">
         <quantity>1</quantity>
         <unitPrice>$39.95</unitPrice>
      </item>

      <item sku="SB-007">
         <quantity>4</quantity>
         <unitPrice>$1.00</unitPrice>
      </item>
   </order>
</orderDigest>
```

Let us assume that you need to create an HTML page displaying this order summary to a customer. To create it, you need to access information in the XML document and create HTML that holds that same information in a different structure. For example, in a simple display the billing address of a customer from the XML document could be turned into an <address> element in the HTML page with lines separated by <br> elements as follows:

```
<address>
   Scott Bonneau<br>
   123 Outatha Way<br>
   Austin<br>
   TX<br>
   78701-1234<br>
</address>
```

The following code shows a way to do this using DOM methods to access the information from the XML document and create the new HTML address:

```
// Parse the address elements
NodeList addressNodeList =
  customerElement.getElementsByTagName("address");

// Identify the billing address
Element billingAddressElement = null;
Element addressElement = null;
String addressType = null;
for (int x = 0, count = addressNodeList.getLength(); x < count; ++x) {
  addressElement = (Element)addressNodeList.item(x);
  addressType = addressElement.getAttribute("type");
  if ("billing".equals(addressType)) {
    billingAddressElement = addressElement;
  }
}

if (billingAddress != null) {
  // Create an address element for the billing address
  htmlAddress = htmlDocument.createElement("address");

  // Access the content of the address element
  NodeList addressContentNodeList =
    billingAddressElement.getElementsByTagName("*");
  Element addressContentElement = null;
  TextNode addressContentText = null;
  TextNode htmlAddressText = null;
  Element brElement = null;
  for (int x = 0, count = addressContentNodeList.getLength();
       x < count; ++x) {
    addressContentElement = (Element)addressContentNodeList.item(x);
    addressContentText = addressContentElement.getFirstChild();
    // Construct text nodes and <br> elements within the address
    htmlAddressText =
      htmlDocument.createTextNode(addressContentText.data);
    htmlAddress.appendChild(htmlAddressText);
    brElement = htmlDocument.createElement("br");
    htmlAddress.appendChild(brElement);
  }
}
```

The preceding code has been simplified by making the assumption that no entities are used in the text held in an address. In DOM, entity references form part of the node tree, which makes it hard to extract the text value of an element.

By comparison, the following XSLT code determines how to treat a billing address by describing a template that should be followed when a billing address is encountered:

```
<!-- Process billing addresses -->
<xsl:template match="address[@type = 'billing']">
  <!-- Create an <address> element -->
  <address>
    <!-- Create a line for each child of the billing address -->
    <xsl:for-each select="*">
      <xsl:value-of select="." /><br />
    </xsl:for-each>
```

```
      </address>
   </xsl:template>
```

The example clearly shows that XSLT has some great advantages. However, XSLT is often used when it isn't necessarily the best tool for the job. The first question we should look at is whether, for a particular task, we should be using XSLT *at all*.

XSLT is designed as a transformation language, rather than as a general-purpose programming language. It's particularly designed as a way of transforming from XML to either another XML-based markup language or HTML. However, it can also be used to transform to or from other formats. Transformations that take a SAX stream generated from a comma-delimited file can be very useful, as can transformations that generate text, such as Java code or SQL instructions. However, if neither the transformation's source nor its result is XML, you should think carefully about whether XSLT is the right tool for the job.

Another point to bear in mind is that XSLT's processing model relies on an in-memory representation of the XML document being used as the source document, known as the **node tree**. Essentially, it's like constructing a DOM for that document. As such, XSLT has some of the same disadvantages as DOM. In particular, the size of the documents that an XSLT processor can cope with depends on the amount of memory on the machine that you're using. We will look at how to mitigate that a little later in the chapter.

The best way to try out a transformation is to use a command-line processor, such as Instant Saxon or MSXML's command line processor. For example, with Instant Saxon from http://saxon.sourceforge.net/ use:

```
> saxon -o output.xml input.xml stylesheet.xsl
```

After performing the transformation you can inspect output.xml to see exactly what the result was.

5.2 XSLT Status

There are currently four versions of "XSLT" in use. In order of emergence, they are:

❑ **WD-xsl**

A version of XSLT that was developed by Microsoft, based on a very early working draft of XSLT, and built into MSXML2, which was in turn built in to Internet Explorer 5 and 5.5.

❑ **XSLT 1.0**

The current version of XSLT, developed by the **World Wide Web Consortium (W3C)**, that reached Recommended status in November 1999. XSLT 1.0 is supported by a range of processors, the most common being MSXML3 (which is built into IE6 but can be installed in "replace mode" to work with IE5+), MSXML4, Saxon, Xalan-J, and Sablotron.

❑ **XSLT 1.1**

The version described in a Working Draft issued by the W3C in December 2000, but on which work ceased in August 2001 so that the Working Group could concentrate on XSLT 2.0. There are a couple of processors that implement the changes that were described in XSLT 1.1, notably Saxon (roughly version 6.1+) and `jd.xslt`.

❑ **XSLT 2.0**

The version currently under development at the W3C, with the latest Working Drafts at time of writing being those issued in November 2002, and partial experimental implementations available in Saxon (version 7.0+) and coming in Xalan-J.

Saxon supports a range of versions of XSLT, but the changes are mostly backwards compatible so you can use XSLT 1.0 with a version of Saxon that supports XSLT 1.1 or 2.0.

Both WD-xsl or XSLT 1.1 are dead ends, as they are languages that are supported in only one or two special implementations, and have features that don't exist in what are, or will be, recommended versions of the language. WD-xsl should be avoided at all costs; since it is poorly documented with little support from either Microsoft or the XSLT community, and lacks many of the features that are necessary to do sophisticated processing. XSLT 1.1 has some very useful features. Most of these have made their way into XSLT 2.0, some (including the `<xsl:script>` element) have not, but the lack of XSLT 1.1 implementations means that it is not a good choice.

Whether or not you use XSLT 2.0 depends on the kind of environment you're working in, and the kind of transformations that you want to use. At time of writing, XSLT 2.0 was not ready for production-level transformations. However, its features can be useful for experimental or one-off stylesheets, and will certainly be useful if you want to make use of information from an XML Schema.

It is undoubtedly worth being aware of the new features of XSLT 2.0 – such as the support for grouping, the lack of "result tree fragments", the ability to create multiple output documents, and the ability to define your own extension functions using XSLT code. Stylesheets you write can be easily upgraded to XSLT 2.0 in the future. In the meantime, most processors have extension functions, elements or other mechanisms for supporting the new features of XSLT 2.0 in XSLT 1.0.

> **Use XSLT 1.0, with extensions if necessary, rather than WD-xsl or XSLT 1.1. Keep an eye on XSLT 2.0 so that you can move to it when the specification has stabilized.**

5.3 Using the XSLT Processing Model

The major difference between XSLT and other programming languages is that XSLT is a **declarative** language like Prolog, rather than a **procedural** language like C. In a declarative language, code describes the *output* you want to create, rather than the *steps* a processor should take to create the output. XSLT also differs from some other declarative languages in that it's primarily a **rule-based** language; the processor locates the code to be executed by matching nodes to templates rather than the code you write pointing at particular code blocks by name.

We looked at this earlier with the example template for processing billing addresses:

```
<!-- Process billing addresses -->
<xsl:template match="address[@type = 'billing']">
  <!-- Create an <address> element -->
  <address>
    <!-- Create a line for each child of the billing address -->
    <xsl:for-each select="*">
      <xsl:value-of select=" " /><br />
    </xsl:for-each>
  </address>
</xsl:template>
```

This template, as a rule, states that when the XSLT processor is told to process an <address> element whose type attribute has the value 'billing', it should do so by creating an HTML <address> element containing lines separated by <br> elements. The code is invoked whenever the XSLT processor is told to process such an <address> element. Consider the following case, where the processor is told to apply templates to the two <address> elements at the same time:

```
<!-- Process customer details -->
<xsl:template match="customer">
  ...
  <!-- Present addresses -->
  <xsl:apply-templates select="address" />
  ...
</xsl:template>
```

Here, the XSLT processor will use the billing address template for the billing address, and another template for the shipping address.

Both of these features of XSLT – being declarative, *and* being rule-based – make XSLT a bit of a strange language to work with, particularly for people used to procedural programming languages such as C++ or Java, or even templating languages such as ASP or JSP. In this section, we'll look at some of the patterns and pitfalls to be aware of when using the XSLT processing model.

186

5.3.1 Use Push and Pull Appropriately

There are two extreme approaches to processing XML using XSLT:

❏ **Push**

Define templates for each element that might be encountered, within which you apply templates to all the children of that element. The source is "pushed" through the stylesheet. The structure of the source determines what the structure of the result look like; the stylesheet just provides mapping rules from source to result.

❏ **Pull**

Create a template for the document element only; use `<xsl:for-each>` to process the content of elements as encountered, and call templates to do particular pieces of processing. The information in the source is "pulled" into the stylesheet. The stylesheet determines what the structure of the result looks like, and the source provides only the raw data to slot into that structure.

An example of using a push style to process the billing address to create the HTML address that we've been looking at, would apply templates to the content of the `<address>` element, and process whatever was found in the order in which it was encountered:

```
<xsl:template match="address[@type = 'billing']">
  <address><xsl:apply-templates /></address>
</xsl:template>
<xsl:template match="name | street | city | state | zip">
  <xsl:value-of select="." /><br />
</xsl:template>
```

Using a pull style, the code for processing the billing address would live in a named template instead, and would explicitly pull in the information from the billing address to create the HTML address:

```
<xsl:template name="processBillingAddress">
  <xsl:param name="billingAddress" />
  <address>
    <xsl:value-of select="$billingAddress/name" /><br />
    <xsl:value-of select="$billingAddress/street" /><br />
    <xsl:value-of select="$billingAddress/city" /><br />
    <xsl:value-of select="$billingAddress/state" /><br />
    <xsl:value-of select="$billingAddress/zip" /><br />
  </address>
</xsl:template>
```

Both extremes have their advantages and disadvantages. The push approach can involve processing more nodes than you really need to. A pure pull approach isn't robust in the face of changes to the structure of the source, and doesn't take advantage of the built-in mechanisms for choosing what to do on the basis of a node's type or name.

187

The best stylesheets use a mix of pull and push styles, depending on the kind of processing that needs to be done. Even when using a particular style, you should adopt a less extreme approach than those characterized. The following two situations describe where one approach is more appropriate than the other.

5.3.1.1 Apply Templates to Only the Nodes that You Want to Process

A sign of push processing being used inappropriately is having templates that match particular elements (or even text nodes), but do nothing with them. For example, you only want the HTML page, which you're generating from the order digest we looked at, to contain information about the customers of each order, not information about the items in the order. One way to do that would be to apply templates to everything within an order, and then filter out anything to do with items by having an empty template that matched text nodes within item elements:

```
<xsl:template match="order">
    ...<xsl:apply-templates />...
</xsl:template>
<xsl:template match="item//text()" />
```

This effectively ignores the text within <item> elements; the items get processed, but no output is generated as a result of that processing. Since the only other content of the <order> element is the <customer> element, this effectively just processes the <customer> element.

Empty templates are often used to filter out information that would otherwise be added to the result; this usually happens because templates are being applied to nodes when they shouldn't. Whenever a template is applied to a node, the processor has to locate an appropriate template for that node. This can be a time-consuming process if there are lots of templates that could match the node, especially if the match patterns include predicates. For this reason, it's a good idea to apply templates only to the nodes that you want to process.

Thus, a better approach than the above, would be to apply templates to only the <customer> element, since that's where all the interesting material lies:

```
<xsl:template match="order">
    ...<xsl:apply-templates select="customer" />...
</xsl:template>
```

In this example, it's easy to list the element that you want to process – the <customer> element. In other situations, it can be easier to list the elements that you *don't* want to process, which means that it's easier to use empty templates to filter out information. If you do so, you should try to make the empty templates match nodes that are as far up the tree as possible. If, in this example, the <order> element contained other things that you *did* want to process, such as payment details, then you would process everything aside from the <item> elements by applying templates to everything and having an empty template that matches the <item> elements (rather than the text within the <item> elements):

```
<xsl:template match="order">
 ...<xsl:apply-templates />...
</xsl:template>
<xsl:template match="item" />
```

As soon as the processor hits an <item> element it knows, it doesn't have to look inside that <item> element to see if there's anything else worth processing. This saves the processor from processing all the descendants of the <item> element.

If you don't want to process a node (if it doesn't contain information you're interested in) then don't apply templates to it.

5.3.1.2 Process Mixed Content Using Templates Rather than xsl:for-each

It's almost always a good idea to use matching templates (in combination with modes as we'll see later) to process nodes, rather than calling templates and using <xsl:for-each>. Using templates enables you to create a more robust stylesheet that adapts to structural changes in the source document.

The extreme pull approach of using <xsl:for-each> is particularly weak in processing mixed content. Usually mixed content is used for document-oriented XML, where a piece of text is marked up with elements that describe the meaning of a particular word or phrase. For example:

```
<p>
  This is some <dfn><term>mixed content</term>: content in which
  elements and text are intermingled</dfn>.
</p>
```

Here, the <p> element contains some text and a <dfn> element, while the <dfn> element contains both text and a <term> element. Imagine trying to change this text so that the term is emphasized and the <dfn> element ignored, to create:

```
<p>
  This is some <em>mixed content</em>: content in which elements and
  text are intermingled.
</p>
```

It's hard to deal with mixed content using a pull approach, but if you had to, the template would look something like this:

```
<xsl:template name="process-mixed">
  <xsl:for-each select="node()">
    <xsl:choose>
      <xsl:when test="self::text()">
        <xsl:value-of select="." />
```

```
      </xsl:when>
      <xsl:when test="self::dfn">
        <xsl:call-template name="process-mixed" />
      </xsl:when>
      <xsl:when test="self::term">
        <em>
          <xsl:call-template name="process-mixed" />
        </em>
      </xsl:when>
    </xsl:choose>
  </xsl:for-each>
</xsl:template>
```

Each possible kind of element would have its own `<xsl:when>`. In comparison, the push approach is much simpler:

```
<xsl:template match="text()">
  <xsl:value-of select="." />
</xsl:template>

<xsl:template match="dfn">
  <xsl:apply-templates />
</xsl:template>

<xsl:template match="term">
  <em><xsl:apply-templates /></em>
</xsl:template>
```

> *Note that the first two templates here are not absolutely necessary as the behavior of these templates is exactly the same as that provided by the built-in templates.*

XSLT processors optimize the discovery of appropriate templates for particular nodes, especially when templates match elements by name, or nodes by node type. Therefore, using templates is usually faster than using an `<xsl:choose>` within an `<xsl:for-each>`. Also, it breaks the code up into simple rules that are easy to add to or detract from in case the structure of the source document changes, and these are easy to customize if your stylesheet is imported and reused by someone else.

Apply templates to nodes rather than using `<xsl:for-each>`, especially when processing mixed content.

5.3.2 Break up your Transformations

XSLT can handle very complex transformations, but stylesheets that carry out complex transformations are often hard to debug and maintain. Rather than create a single stylesheet that does everything at once, it's often a good idea to break up a transformation into several separate, simpler steps that you combine in a **pipeline**.

Each step is individually easier to test and maintain, and can be reused several times in different transformations. If early steps can filter the source document so that it contains less information, or rearrange it so that locating information becomes easier, then splitting up a transformation can also increase its speed and reduce its memory requirements.

For example, the order digest XML file that we've been using may contain many orders, but we're only interested in those that relate to the customer with the `tx78734` ID. We could do both, filter the XML *and* transform it to HTML in the same step. However, it's more modular to do the filtering first, using a simple stylesheet as follows:

```
<xsl:stylesheet version="1.0"
                xmlns:xsl="http://www.w3.org/1999/XSL/Transform">

<!-- $customerID is the ID of the customer we're interested in -->
<xsl:param name="customerID" select="'tx78734'" />

<!-- This template filters the orders in orderDigest so that only
     those involving the customer we are interested in remain. -->
<xsl:template match="orderDigest">
  <orderDigest>
    <xsl:copy-of select="order[customer/@id = $customerID]" />
  </orderDigest>
</xsl:template>
</xsl:stylesheet>
```

and then use the result of this filtering stylesheet as the source for the transformation into HTML.

The simplest way to set up a pipeline is to have completely separate stylesheets, or even other code, such as `SAXFilters`, for each step, and to join them through an external process. This is particularly easy and efficient if you're executing the transformation with server- or client-side code, because it means that there's no need to serialize and re-parse the result of each step in the pipeline (serializing and parsing XML accounts for a significant percentage of the time it takes to do a transformation).

However, if you're only interested in the modularity benefits of using a pipeline, you can also do it using a batch transformation. I often use a batch file that includes the command lines to carry out a series of pipelined transformations, for example, if you use `filter.xsl` on `orderDigest.xml`, and then `summary.xsl` on the result of that transformation, the batch file would look like this:

```
saxon -o filtered.xml orderDigest.xml filter.xsl customerID=tx78734
saxon -o summary.html filtered.xml summary.xsl
```

It's also possible to set up multi-step transformations within a stylesheet. Use a variable to hold the result of the first step, convert the result tree fragment to a node set using a `node-set()` extension function, and use the resulting node set as the source for the next stage of the transformation. The code overleaf shows the general pattern; it splits the transformation into two steps, each of which involves applying templates in a different mode.

191

```
<xsl:stylesheet version="1.0"
                 xmlns:xsl="http://www.w3.org/1999/XSL/Transform"
                 xmlns:exsl="http://exslt.org/common"
                 extension-element-prefixes="exsl">

<xsl:template match="/">
  <!-- First filter the document using the filter mode -->
  <xsl:variable name="filtered">
    <xsl:apply-templates mode="filter" />
  </xsl:variable>
  <!-- Then transform the filtered document using the summary mode -->
  <xsl:apply-templates select="exsl:node-set($filtered)/*"
                        mode="summary" />
</xsl:template>
...
</xsl:stylesheet>
```

The code above uses the `exsl:node-set()` extension function defined in EXSLT.
This is supported by many XSLT processors, the notable exception being MSXML,
which has its own equivalent extension function, `msxsl:node-set()` in the
`urn:schemas-microsoft-com:xslt` namespace. In XSLT 2.0, variables will always
hold node sets rather than result tree fragments. Therefore, extension functions will no
longer be necessary.

> **Breaking down a transformation into separate steps makes it
> easier to maintain, debug, and reuse the individual steps.
> You can pipeline the transformations together within a
> stylesheet or through external code.**

Usually, a pipelined transformation centers on pipelining a source document from one
step to another, with the result of one step becoming the source of the next step. Since
XSLT is XML, it's also possible to put together pipelines in which the result of one step
acts as the *stylesheet* in the next step. This can be useful in three main areas, all of
which fall under the general umbrella of "literate programming":

❑ When the stylesheet's behavior should be determined by a "template"
   document that includes location paths or XPath expressions. Having a
   simple templating language, which you then convert into full XSLT, can be
   useful in that it enables designers to focus on the design or layout of a
   page rather than worrying about XSLT syntax.

❑ When the stylesheet is complex or repetitive, such that it's easier to
   generate the stylesheet automatically rather than write it by hand. An
   example is where every template in the stylesheet needs to have a
   particular set of parameters defined for it. It's easier to write the templates
   without the parameter definitions, and then add those parameter
   definitions programmatically.

❑ When the stylesheet includes embedded documentation that should be
   ignored in the actual transformation.

There are two main ways in which stylesheets can be generated dynamically. First, you create a DOM from a basic stylesheet, and then modify it with the help of DOM methods before using it as the stylesheet in the transformation. Second, you can generate the stylesheet using XSLT.

The latter method is a little tricky unless you're happy using `<xsl:element>` and `<xsl:attribute>` all the time. If you just include XSLT elements as literal result elements in a template, the XSLT processor can't tell which elements it should interpret as instructions, and which as literal result elements. Therefore you have to set up an alias namespace to stand in for the XSLT namespace, and use the `<xsl:namespace-alias>` element to tell the processor to switch namespaces in the result, as follows:

```
<xsl:stylesheet version="1.0"
                xmlns:xsl="http://www.w3.org/1999/XSL/Transform"
                xmlns="http://www.w3.org/1999/XSL/TransformAlias">

<!-- Elements generated in the default namespace should be moved to
     the XSLT namespace -->
<xsl:namespace-alias stylesheet-prefix="#default"
                     result-prefix="xsl" />

<xsl:template match="/">
  <!-- Generate an xsl:stylesheet element -->
  <stylesheet version="1.0">
    ...
  </stylesheet>
</xsl:template>
...
</xsl:stylesheet>
```

> **Since XSLT stylesheets are XML documents, it's not hard to generate an XSLT stylesheet as part of a pipeline, or to adapt an existing stylesheet through DOM manipulation.**

5.3.3 Use XML Lookup Tables Rather than Procedural Code

Whatever language you use, lookup tables are usually a better choice than using procedural code to map from a key to a value. In XSLT, you can create lookup tables using XML and then use all the flexibility of XPath to access information from them. For example, if you had dates in the format `"2002-12-25"` and you wanted to convert them into dates in the format `"25th December 2002"`. You could use the following XSLT to work out a month name from a month number:

```
<xsl:choose>
  <xsl:when test="$month = 1">January</xsl:when>
  <xsl:when test="$month = 2">February</xsl:when>
  ...
  <xsl:when test="$month = 12">December</xsl:when>
</xsl:choose>
```

193

However, it's better to create XML that describes the months, as follows:

```
<months>
   <month abbr="Jan">January</month>
   <month abbr="Feb">Febuary</month>
   ...
   <month abbr="Dec">December</month>
</months>
```

This XML can be reused to carry out other lookups (for example, to get the abbreviation, or to perform the reverse mapping, from month name to month number), and is easier to edit than the procedural code.

There are three choices about where to place this lookup table:

1. You can place it in a separate document (for example, months.xml), which you then access using the document() function:

```
<xsl:value-of
   select="document('months.xml')/months/month[position() = $month]" />
```

This technique is useful if you intend to use the lookup table in a number of stylesheets, as you can reuse it.

2. As the XSLT stylesheet itself is an XML document, you can also place it at the top level of the stylesheet itself, as **data elements**. In this case, you must place the top-most elements within a namespace:

```
<xsl:stylesheet version="1.0"
                xmlns:xsl="http://www.w3.org/1999/XSL/Transform"
                xmlns:m="http://www.example.com/months"
                exclude-result-prefixes="m">

<m:months>
   <m:month abbr="Jan">January</month>
   <m:month abbr="Feb">Febuary</month>
   ...
   <m:month abbr="Dec">December</month>
</m:months>
...
</xsl:stylesheet>
```

To access the data elements, you can take advantage of the fact that document('') accesses the stylesheet itself:

```
<xsl:value-of
   select="document('')/*/m:months/m:month[position() = $month]" />
```

This keeps the lookup table near the code that uses it. It isn't particularly reusable, and can be inefficient since the XSLT processor must read in and store the stylesheet twice – once as a stylesheet and once as a "source document".

194

3. The third technique is to hold the lookup table within a (global) variable. For example:

```
<xsl:variable name="months">
  <month abbr="Jan">January</month>
  <month abbr="Feb">Febuary</month>
  ...
  <month abbr="Dec">December</month>
</xsl:variable>
```

Again you can access the content of this variable either through the document() function:

```
<xsl:value-of select="document('')/*/xsl:variable[@name = 'months']
                      /month[position() = $month]" />
```

or by using a node-set() extension function:

```
<xsl:value-of
   select="exsl:node-set($months)/month[position() = $month]" />
```

This technique enables you to reuse the lookup table since the variable can be defined in a stylesheet that is then imported into other stylesheets, but has the disadvantage of relying on an extension function. In XSLT 2.0, you won't need a node-set() extension function to use this technique.

If you have a large lookup table, you should consider accessing the information it contains using a key. We'll be looking at using keys later in this chapter.

> **Use XML structures as lookup tables rather than procedural code.**

5.3.4 Using Recursion

A process is recursive if it calls itself. In XSLT, as in other declarative programming languages, recursion is used instead of iteration in procedural programming languages, especially when manipulating strings or numbers.

For example, imagine that we wanted to total up the cost of the items in a particular order within the order digest that we've been looking at. The items are held in XML that looks like this:

```
<item sku="TK-421">
  <quantity>1</quantity>
  <unitPrice>$39.95</unitPrice>
</item>
<item sku="SB-007">
  <quantity>4</quantity>
  <unitPrice>$1.00</unitPrice>
</item>
```

The subtotal for each item has to be calculated by multiplying the `<quantity>` by the `<unitPrice>`, and because the `<unitPrice>` is in a currency format, we need to ignore the first character when creating the total. In a procedural language, we'd do this by creating a variable to hold the title and by iterating over the `<item>` elements, calculating the subtotal and adding this to the variable. In pseudo-code:

```
total = 0;
for $i in item {
  total = $total + (substring($i/unitPrice, 2) * $i/quantity);
}
return total;
```

This approach doesn't work in XSLT because once a variable has been assigned a value, you can't update it with a new value. Instead, you need a recursive solution. You can calculate the total for a list of `<item>` elements by calculating the subtotal for the first `<item>` element and adding that subtotal to the total for the rest of the `<item>` elements. Here is a recursive template that does just that:

```
<!-- Template to calculate the subtotal for a list of items -->
<xsl:template name="calculateTotal">
  <!-- $items holds the list of items -->
  <xsl:param name="items" />
  <xsl:choose>
    <!-- When there are items, the total is calculated by adding the
         subtotal for the first item to the total for the rest of the
         items -->
    <xsl:when test="$items">
      <xsl:variable name="first" select="$items[1]" />
      <xsl:variable name="subtotalOfFirst"
        select="substring($first/unitPrice, 2) * $first/quantity" />
      <xsl:variable name="subtotalOfRest">
        <!-- Recursive call -->
        <xsl:call-template name="calculateTotal">
          <xsl:with-param name="items"
                          select="$items[position() > 1]" />
        </xsl:call-template>
      </xsl:variable>
      <!-- Add the two subtotals together to get the result -->
      <xsl:value-of select="$subtotalOfFirst + $subtotalOfRest" />
    </xsl:when>
    <!-- When there aren't any items, the total is zero -->
    <xsl:otherwise>0</xsl:otherwise>
  </xsl:choose>
</xsl:template>
```

Initially this template can be called by passing in all the `<item>` elements from an order as the value of the `$items` parameter:

```
<xsl:template match="order">
  ...
  <xsl:call-template name="calculateTotal">
    <xsl:with-param name="items" select="item" />
  </xsl:call-template>
  ...
</xsl:template>
```

5.3.4.1 Use a Tail-recursive Algorithm when Possible

The previous example is one of a recursive template, but not of a **tail-recursive template**. Tail-recursive templates are those that call themselves as the last thing that they do. A non-tail-recursive template does something more after the recursion (the earlier template adds two numbers together after the recursive call). For example, if you wrote the `calculateTotal` template as follows, it would be tail-recursive because *nothing* happens after the recursive call:

```
<!-- Template to calculate the subtotal for a list of items -->
<xsl:template name="calculateTotal">
  <!-- $items holds the list of items -->
  <xsl:param name="items" />
  <!-- $subtotal holds the total so far; it defaults to 0 -->
  <xsl:param name="subtotal" select="0" />
  <xsl:choose>
    <!-- When there are items, the template recurses with the new
         $subtotal being the old $subtotal plus the subtotal for the
         first item -->
    <xsl:when test="$items">
      <xsl:variable name="first" select="$items[1]" />
      <xsl:variable name="subtotalOfFirst"
        select="substring($first/unitPrice, 2) * $first/quantity" />
      <!-- Recursive call -->
      <xsl:call-template name="calculateTotal">
        <xsl:with-param name="items"
                        select="$items[position() > 1]" />
        <xsl:with-param name="subtotal"
                        select="$subtotal + $subtotalOfFirst" />
      </xsl:call-template>
    </xsl:when>
    <!-- When there aren't any items, the total is the $subtotal -->
    <xsl:otherwise>
      <xsl:value-of select="$subtotal" />
    </xsl:otherwise>
  </xsl:choose>
</xsl:template>
```

It's a good idea to make a template tail-recursive whenever you can, though it's not always possible to find tail-recursive algorithms for certain manipulations, such as multiple search and replace operations. Most good XSLT processors, such as Saxon and MSXML, will optimize tail-recursive templates so that they're treated as if they were written as a loop, which means two things:

❑ **The stack won't overflow**

XSLT processors keep a stack recording of which template has been used to call the current code, so that they know where to go back to, once a template has finished. However, there's a limit to the depth of that stack as that can easily be reached if you have a lot of recursion, and if you reach that limit, the transformation will usually halt with an ugly error. Rewriting a tail-recursive template as a loop means that recursive template calls don't get added to the stack, which means that it's harder to reach the limit of the stack.

❑ **Resources will be reused**

When a template is tail-recursive, the resources used for parameters and variables in one call can be reused in the next call. This helps keep the memory consumption of the transformation down.

5.3.4.2 Use a Divide and Conquer Algorithm if Speed is Important

Another way to increase the speed of recursive templates is to use a **Divide and Conquer (DVC)** algorithm. A DVC algorithm tackles a problem by dividing it in half each time, which results in less recursive depth and usually fewer recursive calls. Therefore using a DVC algorithm can alleviate stack overflow problems and speed up your stylesheet, especially if you have lots of recursive calls.

The following example shows a `calculateTotal` template implemented with a DVC algorithm. Using this algorithm, the list of items is split into two and the `calculateTotal` template called on each half of the list. Note that there are two recursive calls in this template; it is no longer tail-recursive:

```
<!-- Template to calculate the subtotal for a list of items -->
<xsl:template name="calculateTotal">
  <!-- $items holds the list of items -->
  <xsl:param name="items" />

  <!-- $nitems holds the number of items in the list -->
  <xsl:variable name="nitems" select="count($items)" />
  <xsl:choose>
    <!-- When there's more than one item, the template recurses on the
         two halves of the list and adds the results together -->
    <xsl:when test="$nitems > 1">
      <!-- Split the list into two halves -->
      <xsl:variable name="half" select="$nitems div 2" />
      <xsl:variable name="firstHalf"
                    select="$items[position() &lt;= $half]" />
      <xsl:variable name="secondHalf"
                    select="$items[position() > $half]" />

      <!-- Calculate the total for each half -->
      <xsl:variable name="firstHalfTotal">
        <!-- Recursive call -->
        <xsl:call-template name="calculateTotal">
          <xsl:with-param name="items" select="$firstHalf" />
        </xsl:call-template>
      </xsl:variable>
      <xsl:variable name="secondHalfTotal">
        <!-- Recursive call -->
        <xsl:call-template name="calculateTotal">
          <xsl:with-param name="items" select="$secondHalf" />
        </xsl:call-template>
      </xsl:variable>

      <!-- Add the two subtotals together -->
      <xsl:value-of select="$firstHalfTotal + $secondHalfTotal" />
    </xsl:when>
    <!-- When there's one item, the subtotal is calculated from its
         quantity and unit price -->
```

```
      <xsl:when test="$nitems = 1">
        <xsl:value-of select="substring($items/unitPrice, 2) *
                              $items/quantity)" />
      </xsl:when>
      <!-- When there aren't any items, the total is 0 -->
      <xsl:otherwise>0</xsl:otherwise>
    </xsl:choose>
  </xsl:template>
```

Templates that implement DVC algorithms tend to entail a certain amount of overhead for calculating how to divide up the problem and to do the recombination of the results. For the best results, it's a good idea to use basic tail-recursive templates for small amounts of recursion (in the order of 10s of recursive calls) and DVC algorithms for large amounts of recursion (in the order of 1000s of recursive calls). For details, see "Two stage recursive algorithms in XSLT" by Dimitre Novatchev and Slawomir Tyszko at http://www.topxml.com/xsl/articles/recurse/.

When designing recursive templates, use divide and conquer or at least tail-recursive algorithms.

5.3.5 Avoiding Pitfalls

In providing flexibility, XSLT also has a number of pitfalls that are easy to fall prey to. Often, especially to users familiar with procedural programming languages and the functionality of ASP or JSP, the "hard way" is more obvious than the easy way. This section describes some of these pitfalls, and suggests ways to avoid them.

5.3.5.1 XML and HTML are not Text

ASP and JSP lead people to think of converting data to an HTML page as being a matter of taking a template page and substituting parts of that page with instructions that act as macros and are directly substituted when the ASP or JSP page is processed. XSLT takes a very different approach. XSLT stylesheets generate node trees, which are often, but not always, serialized into physical files. When you use XSLT, you are not writing an XML or HTML string, you are creating a node tree.

When you use XSLT, you are creating a result tree, *not* a physical document.

There are three common symptoms of this misunderstanding:

- ❑ Using the text output method when generating XML or HTML
- ❑ Using disable-output-escaping
- ❑ Trying to insert <xsl:value-of> elements within attribute values

199

These three symptoms above come about in two main situations.

1. The first situation is where a user wants to take control of the serialization that's used, for example, to ensure that a `<title>` element is output as `<title></title>` rather than `<title/>`, or that a non-breaking space character is output as ` `. These are serialization details rather than anything that impacts on the actual content of the document that gets generated. As such, they *should* be unimportant to any downstream process. The serialization routines defined for the `xml` and `html` output methods make sure that the serialization of a node tree as XML or HTML follows the appropriate rules.

Most of the ways in which you might want to modify the serialization of a document, are governed by the `<xsl:output>` element. The `<xsl:output>` element controls:

❑   The DOCTYPE declaration that's generated for the result document

❑   The encoding that's used for the result document

❑   Which elements contain CDATA sections

❑   Whether the result is indented or not

Individual XSLT processors often give even greater control through extension attributes on `<xsl:output>`. For example, Saxon defines extension attributes on `<xsl:output>` that give you control over the size of the indentation used in the output, and the kind of character or entity reference used for characters that are outside the encoding used to serialize the result document.

If your processor doesn't give you the control you need, you should use a custom serializer to turn the node tree into a physical document. The easiest way to do this is to create a SAX `ContentHandler` that accepts a stream of SAX events, turns them into a physical document, and then plugs the output of the transformation into that `ContentHandler`. The `org.apache.xml.serialize.XMLSerializer` class is a good starting point.

> `org.apache.xml.serialize.XMLSerializer` *is part of the Xerces distribution, available from* http://xml.apache.org/xerces-j/.

2. A second situation in which users commonly try to create an XML or HTML document as a string, is grouping. For example, you were converting a list of items like below:

```
<list>
  <item>A</item>
  <item>B</item>
  <item>C</item>
  <item>D</item>
  ...
</list>
```

into a table with two columns:

```
<table>
  <tr><td>A</td><td>B</td></tr>
  <tr><td>C</td><td>D</td></tr>
  ...
</table>
```

A procedural approach would be to insert a start tag for the table row before each odd item, and an end tag for the table row after each even item, which would give the XSLT:

```
<xsl:for-each select="item">
  <!-- Open a table row before each odd item -->
  <xsl:if test="position() mod 2 = 1"><tr></xsl:if>
  <td><xsl:value-of select="." /></td>
  <!-- Close the table row after each even item -->
  <xsl:if test="position() mod 2 = 0"></tr></xsl:if>
</xsl:for-each>
```

This isn't allowed in XSLT because it isn't well-formed XML; the `<tr>` element does not properly nest inside the `<xsl:if>` element in which it starts. The XSLT method is to create a row for each odd item, and to create a cell for that item and its immediately following sibling within the row:

```
<!-- Create a row for each odd item -->
<xsl:for-each select="item[position() mod 2 = 1]">
  <tr>
    <!-- The row contains a cell for the odd item, followed by a cell
         for the immediately following (even) item -->
    <td><xsl:value-of select="." /></td>
    <td><xsl:value-of select="following-sibling::item[1]" /></td>
  </tr>
</xsl:for-each>
```

This rest of this section describes the symptoms of treating XSLT like JSP or ASP in more detail.

5.3.5.2 Avoid the Text Output Method

The text output method is for generating text, and should not be used for creating XML or HTML; they have their own output methods. You should always use:

```
<xsl:output method="html" />
<xsl:template match="/">
  <html>
    ...
  </html>
</xsl:template>
```

You should never code something along the lines of:

```
<xsl:output method="text" />
<xsl:template match="/">
  &lt;html&gt;
```

```
    ...
   &lt;/html&gt;
  </xsl:template>
```

or:

```
  <xsl:output method="text" />
  <xsl:template match="/">
   <![CDATA[
   <html>
    ...
   </html>
   ]]>
  </xsl:template>
```

The above code is tedious to write (you have to escape all the angle brackets), and also gives you no guarantees about how well-formed the output that you generate is. It's very easy to create non-well-formed XML if you try to create it as text.

On the other hand, you *should* use the text output method if you are generating something that is not XML or HTML, even if it is very similar to it. For example, a JSP page is usually not XML or HTML as it includes scriptlets in the syntax:

```
  <% code %>
```

This syntax is not well-formed XML. If you're generating JSP, therefore, you should not use the XML or HTML output methods; instead, create the JSP page as text or, if you can, use disable-output-escaping as described in the next section.

> *JSP 1.2 includes an XML syntax in which scriptlets, for example, are included using `<jsp:scriptlet>` elements. An even better way of generating JSP pages using XSLT is to use the XML syntax of JSP.*

5.3.5.3 Avoid Disable-output-escaping

The `disable-output-escaping` attribute resides on `<xsl:text>` and `<xsl:value-of>`, and allows you to tell the XSLT processor to *not* perform any escaping of the text node generated by the `<xsl:text>` or `<xsl:value-of>` instruction.

Normally:

```
  <icecream><xsl:text>Ben &amp; Jerry's</xsl:text></icecream>
```

will be serialized as:

```
  <icecream>Ben &amp; Jerry's</icecream>
```

However, when output-escaping is disabled, the following snippet:

```
<icecream>
   <xsl:text disable-output-escaping="yes">Ben &amp; Jerry's</xsl:text>
</icecream>
```

might lead to the XSLT processor producing:

```
<icecream>Ben & Jerry's</icecream>
```

which is not well-formed XML because the free-standing "&" will be interpreted as the start of an entity reference, when it is not.

As you can see, disabling output-escaping leaves you open to the risk of a non-well-formed output of the transformation. In addition, it is worth bearing in mind that disable-output-escaping only has any effect when the XSLT processor performing the transformation is also responsible for serializing the result of the transformation. This isn't always the case, particularly when the transformation is part of a pipeline. Indeed, an XSLT processor is free to ignore the disable-output-escaping attribute entirely and, thus, using this feature can limit the portability of your stylesheets.

The situations in which disable-output-escaping should be used are few and far between, but there are one or two situations in which disable-output-escaping is the only option. The most common of these arises when an XML document has been designed with embedded XML or HTML within a CDATA section. For example:

```
<doc>
   <![CDATA[<p>Some HTML documentation</p>]]>
</doc>
```

As far as the XSLT processor is concerned, this text appears exactly as if the individual less-than signs had been escaped as follows:

```
<doc>
   &lt;p>Some HTML documentation&lt;/p>
</doc>
```

To extract the HTML, to copy it into the result document, you need to copy the text from the source, unescaped, literally into the result document, for which you need disable-output-escaping:

```
<xsl:value-of select="doc" disable-output-escaping="yes" />
```

In these situations, it's better to try to persuade the designer of the XML document to nest the well-formed HTML properly, using namespaces:

```
<doc>
   <html:p>Some HTML documentation</html:p>
</doc>
```

which enables the XSLT to cleanly copy the HTML into the result tree:

```
<xsl:copy-of select="doc/node()" />
```

5.3.5.4 Use Attribute Value Templates

The final symptom of misunderstanding the way XSLT builds a result tree, is to try to put `<xsl:value-of>` elements within attribute values. For example:

```
<a href="customer?id=<xsl:value-of select="@id" />">
  <xsl:value-of select="@id" />
</a>
```

This is not well-formed XML. All XSLT stylesheets must be well-formed XML documents. The intention of this XSLT snippet is to insert the value of the id attribute into the value of the href attribute being generated so as to create a link to a customer-specific page. The solution is an attribute value template:

```
<a href="customer?id={@id}">
  <xsl:value-of select="@id" />
</a>
```

Within an attribute value on a literal result element, any {}s indicate that some information is being included in the attribute value. The content of the {}s is evaluated and added into the attribute value. An alternative method is to use the `<xsl:attribute>` instruction to create the attribute:

```
<a>
  <xsl:attribute name="href">
    <xsl:text>customer?id=</xsl:text>
    <xsl:value-of select="@id" />
  </xsl:attribute>
  <xsl:value-of select="@id" />
</a>
```

As you can see, the attribute value template is a lot shorter and closer to the appearance of the result document.

5.3.5.5 Be Namespace-aware

XSLT is a namespace-aware tool for processing XML documents, which means that to an XSLT processor, the following documents are the same, both holding `<p>` elements in the XHTML namespace:

```
<p xmlns="http://www.w3.org/1999/xhtml">...</p>
```

```
<html:p xmlns:html="http://www.w3.org/1999/xhtml">...</html:p>
```

However, both of the above are different from the code on the next page, which is a `<p>` element in no namespace:

```
<p>...</p>
```

Importantly, namespace awareness means that the prefix that's used in a source document makes no difference to the way in which that document is processed.

The one exception to this general rule is the `name()` function. The `name()` function returns a qualified name for a node. The prefix used for the qualified name is one of the prefixes used in the source document for the namespace of the node. Usually this means that the `name()` function returns the qualified name used in the source document. If you test that name, your stylesheet will not work if it is used with a document that uses a different prefix.

For example, the location path:

```
*[name() = $name]
```

will only select elements whose qualified name is equal to the value of the $name variable. If $name is "p", it will select the following two elements:

```
<p xmlns="http://www.w3.org/1999/xhtml">...</p>
```

```
<p>...</p>
```

and not:

```
<html:p xmlns:html="http://www.w3.org/1999/xhtml">...</html:p>
```

Namespace awareness is an essential part of XSLT. You should try to make your stylesheet work with namespaces rather than subvert them. To test the name of an element, you should use the `local-name()` function, coupled with the `namespace-uri()` function, as follows:

```
*[local-name() = $name and
   namespace-uri() = 'http://www.w3.org/1999/xhtml']
```

If you know the name of the node that you want to select in advance, then using a normal location path is your best bet. Assuming that the `html` prefix is bound to the XHTML namespace, the following will select the <p> element in the XHTML namespace:

```
html:p
```

If you want to select everything *but* the <p> element in the XHTML namespace, the `self` axis comes in handy:

```
*[not(self::html:p)]
```

> **Do *not* introduce dependence on the prefix used in the source document; your stylesheet should be namespace-aware.**

5.3.5.6 Avoid Using Extension Functions Written in Scripting Languages

XSLT is a Turing-complete language; it can carry out any manipulation of strings and numbers that you might want to carry out. Nevertheless, it's common for users who are familiar with other languages, such as JavaScript or VBScript, to create extension functions in those languages to do things that can be done in XSLT. This is a bad idea for the following reasons.

First, there's currently no standard way of defining extension functions within a stylesheet. Thus, any stylesheet that uses, for example, `<msxml:script>` to create extension functions might not be portable onto another XSLT processor.

Second, using extension functions written in other languages forces the XSLT processor to set up another environment in which that code can be evaluated. This slows down your stylesheet.

Third, other languages don't have the safeguards that are built into XSLT that guarantee that functions don't have side-effects. Being side-effect free is one of the tenets of XSLT; it enables processors to execute pieces of code in parallel, for example, without affecting the result of the transformation, and thus enables optimization. If an extension function has side-effects, it might not work as 'expected in an optimized processor.

Fourth, while the built-in functions in XSLT can't access system resources except through a URI (via the `document()` function), there's no similar guarantee for extension functions. Thus extension functions might not be safe from a security standpoint. If there is system information that you need to access, such as the current date or time, or the file listing from a particular directory, then it's best to pass that information in as a parameter to the stylesheet, or to make that information accessible via a URI accessed by the `document()` function.

Fifth, using an extension function instead of XSLT code is often a sign that there's a gap in understanding how to perform a particular task using XSLT. Consider the code below, which uses three extension functions to count the number of items in a list:

```
<xsl:variable name="reset" select="my:resetCounter()" />
<xsl:for-each select="item">
  <xsl:variable name="increment" select="my:incrementCounter()" />
</xsl:for-each>
Count: <xsl:value-of select="my:getCounter()" />
```

Here, the extension functions are being used to subvert XSLT's rules about variables. In XSLT, variables cannot have new values assigned to them. The previous function calls use a JavaScript variable, which *can* be updated to hold a counter that is reset, incremented, and then retrieved. This enables the programmer to adopt a procedural style of iterating through a set of nodes, adding one to a counter on each iteration, to work out how many nodes there are in a set. However, XPath has a function to deal with this common requirement; a simpler method would be to just use the count() function:

```
Count: <xsl:value-of select="count(item)" />
```

XPath also has a sum() function for the other common example of this pattern – summing the values of a node set. In other situations, you should use recursion (which we looked at earlier in this chapter) rather than iteration.

5.3.5.7 Consider Using ESXLT Modules for Extensions

Extension functions should not be avoided all the time; there are situations in which using an extension function is a good idea.

First, some extension functions are built into several XSLT processors; most of these are defined in the EXSLT modules, which are described at http://www.exslt.org/. These functions are moderately portable (it would still be a good idea to check processor support for a particular function before you use it), have been designed as true functions, without side-effects, and, being built into processors, are just as efficient as normal XPath functions.

Second, extension functions are a lot more flexible than named templates in that they can be called from more places; for example, from the select attribute of <xsl:sort>, or the use attribute of <xsl:key>. It's also much shorter to call an extension function than a named template. Compare the following function call for getting the minimum unit price of a set of items:

```
<xsl:value-of select="math:min(item/unitPrice)" />
```

with the template call:

```
<xsl:template name="math:min">
   <xsl:with-param name="nodes" select="item/unitPrice" />
</xsl:template>
```

If you just want to use these advantages of extension functions, you should try to use XSLT to define the extension function. EXSLT defines a <func:function> element, that goes at the top level of a stylesheet, for defining an extension function. This notion is adopted in XSLT 2.0, which introduces an <xsl:function> element that works in almost exactly the same way. For example, the code overleaf defines an ord:itemSubtotal() function that calculates the subtotal for a particular <item> element by multiplying its unit price by the quantity of the item:

```
<xsl:stylesheet version="1.0"
                xmlns:xsl="http://www.w3.org/1999/XSL/Transform"
                xmlns:func="http://exslt.org/functions"
                xmlns:ord="http://www.example.com/orderDigest"
                extension-element-prefixes="func ord">

<func:function name="ord:itemSubtotal">
  <xsl:param name="item" />
  <func:result
    select="substring($item/unitPrice, 2) * $item/quantity" />
</func:function>
...
</xsl:stylesheet>
```

Third, there are situations where XSLT doesn't have the kind of support that you need to make a task straightforward. For example, XSLT doesn't have support for regular expressions, date arithmetic, or trigonometry. While it's possible to write XSLT to carry out matching against regular expressions, the addition of a date and duration, or the calculation of a cosine, it's not easy. Other languages offer more support, so it makes sense to use them in these situations.

> **Think carefully before using an extension function; if you
> can use XSLT instead of another language, then do so.**

5.4 Speeding up Your Stylesheet

The last section showed how to achieve the transformation that you want within the XSLT processing paradigm. This section is about taking stylesheets that already work, and making them perform better, both in terms of running faster and in terms of taking up less memory.

The discussion in this section is based on general rules of thumb that can help you create stylesheets that run faster. Following these rules will probably make your stylesheets faster, but the performance of a stylesheet can depend on many other factors:

❑ The XSLT processor you're using

❑ The manner in which you invoke the transformation and capture the result

❑ The memory the machine on which you're running the transformation has

❑ The exact details of the structure of the source document that you're working with

If you want to test the performance of your stylesheet, most processors have a verbose output in which they include the time taken by the transformation itself and the various other steps involved in the transformation (such as reading the source document and serializing the result document). CatchXSL! from http://www.xslprofiler.org/ also provides a way of viewing the details of which processing, is taking up time.

5.4.1 Minimize Node Visits

The first rule for increasing the speed of your stylesheets is to limit the number of nodes that your stylesheet visits. This section describes three methods for reducing node visits:

❑ Using keys for doing lookups, particularly when grouping

❑ Using the position() function rather than <xsl:number>

❑ Avoiding the "long" axes that can return large numbers of nodes

However, the basic principle can be applied to many other situations as well – the location path that you use to navigate through a tree, the way a recursive template moves through a node set – and you should bear it mind in other circumstances than the ones described here.

5.4.1.1 Use Keys to Speed Up Multiple Searches

One of the easiest ways to speed up a stylesheet is to introduce keys. Keys are a way of creating lookup tables for nodes, based on some value associated with the node. For example, you had some XML that stored invoices, each of which has an id attribute:

```
<invoices>
  <invoice id="STO-20021024-I">...</invoice>
  <invoice id="CDR-20020816-I">...</invoice>
  <invoice id="STO-20020903-I">...</invoice>
  ...
</invoices>
```

To pick a particular <invoice> out of the document, based on an identifier held in an $invoice variable, you could use a path with a predicate, as follows:

```
/invoices/invoice[@id = $invoice]
```

To find the <invoice>, the processor would search through all the <invoice> elements in the document, looking for the one whose id attribute matched $invoice; every <invoice> element would be visited. If you tried to select an <invoice> element with a different id, the processor would search through them all again, and again each time you tried to find an <invoice> with a particular id. You would end up with a lot of nodes being visited.

A key makes sure that each node is visited just once. On that visit, the processor stores the node and its value (the id in this case) in a lookup table. When you want to search through the list for a second time, the processor just looks up the value and retrieves the nodes that are associated with it. The key definition for this example is:

```
<xsl:key name="invoices" match="invoice" use="@id" />
```

Every <invoice> element is stored in the lookup table alongside the value of its id
attribute. To retrieve the <invoice> elements with the id held in the $invoice
variable, you would use:

```
key('invoices', $invoice)
```

Therefore Keys can save node visits, but they add to memory consumption because the
processor has to store the lookup table. It's worth using keys only if you're doing the
same search multiple times, and if there are lots of nodes that would be visited. If
you're doing a search only a few times, or there are only a few nodes to visit, you
should check the performance to see whether using a key is worthwhile.

5.4.1.2 Use Keys to Speed up Grouping

Along with making basic searches run faster, keys are particularly useful for speeding
up grouping nodes. Suppose we wanted to group the invoices in the previous list,
based on the first segment of their id, which indicates the invoicee, so that we would
get the following:

```
Invoicee: STO
Invoices:
  STO-20021024-I, STO-20020903-I
Invoicee: CDR
Invoices:
  CDR-20020816-I
```

To do this, we need to identify the first <invoice> that relates to a particular invoicee.
One way of doing this, is to search all the preceding <invoice> elements to see if this
one is the first for the invoicee:

```
<!-- Iterate through the invoice elements -->
<xsl:for-each select="/invoices/invoice">
  <!-- $invoicee is the first three letters of the invoice ID -->
  <xsl:variable name="invoicee" select="substring-before(@id, '-')" />
  <!-- Test whether there's already been an invoice that has the same
       invoicee as this one by looking at the preceding siblings -->
  <xsl:if test="not(preceding-sibling::invoice
                       [substring-before(@id, '-') = $invoicee])">
    Invoicee: <xsl:value-of select="$invoicee" />
    Invoices:
    <!-- Create a list of invoices for the invoicee -->
    <xsl:for-each select="/invoices/invoice
                             [substring-before(@id, '-') = $invoicee]">
      <xsl:value-of select="@id" />
      <!-- Add a comma after all but the last invoice in the list -->
      <xsl:if test="position() != last()">, </xsl:if>
    </xsl:for-each>
  </xsl:if>
</xsl:for-each>
```

You can probably see that the nested <xsl:for-each> is a lookup similar to the ones
described earlier, which could be done using a key.

The key needs to index each `<invoice>` element by its invoicee, as follows:

```
<xsl:key name="invoices-by-invoicee" match="invoice"
         use="substring-before(@id, '-')" />
```

Using the key, the same code would look like this:

```
<!-- Iterate through the invoice elements -->
<xsl:for-each select="/invoices/invoice">
   <!-- $invoicee is the first three letters of the invoice ID -->
   <xsl:variable name="invoicee" select="substring-before(@id, '-')" />
   <!-- Test whether there's already been an invoice that has the same
        invoicee as this one by looking at the preceding siblings -->
   <xsl:if test="not(preceding-sibling::invoice
                        [substring-before(@id, '-') = $invoicee])">
   Invoicee: <xsl:value-of select="$invoicee" />
   Invoices:
      <!-- Create a list of invoices for the invoicee -->
      <xsl:for-each select="key('invoices-by-invoicee', $invoicee)">
         <xsl:value-of select="@id" />
         <!-- Add a comma after all but the last invoice in the list -->
         <xsl:if test="position() != last()">, </xsl:if>
      </xsl:for-each>
   </xsl:if>
</xsl:for-each>
```

The key can also be used to identify the first `<invoice>` with a particular invoicee. The key returns the `<invoice>`s with a particular invoicee, in the order in which they appear. You can take the first of these, and then see if the `<invoice>` you're looking at is the same as the one that you've got, in this case by checking their `id`s:

```
<!-- Iterate through the invoice elements -->
<xsl:for-each select="/invoices/invoice">
   <!-- $invoicee is the first three letters of the invoice ID -->
   <xsl:variable name="invoicee" select="substring-before(@id, '-')" />
   <!-- Test whether there's already been an invoice that has the same
        invoicee as this one by retrieving them with the key -->
   <xsl:if test="@id = key('invoices-by-invoicee', $invoicee)[1]/@id">
      Invoicee: <xsl:value-of select="$invoicee" />
      Invoices:
      <!-- Create a list of invoices for the invoicee -->
      <xsl:for-each select="key('invoices-by-invoicee', $invoicee)">
         <xsl:value-of select="@id" />
         <!-- Add a comma after all but the last invoice in the list -->
         <xsl:if test="position() != last()">, </xsl:if>
      </xsl:for-each>
   </xsl:if>
</xsl:for-each>
```

This is much more efficient than checking all the preceding siblings of each `<invoice>`; it results in many fewer node visits. Using keys in this manner for grouping is very common practice and is called Muenchian grouping, after Steve Muench, who first described it. For more details, see http://www.jenitennison.com/xslt/grouping/muenchian.html.

> **Keys provide quick access to nodes, which is useful when you want to look them up by a particular value, especially when grouping.**

5.4.1.3 Consider Using position() Rather than xsl:number

The `<xsl:number>` instruction inserts a formatted number into the result tree. Usually (unless you use the `value` attribute), the number that's used is based on the position of the current node in the source node tree. To work out the number to use, the processor collects together all the preceding siblings of a node (the current node or one of its ancestors) and counts them. For example, taking the invoices that we used in the last section:

```
<invoices>
  <invoice id="STO-20021024-I">...</invoice>
  <invoice id="CDR-20020816-I">...</invoice>
  <invoice id="STO-20020903-I">...</invoice>
  ...
</invoices>
```

We can create a numbered list of the invoices as follows:

```
<xsl:for-each select="/invoices/invoice">
  <xsl:number format="1. " />
  <xsl:value-of select="@id" />
  <br />
</xsl:for-each>
```

The number for the third `<invoice>`, for example, is generated by counting how many preceding siblings that `<invoice>` has. The processor traverses the tree collecting these preceding siblings together, and then counts how many it's found and adds one to get the answer. On the third `<invoice>`, this means visiting two nodes; on the fifty-third `<invoice>`, this means visiting fifty-two nodes (unless the processor is very smart). When iterating through all the `<invoice>` elements, therefore, the number of nodes visited grows exponentially with each extra `<invoice>`.

In this example, however, we're just numbering the `<invoice>` elements in the order that they're being iterated over. As well as looking at the source tree to work out the number of an `<invoice>`, we have an easier way, we could use the `position()` function. The value returned by the `position()` function increments with each `<invoice>` visited. To get the formatting that `<xsl:number>` provides, we can use the `value` attribute on `<xsl:number>`:

```
<xsl:for-each select="/invoices/invoice">
  <xsl:number value="position()" format="1. " />
  <xsl:value-of select="@id" />
  <br />
</xsl:for-each>
```

Along with reducing the number of node visits, using the position() function to give the number of a node is more likely to give you the right number if you change the order in which the nodes are visited. If the <invoice> elements were sorted alphabetically by id, for example:

```
<xsl:for-each select="/invoices/invoice">
  <xsl:sort select="@id" />
  <xsl:number value="position()" format="1. " />
  <xsl:value-of select="@id" />
  <br />
</xsl:for-each>
```

The position() function would still number them incrementally. Using plain <xsl:number> would still base their number on their position in the source tree.

Of course there are times when you can't help using <xsl:number>'s numbering; if you're using the number as an index such that you want the number to be the same no matter how the nodes are sorted, or if you're not visiting the nodes sequentially (for example if you're numbering footnotes that are littered throughout a piece of text). However, the position() function does provide a good, speedy alternative in many cases.

> **When iterating over nodes that you want to number, use the position() function to create numbering rather than <xsl:number>.**

5.4.1.4 Avoid the "Long" Axes

The basic principle that we're exploring in this section is to avoid visiting too many nodes. Within location paths, the easiest way to avoid visiting a lot of nodes is to use axes that only expose a small number of nodes.

For example, using the path:

```
/invoices/invoice
```

will visit the <invoices> element and each <invoice> element.

On the other hand, using the path:

```
//invoice
```

which is a shorthand for:

```
/descendant-or-self::node()/invoice
```

will visit at least *every* element in the document, including all the elements under the `<invoice>` elements. Considering that the `<invoice>` element is likely to have lots of children, this will multiply the number of nodes visited many times.

There are several axes that should usually be avoided in order to reduce node visits:

❑   `descendant`

❑   `descendant-or-self` (`//` shorthand)

❑   `preceding`

❑   `following`

Whether these axes access a lot of nodes, depends on the structure of your document *and* the context node at the time when you use the axis. If you know that the context node can only have two preceding nodes, then using the `preceding` axis isn't a problem; if it could have 100, and especially if you're using the same path for each of those nodes, then using the `preceding` axis would be a bad idea. Unless you're dealing with a very small document, using `//` at the beginning of any path is a bad idea as this entails visiting every element and text node in the document.

> **Consider the number of nodes that are visited with a particular location path, and minimize the number visited, by stepping down to the nodes you're interested in, rather than selecting them all at once.**

5.4.2 Avoid Node Creation

The second rule of thumb for optimizing your stylesheet – actually to reduce memory consumption – is to avoid creating nodes if you can. Nodes take time to create, and are expensive to hold in memory, because the XSLT processor has to keep track of its relationships to other nodes *and* the information about the node itself.

There are three main ways to reduce the number of nodes that are created: using small source documents, stripping unnecessary whitespace from the node trees, and avoiding creating result tree fragments when you don't have to.

5.4.2.1 Use Small Documents

One thing that's perhaps surprising about the performance of XSLT stylesheets, is that one large document is actually slower to use than several small documents. The reason for this is two fold. On the memory front, to speed up movement around the node tree, an XSLT processor will build indices of the nodes that are accessed through different axes. In a large document, where more nodes are visited through a particular axis, these indices are larger than the sum of the similar indexes in small documents. On the speed front, as there are more nodes on a particular axis, there are more nodes to visit, and, as we saw in the last section, the more the node visits, the slower the stylesheet.

Therefore it's a good idea to make the source documents accessed by a stylesheet as small as possible. This can be achieved in two main ways:

- ❑ Filter the source documents so that they only contain the information that you're really interested in. The filter can be another stylesheet (creating a pipeline, as described earlier in this chapter) or a SAXFilter, or can occur at the point the XML document is constructed (if you have control over that).

- ❑ Break up the source document into several smaller files. This is particularly useful if the XSLT processor only needs to access some of those files; for example, if the main source document only references some of them.

Keep the source documents used in a transformation, small.

5.4.2.2 Strip Unnecessary Whitespace

About a third of the nodes in a typical source document can be ignored, whitespace-only, text nodes: whitespace that is added to a document so as to make it more easily human-readable – to indent it – rather than to add any meaning. An easy way, therefore, to cut down on the size of a node tree, is to strip out these whitespace-only text nodes. You can do this with the <xsl:strip-space> element, which goes at the top level of the stylesheet. For example:

```
<xsl:strip-space elements="*" />
```

❗ MSXML strips all whitespace nodes by default, so this instruction will usually not make any difference if you're using MSXML. If you're invoking MSXML from code, you can force MSXML to preserve the whitespace nodes by setting the preserveWhiteSpace property to true when creating a DOM.

Be careful when stripping whitespace-only text nodes, because if you strip all of them, you can end up stripping necessary *as well as* unnecessary whitespace. For example, in the following XML, the space between the <given> and <family> elements is significant:

```
<p>Created by <given>Jeni</given> <family>Tennison</family>.</p>
```

Without the whitespace, the paragraph would read "Created by JeniTennison."

You can preserve whitespace-only text nodes that would otherwise be stripped, by listing the elements in which whitespace-only text nodes should be preserved within the elements attribute of <xsl:preserve-space>. In this example, whitespace-only text nodes should be preserved within the <p> element:

```
<xsl:preserve-space elements="p" />
```

Necessary whitespace usually occurs within mixed-content elements, so it's better to strip whitespace-only text nodes from all elements, and then list those that have mixed content within the `<xsl:preserve-space>` element.

> **Omit whitespace-only text nodes from a node tree by using `<xsl:strip-space>`.**

5.4.2.3 Avoid Creating Result Tree Fragments

We've looked at how to reduce the size of source node trees in the previous two sections. It's also a good idea to limit the number of nodes that a stylesheet generates. The `<xsl:variable>`, `<xsl:param>`, and `<xsl:with-param>` elements, are **variable-binding elements**; they bind a value to a variable. There are two ways of setting the values of variables using these elements: through their `select` attribute, and through their content. Setting a variable using the content of a variable-binding element always creates a **result tree fragment** – a small result tree, whose root node has, as children, whatever nodes are created through the content of the variable.

Therefore, one easy way to cut down on the number of nodes generated by a stylesheet is to use the `select` attribute of `<xsl:variable>`, `<xsl:param>`, and `<xsl:with-param>`, rather than their content. For example, if you set an `$invoicee` variable as follows:

```
<xsl:variable name="invoicee">
  <xsl:value-of select="substring-before(@id, '-')" />
</xsl:variable>
```

then the `$invoicee` variable is actually set to a small result tree fragment consisting of a root node, whose only child is a text node, whose value is the substring before the hyphen in the current node's `id` attribute. Using the content of the `<xsl:variable>` element has meant that two nodes – the root node and the text node – have been created.

It's always a better idea to use the `select` attribute of a variable-binding element where possible as in this example:

```
<xsl:variable name="invoicee" select="substring-before(@id, '-')" />
```

This doesn't create any nodes; it simply sets the variable to the substring before the hyphen in the current node's `id` attribute. The string takes up less memory than the nodes, and as the result tree fragment is likely to be treated as a string anyway, is easier to process because it doesn't have to be converted to a string later on.

> **Avoid using the content of a variable-binding element unless you purposefully want to set it to a result tree fragment.**

Another area to watch out for, in terms of creating unnecessary nodes, is copying existing result tree fragments; particularly in recursive templates. An example is the following `repeat` template, which can be used to create a certain number of empty rows in a table. For instance, the highlighted lines show the unnecessary copying of result tree fragments:

```
<!-- Repeat the value of the $what parameter $count number of times
     -->
<xsl:template name="repeat">
  <!-- $what holds the thing to be repeated -->
  <xsl:param name="what" />
  <!-- $count holds the number of times to repeat $what -->
  <xsl:param name="count" select="1" />
  <!-- $result holds the result so far -->
  <xsl:param name="result" select="$what" />
  <xsl:choose>
    <!-- If we want more than one copy of $what, recurse -->
    <xsl:when test="$count > 1">
      <!-- Recursive call -->
      <xsl:call-template name="repeat">
        <xsl:with-param name="what" select="$what" />
        <!-- $count goes down by one -->
        <xsl:with-param name="count" select="$count - 1" />
        <!-- $what is copied onto the end of the result so far -->
        <xsl:with-param name="result">
          <xsl:copy-of select="$result" />
          <xsl:copy-of select="$what" />
        </xsl:with-param>
      </xsl:call-template>
    </xsl:when>
    <!-- When we only want one copy, give that one copy -->
    <xsl:otherwise>
      <xsl:copy-of select="$result" />
    </xsl:otherwise>
  </xsl:choose>
</xsl:template>
```

In this template, the `$result` parameter keeps track of the result so far. To do so, on each recursion the result gets copied, along with another copy of `$what`, to create the `$result` passed into the next call. In the end, each repetition of `$what` will actually have been copied several times – copies of copies of copies – which is very wasteful. You should use the pattern of having an internally-used parameter to keep track of the current result only if that result is a number or a string, not if it is a result tree fragment. In this case, you should use:

```
<!-- Repeat the value of the $what parameter $count number of times
     -->
<xsl:template name="repeat">
  <!-- $what holds the thing to be repeated -->
  <xsl:param name="what" />
  <!-- $count holds the number of times to repeat $what -->
  <xsl:param name="count" select="1" />
  <!-- If $count is more than 0, copy $what and recurse -->
  <xsl:if test="$count > 0">
    <xsl:copy-of select="$what" />
    <!-- Recursive call -->
    <xsl:call-template name="repeat">
```

```
          <xsl:with-param name="what" select="$what" />
          <!-- $count goes down by one -->
          <xsl:with-param name="count" select="$count - 1" />
      </xsl:call-template>
   </xsl:if>
</xsl:template>
```

> **Avoid copying and recopying the same result tree fragment multiple times.**

5.5 Increasing Modularity and Reusability

The final aspect of XSLT design that we consider in this chapter is the creation of modular and reusable XSLT applications. It's rare that an XSLT application be made up of a single stylesheet that never needs to be revisited. For all but the simplest transformations, an XSLT application will be made up of several stylesheet modules, and will have to be maintained in the face of changes to both the source and result document formats.

This section discusses a few features that aid the modularity, reusability, and maintainability of your XSLT applications. We touched on a few methods earlier in this chapter (such as breaking up a stylesheet into separate transformations that you pipeline together, and using external XML documents to hold lookup tables).

5.5.1 Parameterize your Stylesheet

A stylesheet parameter, declared at the top level of the stylesheet, changes how the stylesheet behaves even when used with the same source document. Stylesheet parameters enable you to use the same stylesheet to create multiple different outputs, which can be very useful for two reasons:

❑   You don't have to repeat the same code in separate stylesheets to get similar effects.

❑   You can load and compile the stylesheet once, and then use it multiple times against the same (or different) source documents. Loading and compiling the stylesheet takes time, so being able to do it just once, is a bonus.

Stylesheet parameters and global variables differ only in that stylesheet parameters can be set in the invocation of the stylesheet, whereas global variables are fixed. If there's any chance that a global variable should be changeable, you may as well declare it as a parameter rather than a global variable.

218

On the other hand, having lots of parameters can make it difficult to invoke the stylesheet, especially from the command line. If you have a stylesheet with lots of parameters, and particularly if they're structured, it may be worth creating an XML document to hold them, rather than having the parameters passed in separately. I usually design such stylesheets as being able to take two parameters; one for the filename of the document, and one that can be passed to the node set directly. For example, in a stylesheet that uses a preferences file, I would have the following two parameters:

```
<!-- $prefs-file is the name of the file in which preferences are held
     -->
<xsl:param name="prefs-file" select="'default.xml'" />
<!-- $prefs is the root node of the preferences document -->
<xsl:param name="prefs" select="document($prefs-file)" />
```

This enables users of the stylesheet to invoke it with a filename from the command line, or to invoke it by passing the preferences XML directly as a DOM, which may itself have been created through some other process.

One aspect of stylesheets that can't be parameterized is the serialization that it uses (XML, HTML, or text format, which encoding is used, and so on). To perform a transformation where these aspects change, you can create separate stylesheets for the different output methods, each importing the stylesheet that does the majority of the work. For example, the following stylesheet creates HTML output using ISO-8859-1:

```
<xsl:stylesheet version="1.0"
                xmlns:xsl="http://www.w3.org/1999/XSL/Transform">
<!-- Import common.xsl -->
<xsl:import href="common.xsl" />
<!-- Set the output method to HTML in ISO-8859-1 encoding -->
<xsl:output method="html" encoding="ISO-8859-1" />
</xsl:stylesheet>
```

while the following stylesheet creates XHTML output in UTF-8:

```
<xsl:stylesheet version="1.0"
                xmlns:xsl="http://www.w3.org/1999/XSL/Transform">
<!-- Import common.xsl -->
<xsl:import href="common.xsl" />
<!-- Set the output method to XML in UTF-8 encoding -->
<xsl:output method="xml" encoding="UTF-8" media-type="text/html"
            cdata-section-elements="script style" />
</xsl:stylesheet>
```

These separate stylesheets can be generated using XSLT and a set of parameters, or within code. JAXP enables you to alter the serialization details when you invoke transformations by setting output properties on a `Transformer` object; it's possible, of course, to create your own custom serializer as we saw earlier.

Add parameters to your stylesheets to make them more reusable; use XML documents to configure your stylesheet if there are many parameters.

5.5.2 Import General Stylesheets into Specific Ones

In the last section, we looked at the serialization of a result tree as being one aspect of a transformation that cannot be controlled by a stylesheet parameter. Another aspect is the actual set of templates and other definitions that are included in the stylesheet – XSLT does not support conditional includes or imports. You cannot determine whether `pretty.xsl` or `default.xsl` has been included, based on a `$view` parameter with something like:

```
<!-- $view says which view we want to have -->
<xsl:param name="view" select="'default'" />
<xsl:choose>
  <!-- When $view is 'pretty', include pretty.xsl -->
  <xsl:when test="$view = 'pretty'">
    <xsl:include href="pretty.xsl" />
  </xsl:when>
  <!-- When $view isn't 'pretty', include default.xsl -->
  <xsl:otherwise>
    <xsl:include href="default.xsl" />
  </xsl:otherwise>
</xsl:choose>
```

The requirement for conditional includes or imports can usually be met by reorganizing an XSLT application so that rather than importing the specific stylesheets (such as `pretty.xsl` and `default.xsl` in the code above) into the more general stylesheet, you import the general stylesheet into the more specific ones. Then, rather than using a parameter to determine the view that gets used, you should select different stylesheets for the different views. For example, both `pretty.xsl` and `default.xsl` would import the general stylesheet `common.xsl`:

```
<xsl:stylesheet version="1.0"
                xmlns:xsl="http://www.w3.org/1999/XSL/Transform">
<xsl:import href="common.xsl" />
...
</xsl:stylesheet>
```

and external code (for example JavaScript or Java) would determine whether `pretty.xsl` or `default.xsl` should be used to transform the source XML:

```
if (view == "pretty") {
  // If view is 'pretty', transform with pretty.xsl
  result = sourceDOM.transformNode(prettyXSLDOM);
} else {
  // Otherwise, transform with default.xsl
  result = sourceDOM.transformNode(defaultXSLDOM);
}
```

Alternatively, you can generate the stylesheet that you want to use, either from scratch or using a basic stylesheet that you adjust with DOM or XSLT manipulations.

220

> **Arrange your stylesheet modules so that general stylesheets are imported into specific stylesheets rather than the other way around.**

5.5.3 Use Modes on your Templates

A simple way of aiding extensibility and maintainability, is to use modes. The principal use of modes is to enable a stylesheet to process the same nodes in different ways, in different circumstances; for example, to process <section> elements once to create a table of contents, again to create the body of the document, and a third time to create an index. However, they are useful in other ways:

- ❏ Use of modes for your templates allows you to merge stylesheets more easily because it lessens the likelihood that the templates will conflict. This is especially true if you use a namespace for the modes in your stylesheet. Merging stylesheets can be useful to enable the same compiled stylesheet to be used multiple times for different transformations, or when building pipelined transformations, as we saw earlier in this chapter.

- ❏ Use of modes, labels your templates to indicate the kind of output that they generate, which is useful as primitive documentation but also as a way of grouping the templates together by the result that they generate, rather than the source nodes that they process.

- ❏ Some XSLT processors, such as MSXML, and more in the future with XSLT 2.0, support invoking a stylesheet with a particular node as the starting node and a specific mode as the starting mode.

If you're used to an object-oriented programming language, it's useful to think of templates as methods that are declared on the nodes (objects) that they match. Templates without an explicit mode can be thought of as a generic "toXML" method; other modes are like more specific methods.

I usually arrange my stylesheet so that every template aside from the template matching the root node, uses a mode. The template matching the root node determines the starting mode for the transformation. For example:

```
<xsl:template match="/">
  <xsl:apply-templates mode="html" />
</xsl:template>

<xsl:template match="invoices" mode="html">
  <html>...</html>
</xsl:template>
```

I also tend to use moded templates, rather than named templates. For example, instead of creating a named template to process an `<invoice>` element to create a total for it:

```
<xsl:template name="totalInvoice">
  <xsl:param name="invoice" />
  <xsl:call-template name="totalItems">
    <xsl:with-param name="items" select="$invoice/item" />
  </xsl:call-template>
</xsl:template>
```

I create a moded template that does just the same:

```
<xsl:template match="invoice" mode="total">
  <xsl:call-template name="totalItems">
    <xsl:with-param name="items" select="item" />
  </xsl:call-template>
</xsl:template>
```

This saves space when invoking the template. Rather than calling the template with a particular invoice as a parameter:

```
<xsl:call-template name="totalInvoice">
  <xsl:with-param name="invoice" select="invoice[1]" />
</xsl:call-template>
```

I can apply templates to that invoice in `total` mode:

```
<xsl:apply-templates select="invoice" mode="total" />
```

Modes are going to be revamped a little in XSLT 2.0 by adding the facility to have the same template be in several modes; this will make using modes even easier.

> **Use modes on your templates to group them together and to indicate the kind of result that they generate.**

5.6 References

This section contains some pointers to resources that are useful for XSLT development.

5.6.1 XSLT Processors

The three major XSLT processors being used at the moment are:

- ❏ MSXML – http://msdn.microsoft.com/xml/
- ❏ Saxon – http://saxon.sourceforge.net/
- ❏ Xalan-J – http://xml.apache.org/xalan-j/

However, there are others available. A complete list can be found at
http://www.xmlsoftware.com/xslt.html.

If you're interested in server-side transformations, it's worth looking at the following:

- ❑ Cocoon – http://xml.apache.org/cocoon
- ❑ AxKit – http://axkit.org/

5.6.2 Recommended Reading

The best sources of information about XSLT and Xpath, are the XSLT and
XPath specifications:

- ❑ http://www.w3.org/TR/xpath
- ❑ http://www.w3.org/TR/xslt

To orient your stylesheets towards adoption of XSLT 2.0 in the future, you should be
aware of the changes in the latest Working Drafts of both XSLT 2.0 and XPath 2.0:

- ❑ http://www.w3.org/TR/xslt20
- ❑ http://www.w3.org/TR/xpath20
- ❑ http://www.w3.org/TR/xquery-operators
- ❑ http://www.w3.org/TR/query-datamodel

Before inventing and coding your own extension functions and elements, check that
they're not already included in XSLT extension libraries:

- ❑ Extension to XSLT – http://www.exslt.org/
- ❑ XSLT Standard Library – http://xsltsl.sourceforge.net/
- ❑ Functional Programming Library for XSLT – http://fxsl.sourceforge.net/

For more "how to" guidance, I recommend the following books:

- ❑ *XSLT Programmers Reference second edition* by Michael Kay, from *Wrox
  Press (ISBN: 1-86100-506-7)*
- ❑ *Beginning XSLT* by Jeni Tennison, from *Wrox Press (ISBN: 1-86100-594-6)*

The following online papers are also useful in terms of understanding how XSLT processors
work and showing the payoffs between different kinds of recursive algorithms:

- ❑ Saxon: Anatomy of an XSLT Processor by Michael Kay.
  http://www-106.ibm.com/developerworks/library/x-xslt2/
- ❑ Two stage recursive algorithms in XSLT by Dimitre Novatchev and
  Slawomir Tyszko. http://www.topxml.com/xsl/articles/recurse/

XML Design

Handbook

6

XML Storage and Archiving

In this chapter, we'll take a look at some of the issues architects face when developing their storage and archiving strategies for XML-enabled systems:

❑ The first section aims to solve the problems associated with using pure XML for storage layers, by presenting a hybrid approach that strikes a balance between relational databases and XML features

❑ The second section discusses storage system design issues and the technique of using customized XML storage structures that directly support XML transmission and presentation requirements

❑ The third section discusses the problems associated with XML decomposition and provides a hybrid solution, using separate approaches for narrative and data-centric documents

❑ The last section deals with archiving strategies and the problems associated with pure XML archiving, and their solutions

6.1 Storing XML

XML is a structured data representation, so it can be used to store and archive data. Like a relational database, the inherent structured nature of XML allows it to describe sophisticated relationships among the various pieces of data that make up a single unit.

As discussed in Chapter 2, *Document Design*, XML documents are divided into two categories: the traditional SGML-for-the-web "narrative" documents, and the increasingly common and important "data-centric" documents. In narrative documents, the data tends to be text with some embedded markup for formatting, indexing, and so forth (such as collections of technical manuals, web pages, or online newspapers and magazines). These documents are typically organized in "articles" or "sections" and other such discrete and self-contained units.

Data-centric XML documents tend to have very little free-form textual data and are usually comprised of familiar data structures such as "records" comprising a number of "fields" (or "rows" and "columns"). These include XML representations of relational databases, XML-RPC messages, and other structured data transactions.

Let's look at a narrative document example. Suppose that surgical technicians are creating medical transcripts using handheld devices. We need to design a system whereby the transcripts can be stored for later retrieval and for sharing with other systems (such as the billing system at the hospital). The enterprise architecture might look something like this:

Figure 1

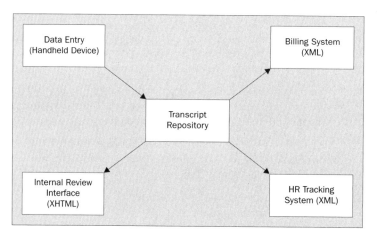

In this example, XML may be used to enter the transcripts into the handheld device, but it would certainly be used for transmission to the repository (where storage might be in XML, a relational database, or some combination thereof). No matter how the transcripts are actually stored, we would likely use XML documents to export data to other sub-systems (billing, medical review, HR, and so on). Each of the arrows in the above diagram represents such XML data exchange documents.

A sample transcript might look something like this:

```
<transcript time="13:42:57">
 <physician id="MD-02488" />
 <patient id="666-43-5030" />
```

```
<procedure>Made two-inch incision in <location>lower left
abdomen</location>with <tool>3-inch scalpel</tool>.
</procedure>
<procedure>Cauterized several <target>severed blood vessels</target>
in <location>lower left abdomen</location> to stop the bleeding.
</procedure>
<procedure>Sutured <target>incision</target> (<qty>5</qty> stitches)
in <location>lower left abdomen</location> with <supply>3-0
silk</supply>.
</procedure>
</transcript>
```

Various options are presented to us, such as:

- ❏ Does it make sense to store this XML document as a bare file in a file system?
- ❏ Should we decompose it into individual sections, or values, and store it in a relational database instead?
- ❏ What about using a native XML database to store the data?

Later in this chapter, we will examine these options and more, using suitable examples.

Now let's change the example a little bit. We'll use the same basic structure, except in this case we'll be creating invoice documents within an e-commerce system. Once again, transaction data (the invoices) needs to be stored for later retrieval and sharing with other systems. The basic architecture is essentially the same, but with different sub-systems:

Figure 2

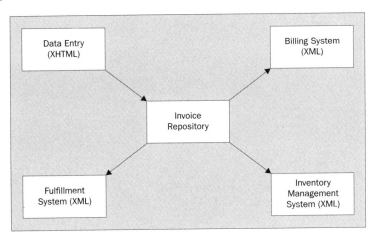

And a sample XML invoice might look like this:

```
<Invoice num="1282373" orderDate="2002-09-17" shipDate="2002-09-19">
    <Customer id="19272" name="John Doe" address1="88 Delta Drive"
         city="Los Angeles" state="CA" zip="79666" />
    <LineItem quantity="1" price="39.98" partnum="123B57" />
    <LineItem quantity="4" price="3.25" partnum="134B22" />
</Invoice>
```

This document is rather different from the one in our first example – it is data-centric, as opposed to the narrative medical transcripts. Also, the tasks we need to perform may differ significantly (we may want to summarize information from many documents at once, or be able to perform fast searches against the invoices we have stored). The basic system architecture for the flow of information is the same, so how can we optimize the sub-systems and data storage architecture for these two quite different types of documents?

If all this is sounding familiar, it should be – as with all of the other design tasks we have examined so far in this book, the combination of technologies used to handle information storage and retrieval depends on the nature of the enterprise model into which they are integrated.

6.1.1 Problems with Creating Pure XML Storage Layers

Once an organization has decided to integrate XML into their enterprise-level architecture, new XML architects often make one mistake which is to create a storage layer that is pure XML (consisting purely of standalone XML files), as shown in the following diagram:

Figure 3

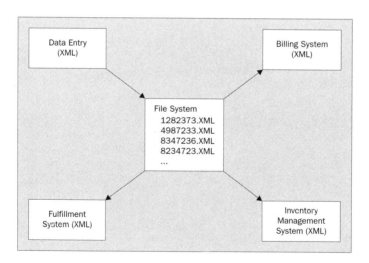

In many circumstances, this might seem to make sense. After all, if the information is entering and exiting the system as XML, and XML is being used to present the information to users (through the application of XSL stylesheets to support multiple media representations of the information), why go through all the trouble of pulling the documents apart and storing them in some other medium, such as a relational database? Why not keep everything in XML?

As it turns out, there are significant limitations to the manipulation of information as XML – in most cases, an XML representation will not be sufficient to handle many of the data processing tasks, which are expected to be done in the original XML files.

6.1.1.1 Searching a Pure XML Storage Layer is Slow

Except for in the most simplistic cases, such a pure XML storage layer will not be sufficient. It is just a set of files in a directory structure, each of which corresponds to an individual XML document:

```
/FileSystem/Xml/Invoices/
./1282373.xml
./4987233.xml
./8347236.xml
./8234723.xml
```

Inherently XML is not an indexed medium – there is no way to quickly identify whether an XML document contains information that is relevant to the programming task at hand. The only way to obtain a specific invoice is to parse the document, looking for the element that matches the search criteria.

In our invoice, we can expect customers to log in and look at their invoice history. For this to happen, the system needs to quickly determine which XML documents correspond to a particular customer and use those documents to drive an XSLT layer that presents the information in those documents to the customer. How does the system determine which XML documents go with a particular customer? The system must parse each document in the storage layer, looking for `<Customer>` elements with `id` attribute values that match the ID of the customer that is currently logged in. Each of these documents can then be styled for presentation. Potentially, every invoice and its customer information must be examined, so in a large system with many customers, parsing documents that are not relevant to the particular task would result in a significant waste of processing time.

Even if a streaming parser, such as SAX, is used, the invoice could easily be at or near the end of the entire document. Basically, without any additional information, this task is virtually impossible (for any reasonable performance), with a pure XML storage layer.

6.1.1.2 Document Aggregation is Difficult

Similarly, there is no simple way to process a set of XML documents to derive aggregate information – they must all be parsed, the relevant information must be read and set aside, and then that information can be summarized if required.

To continue with the previous example, let's say that we have a billing system where we now want to create a single unified bill for all of the invoices submitted for a particular customer. To accomplish this, the billing system has to take our searching problem from the previous example one step further. Not only does the billing system need to determine which invoices are associated with a particular customer ID (and are not yet paid), it then needs to pull the information from each of those invoices relevant to the processing task at hand (in this case, creating the unified bill), and then pull it together into a single form (the total amount due). This is often known as **aggregation processing** or **document aggregation**.

6.1.1.3 Document Manipulation is Inefficient

Another significant concern with pure XML storage is the way XML documents are processed and specific pieces of information are accessed within those documents. Let's say that, in our invoice example, we want to figure out how many units of part number 123B57 were sold in the past month. Once we have identified which XML documents actually contain references to part 123B57, we then need to be able to quickly pull out the quantity attribute for the LineItem element in the document describing part 123B57 and set it aside. This isn't easily done when parsing an XML document directly – the entire document must be read and the information extracted. This is true whether the data is streamed through memory using a SAX parser or completely parsed using DOM Again, there is a lot of wasted processing time with this approach, since most of the information that is read through memory, is simply discarded.

6.1.1.4 Solving the Problems with Indexing

The general solution to the problem is pretty obvious – we need to add some sort of indexing to our XML storage mechanism to enable us to quickly search for, and aggregate, information found in the documents. There are several different approaches that can be taken to index our XML data, including: native XML databases, traditional relational or object-oriented databases, and hybrid combinations thereof.

6.1.2 Native XML Databases

There has been a recent surge of XML products in the marketplace that classify themselves as native XML databases.

> A survey of these products is outside the scope of this chapter, but at the time of writing the leading commercial product was Software AG's Tamino XML Server (http://www.softwareag.com/tamino/). Other options include eXcelon's eXtensible Information Server (http://www.exln.com/products/xis/) and Ipedo's XML database (http://www.ipedo.com/html/products_xml_dat.html). In the open source realm, we have Apache's Xindice (http://xml.apache.org/xindice/).

These products are designed to support the rapid searching of XML data by adding indexing information to the documents, which can then be accessed through the interfaces of the native XML database.

Figure 4

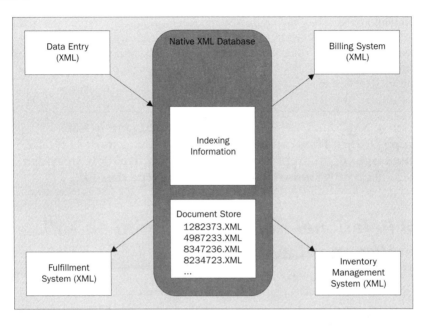

While the specific approach of these native XML databases can differ widely – some actually decompose documents into elements and attributes and store them that way, while others merely augment the existing file repository with indexing data – they all provide the ability to quickly search through the repository for specific documents. In our search example, when a customer wants to see their invoice history, the system first queries the indexing portion of the native XML database to determine which documents pertain to that customer. Depending upon the database, this query might require the use of a proprietary query language, some variant of SQL or perhaps the emerging XML Query language as defined by the W3C. This operation is much quicker than the same operation on a non-indexed XML document because the system only has to examine a list of associated customer IDs and document identifiers to find the documents for that customer. Once the documents are identified, they can be pulled from the repository and processed using XSLT or any other mechanism as per requirements.

Native XML databases are still maturing, and at the time of the publication of this book, not many native XML databases provide good cross-document processing or document manipulation functionality. Also, because these databases were originally designed to primarily support narrative-style XML documents, they provide excellent search capabilities but poor aggregation and document decomposition.

For example, if we were to use a native XML database to create a single unified bill from separate invoices, we would still have to do a significant amount of work. Even though it would be much simpler to identify the invoices pertaining to a particular customer, the code would still have to parse each document completely to pull out the information relevant to the bill we were creating. Some native XML databases have begun to introduce functionality that allows specific portions of documents to be extracted without extracting the entire XML document originally entered into the system; this approach will greatly simplify aggregation-oriented tasks like the one described here. However, even those native databases that decompose the XML data and index it at the element level will still require processing code to traverse the hierarchical element tree to extract specific data.

> **Native XML databases add indexing information to XML repositories. They can be a good choice if you want to retain the original XML representation of the information, provided you need only limited processing of the data therein.**

6.1.3 Relational Repositories with an XML Wrapper Layer

Another approach to the indexing issue is to store most or all of the information in a relational database, and use a wrapper layer to transform the data between the relational representation and XML representations. This same approach can just as easily be used with repositories comprised of spreadsheet files, object-oriented databases, or custom database formats, such as those used in Geographic Information Systems (GIS) or legacy mainframe databases.

> *All of the major relational database vendors provide XML support to a greater or lesser extent. For example, MS SQL Server 2000 provides FOR XML queries for creating XML documents from SQL Server data, and the OPENXML technology to turn XML documents into rowsets (an excellent resource detailing SQL Server's XML support is: SQL Server 2000 XML Distilled, Curlingstone, ISBN: 1904347088). The Oracle 9i database provides similar functionality via its XML SQL Utility (XSU) and, in addition, its XML DB feature provides native XML storage (see http://otn.oracle.com).*

For our invoicing system, the "repository with XML wrapper" architecture might look like this:

Figure 5

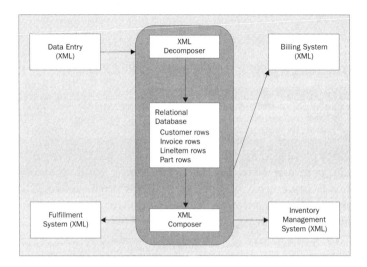

In this approach, XML documents are not stored directly. Instead, information is parsed and then stored in a relational database and simply serialized to or deserialized from XML as circumstances dictate (to drive transmission or presentation layers, for example). This approach can be particularly effective if the information entering the system is not already provided in XML, or if the information needs to be marshaled to non-XML formats as part of the enterprise design. As you will see later in this chapter, the code used to transform the XML data (be it XSLT or some kind of procedural code) is a good candidate for archival storage.

Searches using this architecture couldn't be easier. Since all the information is stored in a relational database, you have access to all of the mechanisms you would normally use to search a relational database: table indexing, key relationships, and so on. To implement our online customer invoice viewer, we would only have to write a SQL query that searches for invoices that have a particular customer ID. The retrieved invoices could then be transformed into XML for presentation, either using built-in XML output support or custom procedural code.

Unlike native XML databases, this approach also facilitates the aggregation and manipulation of data. Since the information is decomposed before it is stored in the database, we can use the well-established SQL aggregation commands to get at the information directly. To create our unified bill, for example, we would only have to write a stored procedure that retrieves the total unpaid amounts for all of the customer's outstanding invoices. An additional benefit is that we can serialize this information into whatever form makes the most sense – **we are not tied in any way to the original XML structure**. This also makes deriving our presentation layer much simpler (as you will see in *Chapter 7*). Of course, some might see this as a disadvantage – but XML is not a panacea, and for many databases the use of the relational storage model may be more appropriate than XML's simple tree structure.

One disadvantage to any such relational-with-wrapper approach is that the XML serialization and deserialization steps take time. If a particular system relies heavily on XML data formats (for example, a particular XML standard used for data transmission), then the pure relational approach will waste a lot of processing time composing and decomposing XML documents. Another drawback is the need for additional programming expertise – instead of just XML and XPath, for example, the developer must now be familiar with RDBMS and SQL. Additionally, in the case of narrative-style XML documents, it may be difficult or even impossible to store the data in a relational database in any usable way.

> **The pure relational storage approach (an XML wrapper around a relational storage layer) can be a good choice when a system is not highly XML-centric, does not involve narrative-style information, or needs to perform significant aggregation processing of the information.**

6.1.4 Hybrid Repositories

The third approach to XML repositories is to add relational indexing to an XML document store, using a true relational database to store the indexing. There are actually two different flavors of hybrid repositories, each of which has its own merit.

6.1.4.1 Storing Complete XML Documents and Relational Data

In the first form of a hybrid repository, the XML documents are stored *exactly* as they enter the system; in other words, any structure in the data that is created, is retained as it is in the XML representation stored in the repository. In addition to storing the XML document, the system also parses the document and makes copies of the indexing information in a relational database. Depending upon a system's requirements, indexing can be minimal (indexing a single key such as the customer ID in our invoice example), or extensive (each and every element, or even attribute, is a separately indexed item). The extracted indexing information is stored in a relational database index, which is used to provide access to the individual documents.

Careful analysis of the system will determine the best balance between minimal indexing and the much more costly "index everything" approach. The requirements that drive this systems' analysis may change in time, hence the indexing process is a prime candidate for the use of XML configuration documents to determine which portions of the data are to be indexed. Therefore, when requirements change and additional indexing is needed, the database may be rebuilt simply by changing an XML document and re-indexing the data. This is another example of how XML can be useful when maintaining complex systems – it is usually much easier to change a textual configuration document than to modify procedural code or proprietary binary registry files. Of course, the use of such XML documents also provides a greater degree of self-documentation whilst still allowing implementation of database design rules in an "executable" form.

This version of our ongoing example would look something like this:

Figure 6

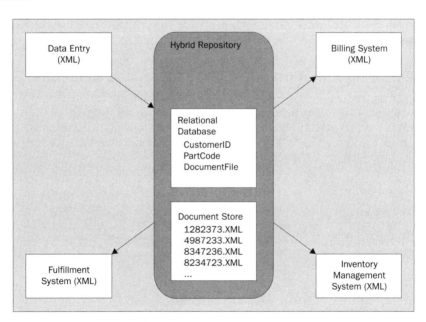

As in the purely relational model, searching is simple in this version of a hybrid repository – provided you have chosen to index the piece of information you want to search against. This is similar to selecting indexes on a relational database – you should index the information that you anticipate the system will need for searching. The indexed database is queried to find the document identifiers for the XML documents that match our customer ID (say, in our online invoice query example). Then, those identifiers are used to extract the XML document(s) for display. Note that this approach allows us to avoid the XML serialization step that would be necessary in a purely relational repository – improving the performance of the presentation step.

The aggregation and document manipulation tasks are also simplified greatly by this approach, provided, you have chosen to index the proper information. In a good design, the information that is used frequently for aggregation and document manipulation, will be *covered* by the index – that is, the necessary information can be retrieved from the relational database without ever needing to open the XML documents themselves. This kind of systems' analysis is very similar to that used for traditional RDBMS index design. As with the purely relational approach, we can take this data and construct our XML document to match our output requirements.

One disadvantage to this approach is the amount of additional storage space consumed by the repository. In essence, you are storing the data twice: once in its (perhaps verbose) original XML form, and again in the relational index. A related disadvantage is the additional complexity of database maintenance – any updates to such data will need to be applied to both the XML document and its copy in the relational index, with attendant difficulties in synchronization and update rollbacks. Here again is a classic tradeoff – the willingness to accept more complex update code and allocate more storage space per document results in faster processing and simpler retrieval code. Whether this is a good choice for a particular programming task will depend on the nature of the application, and the system hardware and software constraints.

6.1.4.2 Storing XML Document Fragments and Relational Data

In the second form of a hybrid repository, all of the indexed content resides in a relational database as in our pure relational example. However, portions of the document that do not need to be indexed (because they will rarely be searched against or aggregated) are stored as XML document fragments, rather than being decomposed into individual elements and attributes.

Figure 7

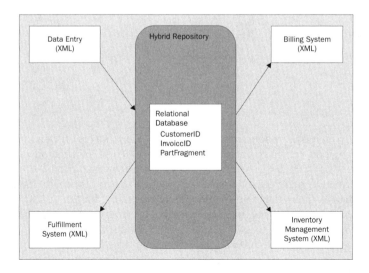

In this form of the repository, appropriate information is still indexed as necessary and pulled out into relational tables; for information that does not need to be indexed, however, XML fragments are stored in our relational database. To understand how this works, let's look at a quick example. Consider the invoice example:

```
<Invoice num="1282373" orderDate="2002-09-17" shipDate="2002-09-19">
    <Customer id="19272" name="John Doe" address1="88 Delta Drive"
            city="Los Angeles" state="CA" zip="79666" />
    <LineItem quantity="1" price="39.98" partnum="123B57" />
    <LineItem quantity="4" price="3.25" partnum="134B22" />
</Invoice>
```

Now let's say that we are receiving invoices in this form to be used to drive an online invoice tracking system. The requirements of the system dictate that it does not need to search against individual line item data, so we can store the invoices in a structure that looks like this:

Figure 8

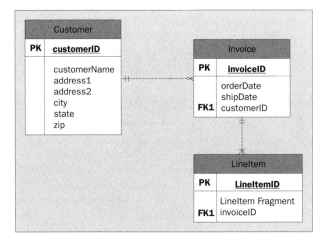

The invoice example above might be stored in the database this way:

```
Invoice:
    invoiceID  = 1282373
    orderDate  = "2002-09-17"
    shipDate   = "2002-09-19"
    customerID = 1

Customer:
    customerID   = 19272
    customerName = "John Doe"
    address1     = "88 Delta Drive"
    address2     = null
    city         = "Los Angeles"
    state        = "CA"
    zip          = "79666"
```

```
LineItem:
  LineItemID    = 1282373.1
  LineItemFragment = '<LineItem quantity="1" price="39.98"
  partnum="123B57" />'
  invoiceID     = 1282373

LineItem:
  LineItemID    = 1282373.2
  LineItemFragment = '<LineItem quantity="4" price="3.25"
  partnum="134B22" />'
  invoiceID     = 1282373
```

If we need to get the specific information for a line item (for presentation purposes, for example), we can simply extract the XML fragment that is stored in the `LineItem` table associated with a particular invoice record.

This approach, like the first hybrid approach, makes it easier to search on fields that are indexed – normal relational database mechanisms can be used to access the indexed fields and identify documents that match particular criteria. Similarly, this approach makes aggregation and document manipulation easier – simply design the indexing to cover the information required for frequently-used aggregation and manipulation tasks, and no XML processing code will be necessary (other than the code that creates XML to drive presentation or transmission).

6.1.4.3 Comparing Hybrid Approaches

So what's the difference between the two hybrid approaches? The first approach requires more storage space (as the data in the original XML document is repeated in the relational indexing), but does not require additional processing time and code to obtain the information in its original form. With the second hybrid approach, less storage space is required since only the non-indexed XML from the original document is retained, and there is no duplication of non-indexing information. The major drawback occurs only if we need to reconstruct the original XML structure – code and processing time are required to rebuild the XML document from the indexed pieces and the XML fragments.

Use a hybrid approach for XML storage when you need to perform indexed operations such as searching and aggregation against the information, but also need to retain the XML form in which the information first entered the system. Use the complete document (first) approach if conservation of storage space is less important than the ability to quickly recreate the original XML document; otherwise, consider the XML fragment (second) approach.

6.2 Storage System Design Issues

Industry standards are becoming more and more prevalent. Pick an industry and a consortium exists for it, defining XML standards that the industry uses to share data among systems. In many cases, architects unfamiliar with XML will design a document repository to simply store the XML as it was received. This is especially true when a system relies on passing information between itself and other partners in a particular XML form. However, there can be some significant disadvantages to simply storing XML documents as they are received.

6.2.1 Problems with Storing XML Documents as Received

As we mentioned earlier in the chapter, the problem with XML standards is that these standards do not directly correspond to an individual business's information representation or presentation requirements. Minor differences in the way particular business processes are approached, can result in major headaches for developers attempting to take advantage of existing standards.

> *As standards mature and support useful extensions for individual business requirements, this concern will diminish. However, it is true at this point in time.*

More significantly, an XML document that works well for one purpose may be completely inappropriate for another. Relying on a single XML representation in a repository can result in increased processing times and code complexity, as well as creating serious problems when trying to maintain or update the software that creates and searches against the repository.

Here's an example. Consider again our invoice system from earlier in the chapter. We want to be able to store the individual invoices as they are submitted by customers (as in a typical "online transaction processing", or **OLTP** system), and allow customers to access that information directly later. In addition, we may want to be able to perform some analysis on the submitted invoices – such as "how much we've billed a particular customer over the years", "how many widgets were ordered in July 1987", etc. These systems are commonly known as "online analysis processing" or **OLAP** systems. We have already defined an XML format for our individual invoices, and we might simply store the invoices as separate XML files:

Figure 9

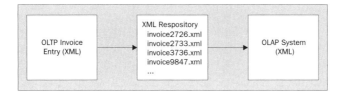

While this will easily support the OLTP side of the system (since the representation is that of the original input), it is less than ideal for the OLAP side. As analysis is required, the system will need to process the document repository to generate that analytical data, and this will result in slower and slower analytical performance as the database grows. One approach to this problem might be to create a database that can be used for both OLTP and OLAP functions. However, this approach is rarely satisfactory for either transaction processing or analysis – one side or the other will almost always be at a disadvantage. There is a different approach we can take – we can design a split XML storage layer to directly support the transaction as well as the analysis needs of the system.

6.2.2 Shaping the Storage to Fit the Task

In this approach, we process the OLTP documents as they enter the system. The information is read from those OLTP documents and used to update OLAP documents that reflect a particular presentation or transmission requirement. For example, we want to show the quantity of each part that has been ordered in our system, aggregated to the monthly level. We could design a document that looks like the following:

```
<PartHistory partCode="125B27">
   ...
   <MonthSummary date="2002-10" totalSold="736" />
   <MonthSummary date="2002-11" totalSold="987" />
   ...
</PartHistory>
```

Then, as invoices enter the system as transactions, they can be processed and relevant information can be used to update the appropriate OLAP document(s):

Figure 10

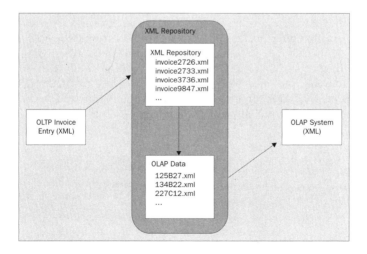

Once we have the OLAP documents, we can simply rely on a file naming convention; that is, we could call the XML document that contains information about part 123B57 something simple like `123B57.xml`, perhaps within a file system sub-directory called `Parts`.

Or we can create a relational index for the documents, something like the following, which could use different, completely arbitrary, filenames:

```
CREATE TABLE PartSummary
(
    partCode varchar(12),
    partFile varchar(1024)
)

PartSummary:
    partCode = "125B27"
    partFile = "/Parts/125series.xml"

PartSummary:
    partCode = "129C82"
    partFile = "/Parts/129series.xml"
```

The downsides are obvious – more storage space is consumed for the repeated information, and additional processing time will be required to extract the appropriate OLAP information from each document as it is received. The benefit is that OLAP processing is much simpler, and the XML documents are directly available in the repository without requiring an XML serialization step.

> **Consider customized XML structures that directly support XML transmission and presentation requirements in the repository. This decision is contingent on which of three criteria (storage space, OLTP processing time, or OLAP processing time) is most critical in your particular architecture and business environment.**

6.2.3 Multiple Repositories for Multiple Purposes

This idea extends naturally to adding more repositories to drive other business requirements. Let's say that now we want to perform two different kinds of analytical processing on the data. In addition to analyzing ordering patterns for various parts, we also want to be able to summarize customer invoice information on a monthly basis. We can add another OLAP document store to our structure to support this second analysis:

Figure 11

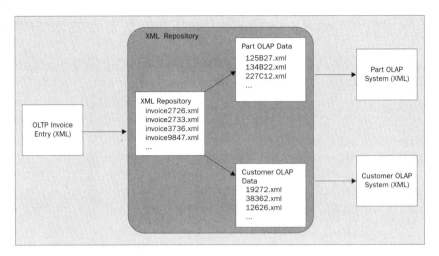

As OLTP documents enter the system, they are used to update the appropriate OLAP documents in each repository – part information is used to update the part documents, and customer information is used to update the customer documents. Again, the tradeoff is clear: more storage space consumed in exchange for better performance on the OLAP side of the system.

> **Store information in multiple forms depending on the requirements of your system. Choose the storage approach that provides the best balance between space consumption and performance, for your particular technical and business needs.**

6.3 Problems with XML Decomposition

Architects with a heavy relational database background often dismiss the notion of storing information in XML. After all, XML documents are just serialized chunks of information – they can't be easily searched on or aggregated across, and working with XML documents tends to be more difficult than writing stored procedures (especially if that's your background).

The advantage of relational databases is that they excel at searching and aggregating related information. The whole point of storing information in a relational database is to allow you to query that database and retrieve particular pieces of information, or aggregate detail information into summary information.

In most cases, the approach taken by the architect is to completely decompose XML documents into elements and attributes as they enter a system, and store that information in a full relational structure that covers the entire source document. However, there are two major issues that arise with wholesale XML document decomposition: excessive and/or unnecessary transformation processing, and difficulty handling unstructured data (as in narrative documents).

6.3.1 Unnecessary Processing

Let's consider the following example, which shows the first three steps of an automobile loan system, from the origination of the process through credit checking to the actual underwriting of the loan:

Figure 12

A sample of the loan document might look like this:

```
<LoanFile>
  <Customer id="19272" name="John Doe" address1="88 Delta Drive"
       city="Los Angeles" state="CA" zip="79666"
       approved="PENDING" />
  <Automobile>
    ... automobile information...
  </Automobile>
  ... other loan data...
</LoanFile>
```

In this example, our transmission requirements oblige us to consume and produce information in a particular XML form (called `LoanFile`). However, the actual processing performed by the credit checking sub-system only interacts with a small portion of the document – the customer information. The rest of the document (the description of the automobile, the automobile dealer information, and so on) is irrelevant to that sub-system. If we were to decompose the entire `<LoanFile>` document and store it in our relational database, we would be wasting processing time and other system resources, to deserialize and then re-serialize the XML document as it passes through our system. While this might not matter for a small system serving a single auto dealer, one can easily see that this becomes a significant problem for a nation-wide credit checking system with millions of customers. This might be a good situation for the use of XML Fragments (once a stable specification evolves and supporting tools mature).

6.3.2 Difficulty Handlin g Unstructured Data

Another problem with decomposing XML documents for storage in relational databases is the question of narrative elements. Consider the medical transcript document example from *Section 6.1* of this chapter:

```
<transcript time="13:42:57">
 <physician id="MD-02488" />
 <patient id="666-43-5030" />
 <procedure>Made two-inch incision in <location>lower left
 abdomen</location>with <tool>3-inch scalpel</tool>.
 </procedure>
 <procedure>Cauterized several <target>severed blood vessels</target>
 in <location>lower left abdomen</location> to stop the bleeding.
 </procedure>
 <procedure>Sutured <target>incision</target> (<qty>5</qty> stitches)
 in <location>lower left abdomen</location> with <supply>3-0
 silk</supply>.
 </procedure>
</transcript>
```

It will be very difficult, if not impossible, to define a relational database structure that describes the many possible variations of this inherently narrative document. While there are islands of structured data within the text, they can appear in so many different combinations and sequences that we would not want to limit them to a specific relational structure. Of course, we can't simply discard text that doesn't fit some pre-defined structure, as this data is likely to be needed further down the processing chain. Clearly, another approach is required.

> **Decomposing an entire XML document into a relational database only makes sense when the document is data-centric without any unstructured text, and the document corresponds directly to the business functions to be performed on that information.**

6.3.3 The Solution: Hyb rid XML-Relational Modeling

In both of these cases, a better approach to the problem is to use a hybrid storage mechanism for the information. As we mentioned earlier in the *Section 6.1.4*, hybrid storage systems provide the best of both worlds: document content is still readily available in XML to drive transmission and presentation layers, while indexing information makes it easy to manipulate specific pieces of information relevant to the task at hand. With this in mind, let's see how the hybrid solution helps address the two examples mentioned.

6.3.3.1 Hybrid Storage for Narrative Documents

In the case of narrative documents, the first hybrid form (storing the complete XML document with a supplemental relational index) makes the most sense. We want to be able to index the contents of the XML document (the tools, procedures, and so on) without needing to reconstitute the document from the indexed information. Hence, copying the indexing information into a separate relational database is the best approach:

Figure 13

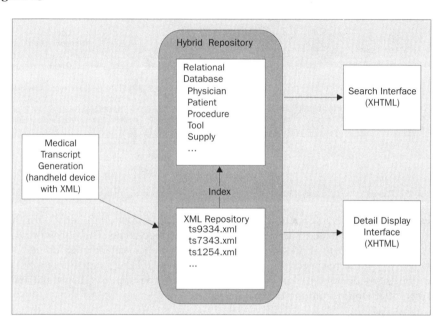

In this example, the original XML documents are readily available for transmission and presentation purposes. Proper design of covering indexes makes it possible to do analysis and aggregation across documents without actually parsing any of the original XML documents, while the entire original document remains available for other sub-systems without the loss of any data or data structure.

6.3.3.2 Hybrid Storage for Data-centric Documents

Remember that the credit checking sub-system requires only a small fraction of the original document to perform its business function. Here we store the pertinent customer information from the document in a relational database, with the remaining unused portions of the original XML document stored as XML fragments (a hybrid solution of the second form):

Figure 14

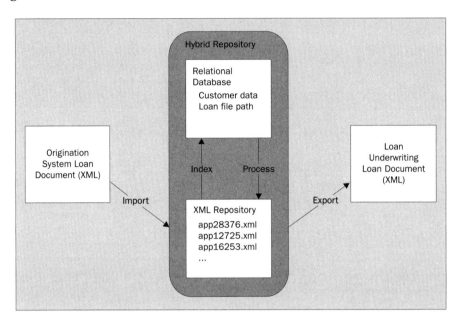

The essential customer information (name, address, ID number, etc.) needed for the credit check is decomposed into a relational form for processing. The unused majority of the original document is preserved within the XML Repository as unmodified fragments. When the results of the credit check are available, we can simply rebuild the <LoanFile> document, with an updated value for the approved attribute and the preserved fragment(s) from the original document:

```
<LoanFile>
   <Customer id="19272" ... approved="YES" />
   ... other loan data ...
</LoanFile>
```

Since the customer information that is to be indexed is relatively small, the storage space required for multiple copies of the data is less of a concern. Even though there is a bit of additional processing time up front to pull out the indexing information, it is minimal compared to the processing time that would be required to decompose, store, and then reserialize the entire document.

Of course, for the sake of this example we're assuming that the credit checking sub-system is interacting with an existing non-XML database of credit histories. One day soon, this kind of legacy system is also likely to be able to handle XML data directly – but for now this example illustrates a good approach to interfacing with such systems.

> **For narrative documents, use a hybrid storage mechanism to allow access to indexed elements within the narrative without decomposing the narrative, while preserving the original form of the document. Alternatively (and for data-centric documents), use hybrid storage with a relational index plus stored XML fragments. Simply discard unused XML data that will not be needed later in the processing chain.**

6.4 Archiving in XML

Another good use of XML in the enterprise is for archiving information. By archiving, we mean the long-term storage of data that no longer needs to be readily available (say for online processing), but cannot be discarded completely (due to business and/or legal requirements, perhaps).

Properly designed XML can provide a complete picture of a specific dataset within a single document. As long as enough meta-information is included (in the form of good element and attribute names), the document can be self-contained and still interpreted outside of the context of any particular processing engine, data dictionary, or schema. In addition, since XML documents are text, they compress very well, making it possible to store many documents and their related meta-information in a single volume for later retrieval. However, a brute-force approach to the archiving of data as XML – particularly when the source information is not in XML already (such as data from a relational database) – can result in difficulties later when the archive needs to be accessed.

6.4.1 Issues with Pure XML Archives

The paramount concern when designing an archiving strategy is making sure that the information can be retrieved in a useable form. In the past, this has usually consisted of dumping relational data to a file that has the structure of the original database, so that the data can easily be loaded (either piecemeal or in bulk) back into the original structure for manipulation. However, with the advent of XML, the opportunity exists to create archiving documents that can stand alone, or in other words are **self-describing**. This is particularly important with the quick turnover of today's technology – no one knows whether the customized system that generated the archive record in the first place will still exist twenty, ten, or even five years from now.

With this in mind, we should focus our archival strategy on designing documents that are self-descriptive and provide all the information that will be needed when the archive is accessed.

6.4.1.1 Retrieval of Archived Information

Individual documents in an XML archive suffer from some of the same issues that individual documents in an XML storage system have to deal with. These documents are just stored as so many files, hence there still needs to be a way to quickly identify the appropriate document or documents for a particular retrieval task. However, relying upon the original search method from the XML document storage system doesn't lend itself to supporting an archive – after all, who knows if Relational Database X or Native XML Database Y will still be available when the archive needs to be accessed? Our archiving strategy needs to take this into account – we need to provide some system-agnostic way to index documents for searching.

6.4.1.2 Recall of Information across Archived Documents

Similarly, we face issues when deciding how we are going to approach the aggregation of information across many documents in our archives. When a customer calls up and requests a summary of how many orders they have placed over the past ten years, we need some mechanism to quickly retrieve the appropriate information or obtain the appropriate XML documents that contain the information. As with searching, the strategy here needs to be system-agnostic – the search mechanism needs to be independent of any particular storage layer, whether it is a native XML or relational database.

Fortunately, we're already familiar with a system-agnostic way to represent information – namely XML itself. We can use XML to provide index, transformation, and summary information as part of our archiving process, reducing the number of documents we need to parse when the archive is accessed, and improving archive search and retrieval performance.

6.4.2 Archiving Document Indexes

When we discussed the various strategies for searching XML documents, they all revolved around indexing – pulling out specific pieces of information from the documents and using them to relate back to the original XML document. For archives, we can adopt a similar strategy – but we'll create our index in XML. Let's look at an example using our invoice sample:

```
<Invoice num-"1282373" orderDate-"2002-09-17" shipDate="2002-09-19">
   <Customer id="19272" name="John Doe" address1="88 Delta Drive"
        city="Los Angeles" state="CA" zip="79666" />
   <LineItem quantity="1" price="39.98" partnum="123B57" />
   <LineItem quantity="4" price="3.25" partnum="134B22" />
</Invoice>
```

As part of our archiving strategy, we have determined that we only need to be able to search each archive by customer ID and date. When we write each volume of the archive, we will just add an index document that looks something like the following:

```
<CustomerHistory>
  <CustomerInvoices id="12626">
    <Invoice invoiceDate="2002-11-11" invoiceFile="74642.xml" />
    <Invoice invoiceDate="2002-11-12" invoiceFile="47462.xml" />
    ...
  </CustomerInvoices>
  <CustomerInvoices id="19272">
    <Invoice invoiceDate="2002-09-17" invoiceFile="78454.xml" />
    <Invoice invoiceDate="2002-11-13" invoiceFile="22544.xml" />
    ...
  </CustomerInvoices>
  ...
</CustomerHistory>
```

Note that we've chosen to use simple relative paths to identify XML documents associated with particular customers. We could also use XLink, but that's probably overkill here – unless we want outside systems to be able to read our archive and properly interpret the references to other files in the archive. When a customer whose ID is "19272" calls in sometime in the year 2005 and asks for a copy of their invoice from September 17th, 2002, we just mount the appropriate archive volume(s) and run a query with the following XPath expression:

```
//CustomerHistory/Customer[@id="19272"]/Invoice[@invoiceDate="2002-09-
17"]/@invoiceFile
```

This returns the name of the file for the customer's invoice on that date (if it exists). Then, we can directly go to that file and retrieve information about that invoice for presentation to the user. Without the index file, we'd have to open each and every document in the archive to see if the customer ID and invoice date matched the ones we were looking for. By taking the time to perform the indexing up front when the archive is created, we've greatly simplified access to the archive later.

6.4.3 Archiving of Summary Information

When creating our archives, we can (and should) design the XML documents in the archive to best match the business requirements for the archive. After all, the archive is intended to be used to easily access information that has aged beyond the day-to-day system – why store data in a form that doesn't suit that purpose well? In particular, pieces of information that are artifacts of the storage medium (such as internal identifiers for rows in a relational database) can be discarded – since our documents have to be complete and self-describing, it doesn't make much sense to store the identifiers in the archive (unless we want to be able to rebuild the database from the archive, in which case XML may not be the best choice).

We can also build archiving documents that provide aggregated information. For example, we might want to create archiving data that allows us to see how many parts were ordered on each day. If the business requirements indicate that this data needs to be available frequently and/or in a timely fashion, we might want to create summary documents for the number of parts ordered for each day in a particular archive. These summary documents could take the place of archived detail documents or (much more likely) sit alongside them in the archive. This is similar to the indexing technique we described earlier in the chapter – the summary XML documents effectively form a covering index for the detail documents, enabling us to retrieve the summary data without needing to drill into individual invoice archives. For example, we might create a document that looks like this:

```
<PartHistory>
  <PartSummary partCode="125B27">
    <DaySummary date="2002-11-11" quantity="37" />
    <DaySummary date="2002-11-12" quantity="22" />
    ...
  </PartSummary>
  <PartSummary partCode="124D22">
    <DaySummary date="2002-11-11" quantity="11" />
    <DaySummary date="2002-11-12" quantity="92" />
    ...
  </PartSummary>
  ...
</PartHistory>
```

When an analysis system needs to determine how many part code 125B27s were ordered for each date over the archive period, it just needs to open the summary document and apply the following XPath to it:

```
//PartHistory/PartSummary[@partCode="125B27"]/DaySummary
```

For each <DaySummary> element that is returned, the analysis program can read the date and quantity attributes to find out how many parts were ordered on which day, and add this to a cumulative sum. Again, by taking the time to calculate and record these daily summaries when the archive is created, later access to the archive is greatly simplified.

> **When creating archives, design additional XML documents to support detail data in the archive. Aggregation documents (that roll up data) and indexing documents (that provide quick access to particular documents in the repository) are both good additions to almost any XML archive.**

6.4.4 Archiving Other Information

Indexing information is almost always stored along with the original database information when archiving data (whether that data is in XML or the cryptic binary backup formats of traditional databases). We've just discussed the possible advantages of retaining (or even constructing) auxiliary indexes and/or summary documents for archival purposes. Yet, another type of related data is often overlooked – the stylesheets, configuration files, stored procedures, and other data and/or code that is required to transform a database for presentation. In many cases, the raw database has little meaning without its physical presentation form as a reference. In some cases, there may be legal or business requirements to maintain documents in certain formats for a period of years. If we take advantage of the desirable separation of semantic content and presentation when we design an XML database, we may no longer have adequate information to recreate a specific form without the addition of a stylesheet. Therefore, it is often imperative to archive any related stylesheet(s) with the main XML document.

6.5 Summary

In this chapter, we've taken a look at some of the issues architects face when developing their storage and archiving strategies for XML-enabled systems. We've seen how pure XML repositories are almost *never* the right approach for storage, and how storing documents in the exact form in which they enter a system can actually be detrimental to a system's performance. We also looked at some alternatives, such as native XML databases and different kinds of hybrid storage layers. Next, we learned strategies for optimizing our XML storage design. Then, we looked at the issues involved with decomposing XML for storage in another medium (such as a relational database), and revisited hybrid database-XML solutions as a good approach to this problem. Finally, we looked at some archiving strategies using XML, and identified ways to can augment our archive approach to increase the value of the archives we create.

XML Design

Handbook

7

7

Presentation Strategies

XML works best when it represents data or information independently of how users view or interact with the data. This leaves the information flexible to a wide range of presentation possibilities. Presentation strategies using XML can be developed in a number of languages and technologies. For web-based applications these include Java servlets, **JavaServer Pages (JSP)**, **Active Server Page (ASP)**/.NET, Perl, Python, PHP, ColdFusion, JavaScript, and VBScript. Standalone or two-tier client-server applications can be developed in any language or environment that provides support for interacting with XML documents, which has wide-spread support. As the concepts that are presented here are, in most cases, not particular to a specific language or technology, the code samples cover many of these options.

This chapter covers how to decide which XML presentation strategies are best, based on the goals of a particular software system. There are a number of factors that will guide you toward the right strategy. The factors covered in this chapter are:

❑   **Configurability** – how the same information can be presented in different ways based on user preferences, roles, or display devices

❑   **Performance** – how quickly data must become available to the user

❑   **Use of Rich Media** – how to handle the larger file sizes and longer download times, when rich media is used in the presentation

❑   **Cross-Platform Support** – how to support multiple server or client platforms

❑   **Working with Third-party and Legacy Data or Software** – how to work with data that is created by third-party or legacy systems, and how to interface with third-party or legacy systems to meet the presentation goals

❑ **Maintainability and Extensibility** – how to develop a presentation strategy that can be modified by others, or that allows easy development of new functionalities

Some other factors that have not been covered here, but may be an important part of your presentation strategy, are those that involve browser-specific features, such as how to use non-standard features like drag-and-drop.

Many issues come into play when developing a good presentation strategy, and they all must be factored into your solution according to their priorities. For instance, presentation strategies that are applicable to subsets of clients supporting an older client environment may be considered a lower priority than providing a faster display. Various factors pull the solution a certain way for which others must compensate because you do not have infinite time or resources to work with.

This chapter presents practical advice for handling presentation issues in the context of various important factors. To best accomplish this goal, we start with an example scenario that will be used throughout this chapter. This will give you a concrete sense of the trade-offs that are involved when different key factors are weighed against each other.

7.1 Example Scenario

To explore the factors that influence XML presentation strategies, first let's start with a sample scenario:

Your project is one of many going on at a large University, with a large variety of computer systems, and many departments performing IT work. Some of this work is coordinated, and some is not. You're a designer on a project that will provide a portal for the various departments and will give easy access to the information that different departments hold in their databases. The project aims at providing access to information about courses that will be available in the coming semester, as well as access to news items drawn from the University daily paper, local news sources, and e-newsletters put out by the various departments.

In our example, there are key factors whose priorities will drive the design for your project. If the priorities of your project are at odds with those of another department, then potentially it becomes a political issue rather than a technical one. You're lucky this time because requirements have been discussed many times and all department heads support your project. The key factors are:

❑ **Configurability** – There are several different user groups that will use that software module, so configurable according to role is important. Less important are features that allow for personalization or interaction with the system from somewhere other than a browser.

❑ **Performance** – This is reasonably important, but not usually the deciding factor when others are taken into account.

❑ **Use of Rich Media** – If news sources are sometimes video, audio, or a synchronized media presentation.

❑ **Cross-Platform Support** – The server environment is well defined. The client environment, however, is not as controlled. The Product Manager on the team has researched the browsers and versions to be supported. These are Internet Explorer 5.5 and higher (5.1 for Macintosh users) and Netscape Navigator 6.0.

❑ **Working with Third-party Data or Software** – The course information is stored in an older relational database. Also, many Professors are comfortable working in Excel, and have requested that there be an option for data to be exported into some format that Excel can load. In addition to the large central database that contains student records, some departments have developed 'home-grown' databases or bought off-the-shelf software to meet specific needs. For example, the Alumni and the Student Housing offices may need to track information that the central database was not able to handle.

❑ **Maintainability and Extensibility** – People don't tend to stay for long periods of time in the IT department at the University, so it's very likely that someone, who has never seen this system before, will be the one to add new features. Since this application is a portal, it's likely to take on new features as the users give feedback.

Developing a strategy will involve making trade-offs that promote priorities and resolve resource contention. To make it clear what the motivating factors are for each strategy, a convention is used where the following aspects are considered:

❑ **Feature** – An informal description of what the software must accomplish

❑ **Design Factors** – Important concepts that will drive the design, such as speed and conservation of storage, or ensure secure access of data

❑ **User** – An informal description of who will be interacting with the feature

❑ **Preconditions** – Anything that is assumed to have already occurred, such as a file exists, or a user has interacted with a different feature prior to this one

❑ **Description of Interaction** – This describes the user (listed above) performing the feature from their perspective

7.2 Configurability

A configurable presentation approach is one where the information to be presented and the conditions under which the presentation can vary, depend on a number of factors, such as the role of the user, personal preferences, and the current display device. Configurability anticipates different uses for the same functions or data, without having to develop specialized software for each new use.

7.2.1 Role-based Configurability

Role-based configurability guides users through appropriate workflows, based on the way the users interact with the system, increasing the system's overall usability, as well as providing elementary means of security to data and functionality. Role-based configurability is accomplished by predetermining what functions or data will be under role-based control (thus creating a set of maintenance features for the creation and assignment of roles to users), and then verifying the required role just before processing a function or before interacting with data that is under role-based control.

Upon login, the role of the active user is accessed. Based on this role, the presentation of data and features can be manipulated, by applying a style that produces the desired data and access to functions before the data is delivered to the client.

The following list describes a feature from our example scenario:

❑ **Feature** – View course information.

❑ **Design Factors** – Provide course information based on the current role of the user.

❑ **User** – Faculty members and students who want to view the course information for different purposes.

❑ **Preconditions** – The user has to be logged in. During the login procedure, the system looked up the role of the user.

❑ **Description of Interaction** – The user selects the desired course, and the information appropriate to their role is displayed.

7.2.1.1 Develop Role-specific Stylesheets and Run from a Common Framework

XSLT stylesheets are capable of different complex manipulations of the same XML documents, and can present data in a particular way to users based on their role, or hide data completely by not including it in the transformed result. If one of the roles needs to change, then we simply need to change the stylesheet. If a new role is needed, then we need to create a new stylesheet for that role. As new people gain access to the system, it is easy to set their roles, and if users' responsibilities expand (or shrink), they must be assigned different roles to reflect those changes.

This type of approach to role management means that you can generate menus dynamically, based on what the user is allowed to do. However, this doesn't preclude the need for a system that ensures secure access to features and data. In browser-based and other types of user interfaces, it's possible to understand how to access restricted features even when no menu items are provided. The system should validate the user's privileges on the server at every client request.

In this example, the English 220 course has been selected, and the server will now process the request. First, the server will access the XML document. Then, the XSLT stylesheet will be selected and applied to the XML document depending on the user's role, which was determined when the user first logged in. The result is returned as the request response.

The following shows the XML document, `courseEng220.xml`, which we will use to define the specific data for the English course:

```
<course id="eng220">
  <title>English Literature</title>
  <class_size_limit>20</class_size_limit>
  <description>An exploration of 10 works of English literature from
  the early 1800's through mid 1900's.</description>
  <syllabus>
    <!-- syllabus details here -->
    <textbook>'Selections from English Literature' by Deborah Collen
    </textbook>
    <textbook>'More English Literature' by Deborah Collen
    </textbook>
    <grade_component contribution="20%">Term Paper - compare and
    contrast works from two different historical periods.
    </grade_component>
    <grade_component contribution ="20%">Term Paper - compare and
    contrast works from two different authors from the same historical
    period.
    </grade_component>
    <grade_component contribution ="20%">Mid-term on works from first
    half of course.
    </grade_component>
    <grade_component contribution ="20%">Final on works from first half
    of course.
    </grade_component>
    <grade_component contribution ="20%">Class participation through
    discussion of works is expected.
    </grade_component>
  </syllabus>
  <prerequisites>
    <prerequisite id="eng101"><title>English Comp 1</title>
    </prerequisite>
    <prerequisite id="eng120"><title>English Comp 2</title>
    </prerequisite>
    <prerequisite id="eng201"><title>American Literature</title>
    </prerequisite>
  </prerequisites>
</course>
```

A student reviewing course prerequisites would use the `course_student.xsl` stylesheet, and a department head reviewing or verifying outlines and course descriptions would use the second stylesheet called `course_admin.xsl`. For each new role that was created, a specific stylesheet would be needed to tailor the presentation according to the needs of the position.

The following XSL stylesheet, `course_shell.xsl`, would serve as the starting point from which the other role-based versions would extend. This example shows the stylesheets outside of a processing framework. Later examples show how you might apply the XSLT stylesheet to the XML data.

```
<?xml version="1.0" encoding="iso-8859-1"?>
<xsl:stylesheet version="1.0"
  xmlns:xsl="http://www.w3.org/1999/XSL/Transform">

<xsl:template match="/course">
 <html>
 <body>
  <xsl:call-template name="common_header"/>
  <xsl:call-template name="initiate"/>
 </body>
 </html>
</xsl:template>

<xsl:template name="common_header">
   <!-- html common to all roles -->
   <img src="banner.gif"/><br/>
</xsl:template>

</xsl:stylesheet>
```

The student will see the result of the following stylesheet, `course_student.xsl`, when applied to the XML course data:

```
<?xml version="1.0" encoding="iso-8859-1"?>
<xsl:stylesheet version="1.0"
  xmlns:xsl="http://www.w3.org/1999/XSL/Transform">
<xsl:include href="course_shell.xsl"/>

<xsl:template name="initiate">
 <h1>Course Prerequisites for <xsl:value-of
 select="/course/title"/></h1>
  <p><xsl:value-of select="/course/description"/></p>
   <xsl:apply-templates select="/course/prerequisites"/>
</xsl:template>

<xsl:template match="prerequisites">
 <table>
  <tr><th>Course ID</th><th>Title</th></tr>
  <xsl:apply-templates select="prerequisite"/>
 </table>
</xsl:template>

<xsl:template match="prerequisite">
 <tr>
  <td><xsl:value-of select="@id"/></td>
  <td><xsl:value-of select="title"/></td>
```

```
      </tr>
    </xsl:template>

    <!--these templates produce no output -->
    <xsl:template match="title"/>
    <xsl:template match="description"/>
    <xsl:template match="syllabus"/>

</xsl:stylesheet>
```

Based on the above stylesheet, the course prerequisites for English Literature are as rendered below:

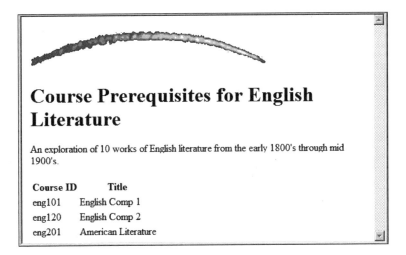

The administrator would see the result of the following stylesheet, course_admin.xsl, when applied to the XML course data:

```
<?xml version="1.0" encoding="iso-8859-1"?>
<xsl:stylesheet version="1.0"
xmlns:xsl="http://www.w3.org/1999/XSL/Transform">
  <xsl:include href="./course_shell.xsl"/>

<xsl:template name="initiate">
  <h1><xsl:value-of select="/course/title"/></h1>
  <p><xsl:value-of select="/course/description"/></p>
  <xsl:apply-templates select="/course/syllabus"/>
</xsl:template>

<xsl:template match="syllabus">
  <table>
    <tr><th>Textbook</th></tr>
      <xsl:apply-templates select="textbook"/>
    </table>
    <br/>
    <table>
    <tr><th>% of grade</th><th>Description</th></tr>
      <xsl:apply-templates select="grade_component"/>
```

```
  </table>
</xsl:template>

<xsl:template match="textbook">
 <tr><td><xsl:value-of select="."/></td></tr>
</xsl:template>

<xsl:template match="grade_component">
 <tr>
  <td><xsl:value-of select="@contribution"/></td>
  <td><xsl:value-of select="."/></td>
 </tr>
</xsl:template>

<!--these templates produce no output -->
<xsl:template match="title"/>
<xsl:template match="description"/>
<xsl:template match="prerequisites"/>

</xsl:stylesheet>
```

Based on the above stylesheet, the following information is rendered:

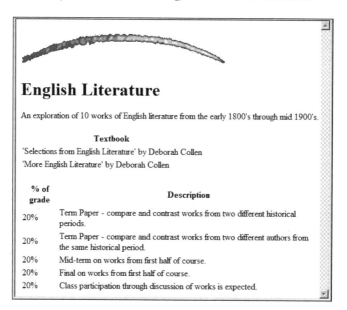

7.2.2 Device-dependent Configurability

Device-dependent configurability extends the reach of your system to people and places that it might not otherwise have access to, such as mobile users with wireless PDAs and automotive telematics. Also, your system could become more accessible to those who might not be able to use the software, such as blind or low-vision users and those physically unable to interact with a mouse or keyboard.

The following list describes a feature from our example scenario:

❑ **Feature** – All pages are accessible to audio devices that use voiceXML, to serve the needs of users with low or no vision

❑ **Design Factors** – Provide the same information in a manner that is appropriate for the target device

❑ **Preconditions** – None

❑ **Description of Interaction** – The target device will render the voiceXML data into verbal prompts

7.2.2.1 Develop Device-specific Stylesheets to be used in a Device-Independent Framework

The device-dependent aspects of the presentation should be encapsulated into a single entity (XML document, object, table row, etc.), and designed to work in a device-independent framework. Modifying existing device-dependent information or adding new portions, doesn't become overly complex when the device-specific information is handled separately from the main display paradigm.

The following XML sample, called `portalMenu.xml`, contains the main menu options for the current user:

```
<options>
  <topic id="100" name="News">
    <source id="10217">On-Campus Daily</source>
    <source id="10218">Smallville Times</source>
    <source id="10288">
            Poetry and Prose: English Dept. Newsletter</source>
    <source id="10090">
            The Journal - Communications Newsletter</source>
  </topic>
  <topic id="101" name="Curriculum">
    <action id="10219">Add a New Course</action>
    <action id="10225">Delete a Course</action>
    <action id="10247">Edit a Course</action>
    <topic name="departments"></topic>
    <topic name="professors"></topic>
    <topic name="courses"></topic>
  </topic>
  <topic id="102" name="People">
    <source id="10300">Student Directory</source>
    <source id="10301">Faculty Directory</source>
    <source id="10302">Administrative Directory</source>
    <action id="10303">Search all Directories</action>
  </topic>
  <articles>
    <keyword value="basketball"/>
    <keyword value="astronomy"/>
    <source id="44054">
            Big win in hoops last night...</source>
    <source id="988">
            New course: Basketball 101 to be ...</source>
    <source id="12435">
            Physicists now believe that ...</source>
```

261

```
      </articles>
    </options>
```

When rendered into HTML and viewed in a browser, we would see the following display:

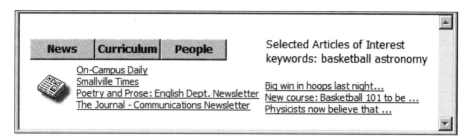

Here is the corresponding HTML source:

```
<HTML>
<BODY>
<form action="http://www.univ.edu/portal/dispatch">
<table>
  <tr>
    <td><table>
      <tr><td colspan="2">
        <button id="100">News</button>
        <button id="101">Curriculum</button>
        <button id="102">People</button>
      </td></tr>
      <tr><td>
      <img src="news.gif"/></td><td>
        <a href="dispatch?src=10217">On-Campus Daily</a><br/>
        <a href="dispatch?src=10218">Smallville Times</a><br/>
        <a href="dispatch?src=10288">
          Poetry and Prose: English Dept. Newsletter</a><br/>
        <a href="dispatch?src=10090">
          The Journal - Communications Newsletter</a><br/>
      </td></tr></table>
      </td>
      <td valign="top">Selected Articles of Interest<br/>
        keywords: basketball astronomy <br/><br/>
        <a href="dispatch?src=44054">
          Big win in hoops last night...</a><br/>
        <a href="dispatch?src=988">
          New course: Basketball 101 to be ...</a><br/>
        <a href="dispatch?src=12435">
          Physicists now believe that ...</a><br/>
      </td></tr>
  </table>
</form>
</BODY>
<HTML>
```

Next, the XSLT stylesheet, `portalToHtml.xsl`, to create the HTML page:

```
<?xml version="1.0"?>
<xsl:stylesheet version="1.0"
xmlns:xsl="http://www.w3.org/1999/XSL/Transform">
  <xsl:param name="currentSelection" select="News"/>

  <xsl:template match="/options">
    <link href="sample.css" rel="stylesheet"/>
    <form action="http://www.univ.edu/portal/dispatch">
      <table>
        <tr><td>
        <table>
          <tr><!-- controls -->
          <td colspan="2"><xsl:for-each select="topic">
            <button>
              <xsl:attribute name="id">
                  <xsl:value-of select="@id"/>
                </xsl:attribute>
              <xsl:value-of select="@name"/></button>
              <xsl:text> </xsl:text>
            </xsl:for-each></td>
          </tr>
          <xsl:apply-templates select="topic[@name='News']"/>
        </table>
      </td>

      <td valign="top">Selected Articles of Interest<br/>
        keywords:
          <xsl:for-each select="articles/keyword">
            <xsl:value-of select="@value"/><xsl:text> </xsl:text>
            </xsl:for-each>
            <br/><br/>
            <xsl:apply-templates select="articles/source"/>
        </td></tr>
      </table>
    </form>
  </xsl:template>

<xsl:template match="topic">
  <tr><td><img src="news.gif"/></td><!-- control options -->
  <td> <xsl:apply-templates select="source"/>
  </td></tr>
</xsl:template>

<xsl:template match="source">
  <xsl:variable name="url">
    <xsl:text>dispatch?src=</xsl:text>
    <xsl:value-of select="@id"/>
  </xsl:variable>
  <a><xsl:attribute name="href">
      <xsl:value-of select="$url"/>
    </xsl:attribute>
    <xsl:value-of select="."/>
  </a><br/>
</xsl:template>
</xsl:stylesheet>
```

Now we want to create the same menu options for a voiceXML browser. Here is what the resulting VXML form would render to:

```
<?xml version="1.0" encoding="utf-8" ?>
  <vxml version="2.0">
    <menu>
      <prompt>
        Say one of <enumerate />
      </prompt>
    <choice next="http://www.univ.edu/vxmlportal/dispatch?id=100">
      News</choice>
    <choice next="http://www.univ.edu/vxmlportal/dispatch?id=101">
      Curriculum</choice>
    <choice next="http://www.univ.edu/vxmlportal/dispatch?id=102">
      People</choice>
    <noinput>
      Please say one of <enumerate />
    </noinput>
  </menu>
</vxml>
```

And here's the XSLT stylesheet, `portalToVxml.xsl`, to create the voiceXML page:

```
<?xml version="1.0" encoding="iso-8859-1"?>
<xsl:stylesheet version="1.0"
xmlns:xsl="http://www.w3.org/1999/XSL/Transform">
  <xsl:output method="xml"/>

  <xsl:template match="/options">
    <vxml version="2.0">
      <menu>
        <prompt>Say one of <enumerate/> </prompt>
        <xsl:apply-templates select="topic"/>
        <noinput>Please say one of <enumerate/></noinput>
      </menu>
    </vxml>
  </xsl:template>

<xsl:template match="topic">
  <xsl:variable name="url">
    <xsl:text>http://www.univ.edu/vxmlportal/dispatch?id=</xsl:text>
    <xsl:value-of select="@id"/>
  </xsl:variable>
  <choice>
    <xsl:attribute name="next">
      <xsl:value-of select="$url"/>
    </xsl:attribute>
    <xsl:value-of select="@name"/>
  </choice>
</xsl:template>
</xsl:stylesheet>
```

Refer to http://www.w3c.org/Voice for the latest status on voiceXML browsers and the state of this XML format.

7.2.3 Personalization

Personalization gives users the ability to control their experience thus increasing their sense of ownership of the system, and in turn, encourages further use, and the overall usability of your system. Personalization is accomplished by giving choices to the users from a fixed set of pre-determined attributes, drawn about their environment. A user's preferences for these attributes are stored in a place (a file, an XML document, a database table, etc.) that is loaded when the user logs in.

Preferences, like role-based configuration, can limit the amount of data a person sees, can influence how they see the data, and what they can do to the data. It's important to remember that role- and preference-based configuration can happen at the server or the client. If it is done at the client, then potentially sensitive information could travel the network and become accessible at the client, even if the data is not viewable from the user interface. The security policy of the system should always verify at the server, before any data is released to the network.

The following list describes a feature from our example scenario:

❏ **Feature** – Users can pre-select keywords for articles of interest that will display in the main portal page. The user can also select from a set of predefined display themes.

❏ **Design Factors** – Provide a personalized user experience.

❏ **User** – All.

❏ **Preconditions** – None.

❏ **Description of Interaction** – The user logs in. Based on the set of keywords provided when the account personalization was configured, a set of articles drawn from the University-wide paper, local town paper, and various newsletters put out by some departments, appear as article hyperlinks in a sidebar on the main portal page. From the same setup screen, let's say the user selects the 'flying toasters' theme. Upon submitting the page, the background changes to the flying toasters wallpaper and the font size, color, and face change. The menus and buttons become white, and are filled with thick lettering.

7.2.3.1 Pass Personalization Parameters into your Stylesheets

Personalization parameters are bits of information that are maintained with a user's record. When a person logs in, these parameters are acquired from their datastore, and used during the session. You can think of personalization parameters as functions to an argument, as they are variables associated with a person. You can build a presentation framework such that these parameters are passed into the XSLT stylesheet which uses them to produce the personalized output:

```
<html>
 <body>
  <h1>Check the items you want to see as your personalized
  settings</h1>
  <form action="CreatePersonalizedView/" method="post">
  <input type="hidden" id="user_id" value="1234"/>
  <input type="checkbox" id="title">Course Title<br/>
  <input type="checkbox" id="classSize">Maximum Class Size<br/>
  <input type="checkbox" id="description">Description<br/>
  <input type="checkbox" id="textbooks">Textbooks<br/>
  <input type="checkbox" id="grade">Grading Components<br/>
  <input type="checkbox" id="prerequisites">Prerequisites<br/>
  <input type="submit" value="Personalize the Display">
 </form>
 </body>
</html>
```

The server process at `CreatePersonalizedView` could be a Java Servlet, an ASP page, a Perl script, or any number of web server-supported languages. The list of selected items could be stored in a record in a relational database or in an XML document.

If user `1234` worked in the University bookstore and was going to use the data to verify whether adequate supplies of books for each course were ordered, he/she might check off 'Course Title', 'Maximum Class Size, and 'Textbooks'. If the personalization parameters are stored in an XML document, then the following xml file, `config1234.xml`, is produced at this point:

```
<?xml version="1.0"?>
<config user_id="1234">
  <title display="yes"/>
  <class_size_limit display="yes"/>
  <textbooks display="yes"/>
</config>
```

The resulting XSL file (called `course_shell.xsl`) is created, and saved as part of user `1234`'s record:

```
<?xml version="1.0"?>
<xsl:stylesheet version="1.0"
xmlns:xsl="http://www.w3.org/1999/XSL/Transform">
  <xsl:output method="text"/>

<xsl:param name="configFile" select="'configDefault.xml'"/>
<xsl:variable name="config" select="document($configFile)"/>

<xsl:include href="all_course templates.xsl"/>

<xsl:template match="/">
  <html>
  <body>
    <xsl:if test="$config/config/title/@display = 'yes'">
      <xsl:apply-templates select="/course/title"/>
    </xsl:if>

    <xsl:if test="$config/config/class_size_limit/@display = 'yes'">
      <xsl:apply-templates select="/course/class_size_limit"/>
    </xsl:if>
    <xsl:if test="$config/config/description/@display = 'yes'">
```

```
      <xsl:apply-templates select="/course/description"/>
      </xsl:if>

      <xsl:if test="$config/config/textbooks/@display = 'yes'">
        <xsl:apply-templates select="/course/syllabus/textbook"/>
      </xsl:if>

      <xsl:if test="$config/config/grade_component/@display = 'yes'">
        <xsl:apply-templates select="/course/syllabus/grade_component"/>
      </xsl:if>

      <xsl:if test="$config/config/prerequisites/@display = 'yes'">
        <xsl:apply-templates select="/course/prerequisites"/>
      </xsl:if>
  </body>
  </html>
  </xsl:template>

</xsl:stylesheet>
```

This file, `all_course_templates.xsl`, contains all the templates that might be used to display course information:

```
<?xml version="1.0" encoding="iso-8859-1"?>
<xsl:stylesheet version="1.0"
xmlns:xsl="http://www.w3.org/1999/XSL/Transform">

<xsl:template match="title">
 <p>Title: <xsl:value-of select="."/></p>
</xsl:template>

<xsl:template match="class_size_limit">
 <p>Class Size Limit: <xsl:value-of select="."/></p>
</xsl:template>

<xsl:template match="description">
 <p>Description: <xsl:value-of select="."/></p>
</xsl:template>

<xsl:template match="syllabus">
 <p>Syllabus</p>
 <p>Textbooks: <xsl:apply-templates select="textbook"/></p>
 <p>Grading: <xsl:apply-templates select="grade_component"/></p>
</xsl:template>

<xsl:template match="textbook">
 Title: <xsl:value-of select="."/><br/>
</xsl:template>

<xsl:template match="grade_component">
   <xsl:value-of select="."/> accounts for <xsl:value-of
select="@contribution"/> of the final grade.<br/>
</xsl:template>

<xsl:template match="prerequisites">
 <p>Prerequisites: <xsl:apply-templates select="prerequesite"/></p>
</xsl:template>

<xsl:template match="prerequisite">
 <xsl:value-of select="."/><br/>
</xsl:template>
</xsl:stylesheet>
```

When the stylesheet is applied to the XML data, the user's configuration parameter is passed in as part of the call to the transform engine. When a configuration file is not passed in, a default file is used instead, as shown in the select attribute in the `<xsl:param>` statements at the beginning of `course_shell.xsl`. Here, the XML document and XSLT stylesheet is processed via a command line using James Clark's XSLT transform engine:

```
xt.exe courseEng220.xml course_shell.xsl configFile=config1234.xml
```

7.3 Performance

Performance involves strategies that get the results presented in the desired format in a timely manner, or where the user is not left idle or waiting for data too long before it appears. Performance is important when users are providing information during data entry, or selecting options, as while setting up a report. Large files that need downloading to the client, competition for resources on the server, or complex processing times at the server, are the typical causes for performance delays.

When such processing bottlenecks are encountered, and the user is told how long to wait, then this time can be factored into the user's workflow, provided it's not too long. For pages that involve complex queries or calculations, you can pre-construct pages at an earlier time so as to have the information ready to deliver to the client when it is requested. The trade-off is that the data will not always be up-to-date, but accurate as of the last time the page was constructed.

Style can be applied to data in various ways, such as:

- ❑ at runtime, at the server
- ❑ at runtime, at the client
- ❑ offline, at the server, whenever data as changed
- ❑ offline, at the server, at specific predefined intervals

Performance is XML's weak area because of the amount of processing that XML parsers are required to do when loading a document and constructing the internal tree-like representation for DOM processing. If speed is of very high importance, then XML might not be the best solution. Relational databases benefit from many years of use and incremental improvements, and generally outperform XML parsers in a time-to-display race. Relational databases are also equipped with highly optimized query languages like SQL, providing faster data manipulations. On the other hand, XML querying technologies like XPath are relatively less mature. As XML technology matures and usage becomes more pervasive, XML parsers have started to benefit from performance improvements.

The following list describes a feature from our example scenario:

- ❏ **Feature** – Show course requirements and course prerequisites for a selected major, as a tree diagram that reveals prerequisite dependencies

- ❏ **Design Factors** – The page should display within 5 seconds – which is the general page display guideline for the portal application

- ❏ **User** – Any student, faculty, or administrator of the University

- ❏ **Preconditions** – None

- ❏ **Description of Interaction** – The user selects the major from the list of all the majors and the page with the tree diagram displays

7.3.1.1 Anticipate Presentation Needs by having Information Ready to Deliver, or Pre-parse XML and XSLT Stylesheets

If the data doesn't change frequently or the users can accept that the information feeding the page might not be completely up-to-date, then creating the pages before they are requested and having them ready to deliver upon request will remove the processing delay. The trade-off for pre-constructing and caching pages is that options for personalization, device dependencies, and other run-time specific factors will be harder to support. One approach is to predict the various versions that people will request and have them all cached. The trade-off is that of storage for possibly many different versions of every cached page. Also, it's not always possible to predetermine all possible variations of a page. In these circumstances, it makes sense to prepares and cache the pieces that won't vary.

Data latency may be an important design decision in these circumstances, as the age of the data should be clear to the viewer. If a complex report is run overnight, then its 'create time' should be included in the report. Latency is not an issue in cases where the data changes infrequently. If this is the case, then offline styling should be taken advantage of because whenever the page is requested, it appears in the time it takes to fulfill the page request.

In our example, to construct the diagram of the courses and their prerequisites, queries pull the course data from the University's main relational database, construct an XML document, and then apply a transform to display the course and dependencies in a tree diagram. Two factors make this a good candidate for offline styling:

- ❏ The data changes infrequently; on an average about twice a year

- ❏ The page takes an average of 15 seconds to construct

The following example, updateMajors.py, is a python script that runs after major course requirements are changed. This could be implemented in a number of ways including using a "modified flag" on each record, or by recording the update event to a log file. A process that is executed at regular intervals would monitor the modified flag field or the log for changes. The result from the XSL transform should be saved to a file in a location where a user via a browser can access it. This can be done very simply, by saving the results to a predefined file name and location, to which a webpage contains a link:

```python
import libxml2
import libxslt

# check for the right number of input arguments
if len(sys.argv) != 4:
    print "usage: updateMajors <updated dir> <xslt stylesheet> <target
dir>"
    sys.exit(0)

# get the command line arguments
updatedDir = sys.argv[1]
xsltFile   = sys.argv[2]
targetDir  = syst.argv[3]

# get all updated files
updatedXMLFiles = os.listdir(updatedDir)

# Apply the same stylesheet to update XML files
styleDoc = libxml2.parseFile(xsltFile)

# for each updated XML file, do the following
for updatedXML in updatedXMLFiles:

    # load the file into an internal XML document
    doc = libxml2.parseFile(updatedXML)
    # transform the data, passing no parameters
    result = styleDoc.applyStylesheet(doc, None)
    # generate the output filename and save the results
    resultFile = targetDir + os.path.basename(sourceFile) + ".html"
    # save the results to a file
    style.saveResultToFilename(resultFile, result, 0)

# release memory
style.freeStylesheet()
doc.freeDoc()
result.freeDoc()
```

To run this script, apply the python interpreter along with the script arguments as shown below. The resulting files in the target directory can then be moved to their proper location in the web server directory during the next portal upgrade:

```
python updateMajorReqs.py d:\updatedMajorReqs\
d:\transforms\majorReqsTree.xsl d:\updatedMajorWebPages\
```

7.3.1.2 Use Runtime Styling when Data Accuracy is Important

Sometimes, the integrity of the data being displayed far exceeds the need for timeliness. In these cases, it's best to render the XML into HTML (or the target format of the XSLT stylesheet).

In a system with fairly weak performance constraints, but with a strong requirement for up-to-the-minute results, you should consider using runtime styling. This approach is slower, as the server will perform the transformation of the data every time the data is to be displayed.

This example shows a Java Servlet returning a requested page after it has been dynamically generated at the server:

```
import java.io.*;
import javax.servlet.*;
import javax.servlet.http.*;
import javax.xml.transform.*;
import javax.xml.transform.stream.*;

public class RuntimeStyleServlet extends HttpServlet {

  public void doGet( HttpServletRequest req, HttpServletResponse res )
        throws IOException, ServletException {

    File xmlSource = "JournalismMajor.xml";
    File xslStyle = " majorReqsTree.xsl";

    TransformerFactory factory = TransformerFactory.newInstance();
    Transformer t = factory.newTransformer(
      new StreamSource(xslStyle));
    t.transform(new StreamSource(xmlSource),
          new StreamResult(res.getOutputStream()));
    }
}
```

The client would access this data via an HTTP request to the servlet, such as http://www.mysite.com/servlets/RuntimeStyleServlet.

7.3.1.3 For Rapid Development, Perform the XSL Transforms at the Client

Some browsers, including Internet Explorer 5.0 and higher, or Netscape Navigator 6.0 and higher, which have a built-in XSL transform engine, are capable of displaying XML in an interactive tree format. This is a way to apply XSL stylesheets, very quickly, to XML data without having to create a framework to provide server-side code to start prototyping. The disadvantage is that it is not a flexible display approach, as the XML data is bound to the XSL stylesheet. If you want to change the stylesheet, you must edit the XML document.

To have style applied to XML at the client, the XML will need a reference to the XSL stylesheet in the XML document with a <xml-stylesheet> command. For other browsers that do not support this operation, the XML will display without style.

271

This example adds the stylesheet command to `courseEng220.xml`, from a previous example:

```
<?xml version="1.0"?>
<?xml-stylesheet type="text/xsl" href="course_student.xsl"?>

<course id="eng220">
  <title>English Literature</title>
  <description>An exploration of 10 works of English literature
      from the early 1800's through mid 1900's.</description>
  <syllabus>
   <!-- shown in earlier example -->
  </syllabus>
</course>
```

7.3.1.4 For Simple Styling Requirements, use Cascading Stylesheets (CSS)

If the XML data is not manipulated but needs to be presented as it is specified in the XML file, then consider creating a cascading stylesheet to specify how the XML data items will be displayed.

Support of client-processed CSS is widespread, and as this example shows, is specified with the XML document using the `<xml-stylesheet>` command:

```
<?xml version="1.0"?>
<?xml-stylesheet type="text/css" href="syllabus.css"?>

<course id="eng220">
  <title>English Literature</title>
  <description>An exploration of 10 works of English literature
      from the early 1800's through mid 1900's.</description>
  <syllabus>
   <!-- shown in earlier example -->
  </syllabus>
</course>
```

The corresponding CSS file, called `syllabus.css`, would be:

```
course  { background-color: #cccccc; border: none; width: 300;}
title { display: block; font-size: 20pt; margin-left: 0; }
description { display: block; margin-left: 20pt;}
syllabus { display: block; font-family: monospace; margin-left: 20pt;}
```

7.4 Use of Rich Media

Rich media is video, audio, animation, or any other type of media form that provides a richer experience to the user. Rich media files are typically larger in size than those containing plain or formatted text, and therefore, can have an impact on performance. Adding some animation or video with or without associated timed text, can make you either stand out from the crowd and give a polished, innovative look, or can ruin the presentation for the user because of long download times.

7.4.1 Synchronized Media

Synchronized media presentations involve multiple sources of rich media, such as video, audio, animation, etc. that are rendered within some type of relationship framework, such as audio soundtrack over video or timed text synchronized with a PowerPoint presentation. Rendering synchronized media in browser environments means that the presentation scheme must handle issues of media formats and their playback processes, and bandwidth slowdowns for large rich media files over bandwidth constrained lines.

There are two formats designed to synchronize multiple-sourced rich media presentations, taking somewhat polarized approaches. One approach started from the ground up with a new XML format for the specification of synchronized media, known as **Synchronized Multimedia Integration Language (SMIL)**, pronounced "smile". The other started with HTML and extended it to incorporate aspects of the SMIL standard that fit within the HTML model, known as **XHTML+SMIL**.

SMIL is a W3C controlled XML standard that specifies interaction, timing dependencies, and interrelationships between different types of rich media including images, audio, video, and text, for the specification and playback of rich media presentations. To playback a SMIL presentation, you must use a media player or plug-in that supports it, such as Real's RealOne media player or Apple's QuickTime. Refer to http://www.w3.org/AudioVideo/ for the latest information on media players and browsers that support SMIL 2.0.

XHTML+SMIL augments XHTML with a subset of SMIL commands to handle the most common functions used in multimedia presentations. Rather than a plug-in or media player for rendering, a browser that supports XHTML+TIME commands is used; the primary choice is Microsoft's Internet Explorer 6.0 or higher.

7.4.1.1 Determine how the Client will Playback the Rich Media Presentation so as to Decide on the Format

Media players have been looking more like browsers over the years and browsers have been looking more like media players, and someday they will probably meet in the middle. Until then, one format cannot go to both browser and media player. Refer to *Section 1.4.1* on how to handle multiple rendering targets if you need to support both. Otherwise, the client playback environment will drive the decision on which format to use.

7.4.1.1.1 For Playing Synchronized Rich Media in a SMIL 2.0-compliant Media Player or Plug-in, Represent your Presentation in SMIL

SMIL is a rich standard for controlling where, when, how long, and which triggers initiate various types of media sources. To take full advantage of the SMIL functions, you will need to commit to one of the players or plug-ins that supports SMIL 2.0. The disadvantage is that the client should either have the plug-in present, or the media player installed, which often is not the case, versus one of the major browsers that are ubiquitous.

The following file, campus.smi, shows a SMIL presentation on campus life:

```
<?xml version="1.0" encoding="ISO-8859-1"?>
<smil>
  <head>
    <meta name="title" content="Slideshow"/>
    <layout>
      <root-layout id="Player-Window" background-color="#c0c0c0"
        width="540" height="300"/>
      <region id="audioChannel"/>
      <region id="backgroundArea" width="540" height="300"
        z-index="0"/>
      <region id="slideShowArea" left="10" top="10" width="530"
        height="280" z-index="0"/>
    </layout>
  </head>
  <body>
    <par id="SlideShow_Presentation">
      <seq id="Background">
        <img id="bk1" region="backgroundArea" src="bkgrd.gif"
          fill="freeze"/>
      </seq>
      <seq id="slideShowSequence">
        <video id="im1" region="slideShowArea" src="im1.jpg"
          dur="3s"/>
        <video id="im2" region="slideShowArea" src="im2.jpg"
          dur="3s"/>
        <video id="im3" region="slideShowArea" src="im3.jpg"
          dur="3s"/>
        <video id="im4" region="slideShowArea" src="im4.jpg"
          dur="3s"/>
        <video id="im5" region="slideShowArea" src="im5.jpg"
          dur="3s"/>
        <video id="im6" region="slideShowArea" src="im6.jpg"
          dur="3s"/>
      </seq>
    </par>
  </body>
</smil>
```

274

7.4.1.1.2 If your Primary Client Environment is IE 6.0 and higher, you can represent your Presentation in XHTML+SMIL

When the client environment is controlled and known to be IE 6.0 or higher, you can choose to represent your presentation in XHTML+SMIL. The advantage is that no plug-in media player is required. The disadvantage is that this format is a subset of SMIL, and therefore, will not offer all the rich features and won't be portable if the client environment should become less controlled.

The following file, `campus.html`, shows a XHTML+ SMIL presentation using the same image content as in the SMIL example:

```
<!DOCTYPE HTML PUBLIC "-//W3C//DTD HTML 4.0 Transitional//EN"
    "http://www.w3.org/TR/REC-html40/loose.dtd">
<html>
<head>
<title>Campus Life</title>
</head>
<body>
    <h1>Campus Life</h1>
    <hr>
    <div>

    <XML:NAMESPACE PREFIX="t"/>
        <style>
        /* IE5 specific code */
        .time  { behavior: url(#DEFAULT#TIME);}
        t\:seq { behavior: url(#DEFAULT#TIME);}
        t\:par { behavior: url(#DEFAULT#TIME);}
        t\:img { behavior: url(#DEFAULT#TIME);}
        </style>
        <t:par>
        <ul>
            <li style="color:blue;font-size:16pt" CLASS="time"
                t:BEGIN="0">Music</li>
            <li style="color:lime;font-size:16pt" CLASS="time"
                t:BEGIN="3">Art</li>
            <li style="color:blue;font-size:16pt" CLASS="time"
                t:BEGIN="6">Fun</li>
            <li style="color:lime;font-size:16pt" CLASS="time"
                t:BEGIN="9">Work</li>
            <li style="color:blue;font-size:16pt" CLASS="time"
                t:BEGIN="12">Thinking Outside the Box</li>
            <li style="color:lime;font-size:16pt" CLASS="time"
                t:BEGIN="15">Friendships</li>
        </ul>
        <t:SEQ t:BEGIN="0" t:TIMEACTION="display">
            <img CLASS="time" alt="campus life image 1" ID="img1"
                t:TIMEACTION="display" SRC="im1.jpg" t:DUR="3" />
            <img CLASS="time" alt="campus life image 2" ID="img2"
                t:TIMEACTION="display" SRC="im2.jpg" t:DUR="3" />
```

275

```
               <img CLASS="time" alt="campus life image 3" ID="img3"
                   t:TIMEACTION="display" SRC="im3.jpg" t:DUR="3" />
               <img CLASS="time" alt="campus life image 4" ID="img4"
                   t:TIMEACTION="display" SRC="im4.jpg" t:DUR="3" />
               <img CLASS="time" alt="campus life image 5" ID="img5"
                   t:TIMEACTION="display" SRC="im5.jpg" t:DUR="3" />
               <img CLASS="time" alt="campus life image 6" ID="img6"
                   t:TIMEACTION="display" SRC="im6.jpg" t:DUR="30" />
           </t:SEQ>
         </t:par>
     </div>
   </body>
   </html>
```

7.5 Cross-Platform Support

Cross-platform support allows your system to be independent of a particular set of computers or operating system vendors. Languages such as Java, scripting languages such as Python and Perl, and implementations, such as JAXP and TraX, have grown in popularity since their introduction, as they facilitate the support of multiple environments.

Providing a presentation strategy that supports multiple servers, means that you will need to provide a layer of abstraction around system-specific libraries, such as the XML parser and XSLT transform engine.

In our sample scenario, the server environment is not expected to change, and neither is it expected to support different environments, so this design factor would not be a significant one for us. However, in this case, it is good to plan defensively for the future, as the libraries that are OS-specific are more likely to change or expand their APIs, so a layer between these libraries and your software is prudent.

7.5.1.1 Use the JAXP and TRaX API for Cross-Platform Support

Java API for XML Parsing (JAXP) adds a layer of abstraction over any particular XML parser, thus letting you develop Java code that is independent of the XML and XSLT processor. This means that you can move your server-side code to another environment where a different parser and transform engine might be used for the direct XML and XSLT interaction, without having to modify your code.

The following JAXP implementations support both XML parsing and XSL transforms:

❏ Apache Xalan-J

❏ JAXP Reference Implementation

❏ Java 2 Platform, Standard Edition 1.4

❏ Saxon

The following example shows a Java Servlet that uses the JAXP interface. The actual XML parser and XSLT transformer being used is not apparent here. For the Xalan-J implementation, you would set the specific processor classes via a system property. Check the JAXP implementation for specifics on how this is done:

```
import java.io.*;
import javax.servlet.*;
import javax.servlet.http.*;
import javax.xml.transform.*;
import javax.xml.transform.stream.*;

public class RuntimeStyleServlet extends HttpServlet {

    public void doGet( HttpServletRequest req, HttpServletResponse res )
            throws IOException, ServletException {

        File xmlSource = "courseEng210.xml";
        File xslStyle = "basicSyllabus.xsl";

        TransformerFactory factory = TransformerFactory.newInstance();
        Transformer t = factory.newTransformer(new
                StreamSource(xslStyle));
        t.transform(new StreamSource(xmlSource),
                new StreamResult(res.getOutputStream()));
        }
    }
}
```

Having the XSLT engine arguments set as constants within this servlet is not ideal, but is shown to simplify the example. These arguments should be passed in through the servlet's request object.

7.6 Working with Third-party and Legacy Data or Software

Working with data that has been created by other systems or making your data accessible to other systems, allows your software to connect with others and become part of a larger and more powerful solution. Your system may also have requirements that indicate that it must work with data that was created from older corporate systems, for downward compatibility.

By giving access to your data to third-party or legacy software as part of your strategy, your system can leverage the presentation strengths of other applications. This is accomplished through export facilities from the internal schema to an XML or non-XML compatible format of the third-party software.

The following list describes a feature from our example scenario:

- ❏ **Feature** – Export data into Excel so that it can be viewed and interacted with as a spreadsheet.
- ❏ **Design Factors** – Make data accessible to third-party software.
- ❏ **User** – Any.
- ❏ **Preconditions** – None.
- ❏ **Description of Interaction** – The user has an 'export' option, which when selected, must be provided with a local file location for the exported results. Once the data has completed exporting, the user can start Excel and open the file.

7.6.1.1 Use XSL to Convert between Older and Newer Formats

Rates of companies adopting XML for input and output into future and current projects has grown and accelerated across all IT-related industries. It is common for existing systems to have added functionality to be able to import and export data in an XML format, including applications like Excel, databases like Oracle, Avid's MetaSync for film/video editing, QuarkXPress for publishing, and Quickbooks for business accounting. XSL stylesheets can capture all the text-based particulars in a presentation, for both XML-to-XML transformation and XML-to-text transformations. For example, an XML-to-XML transformation is going from the internal XML data representation, an internal specification, to DocBook for print publication or to XHTML for publication to a web site. Now that XML is ubiquitous, new standards, with very few exceptions, are represented solely in XML or include an XML option.

In our example, the `courseEng220.xml` file is transformed with the following stylesheet, `excel.xsl`, to produce a new XML file that can be loaded into Excel:

```
<?xml version="1.0" encoding="iso-8859-1"?>
<xsl:stylesheet version="1.0"
xmlns:xsl="http://www.w3.org/1999/XSL/Transform">
<xsl:output method="xml" media-type="application/msexcel"/>

<xsl:template match="title">
 <Row>
  <Cell><Data>Title</Data></Cell>
  <Cell><Data><xsl:value-of select="."/></Data></Cell>
 </Row>
</xsl:template>

<xsl:template match="class_size_limit">
 <Row>
  <Cell><Data>Class Size Limit</Data></Cell>
  <Cell><Data><xsl:value-of select="."/></Data></Cell>
 </Row>
</xsl:template>

<xsl:template match="description">
 <Row>
```

```
  <Cell><Data>Description</Data></Cell>
  <Cell><Data><xsl:value-of select="."/></Data></Cell>
 </Row>
</xsl:template>

<xsl:template match="syllabus">
 <Row>
  <Cell><Data>Syllabus:</Data></Cell>
 </Row>
 <xsl:apply-templates select="textbook"/>
 <xsl:apply-templates select="grade_component"/>
</xsl:template>

<xsl:template match="textbook">
 <Row>
  <Cell><Data>Textbook</Data></Cell>
  <Cell><Data><xsl:value-of select="."/></Data></Cell>
 </Row>
</xsl:template>

<xsl:template match="grade_component">
 <Row>
  <Cell><Data>Grade</Data></Cell>
  <Cell><Data><xsl:value-of select="@contribution"/></Data></Cell>
  <Cell><Data><xsl:value-of select="."/></Data></Cell>
 </Row>
</xsl:template>

<xsl:template match="prerequisites">
 <Row>
  <Cell><Data>Prerequisites</Data></Cell>
 </Row>
 <xsl:apply-templates select="prerequisite"/>
</xsl:template>

<xsl:template match="prerequisite">
 <Row>
  <Cell><Data></Data></Cell>
  <Cell><Data><xsl:value-of select="."/></Data></Cell>
 </Row>
</xsl:template>
</xsl:stylesheet>
```

Here, the XML document and XSLT stylesheet is processed via a command line using James Clark's XSLT transform engine:

```
xt.exe courseEng220.xml excel.xsl > courseEng220_excel.xml
```

7.7 Maintainability and Extensibility

Maintainability involves system design such that making modifications or enhancements to features can be accomplished easily without significant reworking of the code. Extensibility involves system design such that the software can be used in new ways, or new modules can be developed, which integrate easily with the existing software. Extensibility is similar to maintainability in that both should be carried out without reworking low-level or framework code.

The person or group performing software maintenance is often different from the original code team. This means that rather than having to design code from scratch, the existing code must first be comprehended, before architecture can be developed that works well with the current architecture.

7.7.1.1 Break Units down into Smaller, Less Complicated Pieces

The project will gain a small amount of complexity in having to manage more files, but this will allow for the smaller system pieces to be understood more easily.

The example from *Section 7.2.3* used an XSLT file called `all_course_templates.xsl`. If each template in this file became more and more expanded for each piece of information that can be displayed, then it makes sense to create an XSLT file for each top level item. Since there are no dependencies among the various templates, this would create a maintainable and modular set of templates.

The following three files, `Title.xsl`, `ClassSizeLimit.xsl`, and `Description.xsl`, would each contain templates that produced their respective topic. In practice, it would only make sense if the complexity of each topic justified as a separate file, as opposed to this example.

`Title.xsl` is as follows:

```
<?xml version="1.0" encoding="iso-8859-1"?>
<xsl:stylesheet version="1.0"
xmlns:xsl="http://www.w3.org/1999/XSL/Transform">

<xsl:template match="title">
    <p>Title: <xsl:value-of select="."/></p>
</xsl:template>
```

`ClassSizeLimit.xsl` is given as follows:

```
<?xml version="1.0" encoding="iso-8859-1"?>
<xsl:stylesheet version="1.0"
xmlns:xsl="http://www.w3.org/1999/XSL/Transform">

<xsl:template match="class_size_limit">
   <p>Class Size Limit: <xsl:value-of select="."/></p>
</xsl:template>
```

`Description.xsl` is as follows:

```
<?xml version="1.0" encoding="iso-8859-1"?>
<xsl:stylesheet version="1.0"
xmlns:xsl="http://www.w3.org/1999/XSL/Transform">

<xsl:template match="description">
  <p>Description: <xsl:value-of select="."/></p>
</xsl:template>
```

7.8 Summary

XML gives you many options when developing a presentation strategy, ranging from the simple application of cascading stylesheets, to complex XSLT transforms for extracting the data based on the user's role or preferences. The important thing to remember is that when the content, or the important pieces of information, is kept separate from the way in which it's presented, you will greatly increase your presentation strategy options when using XML as part of the solution.

This chapter showed you how to use XML to develop a scheme where various rendering devices could be given device-dependent formats created from the same XML-based information and a common framework. XML allows for solid maintenance plans and eases issues of extensibility when both these are considered important. XML also supports rich media in your presentations through the use of XML standards that work with video, images, audio, and graphics.

Most importantly, through many examples we presented that XML is a flexible tool where you can build your presentation strategy based on requirements that are important to your application.

XML Design

Handbook

Appendix

Parser Performance

Implementation does Matter

One of the questions that always comes up at some point when people are designing XML parsing code for the first time is this: "Does the parser implementation matter?" The short answer is: of course, the implementation always matters, whether you're talking about XML parsers, or network protocol stacks, or 3D graphics engines. In the XML parsing world, the standardization on SAX as the API for push-based streaming parsers and DOM as the API for all-in-memory parsers has made our jobs as developers and designers a bit easier. Since these APIs are standardized and many different implementations are available, it takes a lot of the worry out of the game at design time. Instead of concerning yourself with the intricacies of this implementation versus that implementation, you can focus instead on making the right parsing technology decisions (DOM or SAX) and making sure that your parsing code is implemented as efficiently as possible using that technology; for example, turning off validation when it's not necessary for your application.

This is not to say that you should ignore the performance of your XML parser implementation; in fact, quite the contrary. Having standardized APIs doesn't absolve us, as developers, from concerning ourselves with performance. What it does do is allow us to write our code against a standard API, and if there happen to be performance issues that are actually at the level of the parser implementation, then we're free to drop in a different implementation of the API that has better performance characteristics. This is a case where interface-driven programming works out as well in practice as it does in principle.

Java's JAXP provides interfaces to both the SAX Level 2 and DOM Level 2 APIs, and it is the recommended way for interacting with SAX and DOM from Java. Luckily for us, the developers who designed JAXP had the foresight to assume that parser implementations would evolve at a more rapid rate than the parsing APIs would, and they designed the framework accordingly. The parser implementation can be switched out without any compile-time changes; the JAXP parser factory classes read the value of a system property to determine the parser implementation to load at runtime.

While the implementation does matter, the reality of the world today is that the popular implementations available today have all been through multiple revisions and are all fairly well tuned at this point. This means that you're not likely to see a very large deviation in terms of behavior from one implementation to the next. Nevertheless, it is a good academic exercise to take a look at how some of the more popular parsers out there today handle some of the more taxing examples that we covered in the book.

The Examples

In two of the chapters (*Chapter 2, Basic Document Design* and *Chapter 4, Parsing Strategies*), we explored a variety of examples that used SAX, DOM, and pull-parsing technology to implement parsing solutions for a set of example documents. With the exception of the pull-parser code from *Chapter 4*, all of the examples were written to the standard SAX Level 2 and DOM Level 2 interfaces using the JAXP 1.2 APIs in Java. (As was mentioned in *Chapter 4*, at the time of this writing there is not yet a standard for pull parsing in Java, although there is a JSR for one called StAX: **St**reaming **A**PI for **X**ML.)

Since the examples in Chapters 3 and 5 were all written using the JAXP framework, changing the parser implementation is as simple as setting a system property.

The Parser Implementations

For the purposes of this appendix, we'll be taking a look at three of the most common and popular JAXP implementations available today:

❏ **Apache's Crimson**: The default parser implementation that ships with the JDK 1.4. You can get it at http://java.sun.com/j2se/1.4/download.html.

❏ **Apache's Xerces**: Perhaps the most popular parser implementation in use at the time of this writing. You can get this at http://xml.apache.org/xerces2-j/index.html.

❏ **GNU's Ælfred2**: A SAX2/DOM2 parser implementation from GNU. You can get it at http://www.gnu.org/software/classpathx/jaxp/jaxp.html.

You can find the JAR files containing the implementations in the lib directory of the zip file that contains the example source code.

Running the examples

In order to run the examples yourself, the first thing you'll need to do is download and unzip the examples. (For information on where to go to download the examples, please refer to the *How to download the source code for the book* section in the *Introduction* chapter.)

The Directory Structure

When you unzip the samples, you should see three sub-directories: classes, lib, and src. The classes directory contains pre-built versions of all of the examples; the lib directory contains some third-party JARs that the examples make use of, including the different parser implementations that will be used in this appendix; and finally the src directory is where the entire source for the examples resides.

Using the Predefined Batch Files

In the root directory where you unzipped the examples there are three Windows batch files: aelfred.bat, crimson.bat, and xerces.bat, each corresponding to one of the three parser implementations that we're examining here. Each of these batch files is just a simple wrapper that calls through to the JVM with the appropriate classpath and system properties that ensure that the correct parser implementation is loaded at runtime. Let's take a look at xerces.bat to see exactly what these batchfiles do:

```
@echo off

set example_cp=classes;lib\xmlParserAPIs.jar;lib\xercesImpl.jar;
set sax_driver=org.apache.xerces.parsers.SAXParser
set dom_driver=org.apache.xerces.jaxp.DocumentBuilderFactoryImpl

java -Xmx256mb -classpath %example_cp%  (cont'd)
        -Dorg.xml.sax.driver=%sax_driver%  (cont'd)
        -Djavax.xml.parsers.DocumentBuilderFactory=%dom_driver%  (cont'd)
        %1 %2 %3 %4 %5 %6 %7 %8 %9
```

-Xmx256mb limits the file size that DOM can handle. You could increase this limit to get the larger files to run.

The batch files are all designed the same way; there are three variables that are set that control the behavior of the VM:

❑ example_cp: This is the classpath for the examples. In each batch file it includes the classes' directory (which contains the classes for the examples) and the JAR lib\xmlParserAPIs.jar, which contains the standard JAXP interfaces. Each batch file then includes whatever else is required for that specific parser implementation.

❑ sax_driver: This is the fully-qualified name of the class that implements the XmlReader interface for this parser implementation.

❏ dom_driver: This is the fully-qualified name of the class of the DocumentBuilderFactory for this parser implementation.

To run the examples using these batch files, you just need to pass the example class name and the source document as parameters to the batch file. For example, if you want to run the "order digest in SAX" example from *Chapter 4* with the source document that has 10,000 orders, you'd type the following:

```
[c:\xmldesign] xerces.bat com.wrox.xmldesign.chapter4.OrderDigestSAX
"src\xml\Chapter 4\4.2.1.10000orders.xml"
```

All of the data for this appendix was gathered by running these batch files in precisely this fashion.

Plugging in your Favorite JAXP Implementation to the Examples

If you're interested in running some of the examples with a JAXP implementation that we haven't covered here, you're in luck; it's very easy to do. You can use the batch files that are supplied with the examples as a starting point, and all you have to do is make three easy modifications:

❏ Update the example_cp variable to include whatever classes or JARs are required for your parser implementation to run (such as xercesImpl.jar for Xerces).

❏ Set the sax_driver variable to be the implementer of the XmlReader interface for your parser implementation.

❏ Set the dom_driver variable to be the DocumentBuilderFactory for your parser implementation.

And that's it! Just run your new batch file like you would any of the predefined ones, and the examples will be run using your favorite JAXP implementation.

The Test Environment

All of the tests documented in this appendix were run using the following machine configuration:

❏ AMD Athlon 1.67GHz Processor

❏ 512MB RAM

❏ Microsoft Windows 2000

❏ Sun's JDK 1.4.0_01

How the Tests Were Conducted

All of these tests were run in the following manner:

- ❑ On a dedicated machine. No other user-level applications were being run at the time the tests were run, except for a word processor and Windows Performance Monitor.

- ❑ Memory stats from PerfMon. All memory usage statistics were gathered using Windows Performance Monitor, reading the Private Bytes performance counter on the VM's process.

- ❑ Average of 20 runs. All of the results in here are an aggregate of 20 counted runs of the program; the first (non-counted) run is ignored, to allow for the HotSpot VM to "warm up".

Now let's move on and see the results of the tests.

Examples From Chapter 2

The following are the results of running selected examples from *Chapter 2* against the documents that were presented or described for each of those examples in the text of the chapter.

Performance of Elements vs. Attributes (Section 2.2.2.1.1)

SAX

Java class: com.wrox.xmldesign.chapter2.GenericParserSAX

File: src\xml\Chapter 2\2.2.2.1.1.10000.10.attributes.xml
Size: 2,940,025 bytes
Ælfred2: 0.4953 seconds, 6,884,631 bytes
Crimson: 0.4781 seconds 7,504,691 bytes
Xerces: 0.4547 seconds, 9,666,560 bytes

File: src\xml\Chapter 2\2.2.2.1.1.10000.10.elements.xml
Size: 4,770,025 bytes
Ælfred2: 0.6461 seconds, 6,797,897 bytes
Crimson: 0.5727 seconds, 7,089,493 bytes
Xerces: 0.5867 seconds, 8,404,677 bytes

File: `src\xml\Chapter 2\2.2.2.1.1.10000.10.mixed.xml`
Size: 4,470,025 bytes
Ælfred2: 0.7656 seconds, 6,827,008 bytes
Crimson: 0.76405 seconds, 6,875,247 bytes
Xerces: 0.7344 seconds, 8,318,720 bytes

File: `src\xml\Chapter 2\2.2.2.1.1.50000.10.attributes.xml`
Size: 14,700,025 bytes
Ælfred2: 2.47345 seconds, 6,763,678 bytes
Crimson: 2.47345 seconds, 6,751,232 bytes
Xerces: 2.2406 seconds, 7,943,936 bytes

File: `src\xml\Chapter 2\2.2.2.1.1.50000.10.elements.xml`
Size: 23,850,025 bytes
Ælfred2: 3.24845 seconds, 6,737,148 bytes
Crimson: 2.85075 seconds, 6,714,821 bytes
Xerces: 2.9367 seconds, 7,750,412 bytes

File: `src\xml\Chapter 2\2.2.2.1.1.50000.10.mixed.xml`
Size: 22,350,025 bytes
Ælfred2: 3.7758 seconds, 6,775,142 bytes
Crimson: 3.83515 seconds, 6,722,750 bytes
Xerces: 3.66565 seconds, 7.801,147 bytes

Notes

Looking at these examples, you can see that even though the sizes of the input files vary dramatically, the amount of RAM that is taken up by the SAX parsing code remains relatively constant. This should not come as a surprise, since SAX is a forward-only parser.

You can also see that the three JAXP implementations are all fairly close in terms of both processing time and memory usage, with Ælfred2 being slightly slower than the other two, and with Xerces requiring on average slightly more memory than the others. This memory usage statistic is slightly misleading for the smaller documents, however; there is a steep drop-off in memory usage shortly after the application begins that affected these numbers. Even still, Xerces appears to require slightly more memory usage than the other two.

DOM
Java class: com.wrox.xmldesign.chapter2.GenericParserDOM

File: `src\xml\Chapter 2\2.2.2.1.1.10000.10.attributes.xml`
Size: 2,940,025 bytes
Ælfred2: 4.0297 seconds, 36,255,102 bytes
Crimson: 0.8047 seconds, 30,022,770 bytes
Xerces: 0.9664 seconds, 31,806,185 bytes

File: `src\xml\Chapter 2\2.2.2.1.1.10000.10.elements.xml`
Size: `4,770,025 bytes`
Ælfred2: 6.7539 seconds, 55,7760,145 bytes
Crimson: 1.55545 seconds, 53,481,954 bytes
Xerces: 1.47035 seconds, 57,553,408 bytes

File: `src\xml\Chapter 2\2.2.2.1.1.10000.10.mixed.xml`
Size: `4,470,025 bytes`
Ælfred2: 5.6078 seconds, 73,546,032 bytes
Crimson: 1.8914 seconds, 60,399,923 bytes
Xerces: 1.97655 seconds, 79,153,962 bytes

File: `src\xml\Chapter 2\2.2.2.1.1.50000.10.attributes.xml`
Size: `14,700,025 bytes`
Ælfred2: 79.846 seconds, 171,767,867 bytes
Crimson: 3.84925 seconds, 135,746,075 bytes
Xerces: 4.72815 seconds, 137,456,085 bytes

File: `src\xml\Chapter 2\2.2.2.1.1.50000.10.elements.xml`
Size: `23,570,025 bytes`
Ælfred2: 89.144 seconds, 256,100,393 bytes
Crimson: 7.71955 seconds, 274,083,981 bytes
Xerces: 6.9664 seconds, 217,264,914 bytes

File: `src\xml\Chapter 2\2.2.2.1.1.50000.10.mixed.xml`
Size: `22,350,025 bytes`
Ælfred2: 88.735 seconds, 274,246,375 bytes
Crimson: 8.72105 seconds, 274,060,820 bytes
Xerces: 8.7945 seconds, 253,735,854 bytes

Notes

Looking at these examples, it becomes clear that the larger the input file, the more memory is required to parse the document. If you look at the sizes of the files and compare them to the amount of memory required by the VM during parsing, you can see that for each 1MB of input text, there is about a 5MB to 10MB cost associated with the DOM. This should reinforce the fact that DOM is not the best choice for very large files.

You can also see that Ælfred2 is lagging quite far behind the other two JAXP implementations in terms of processing time, by upwards of a factor of ten in the most extreme cases.

Books (Section 2.2.3)

Java class: com.wrox.xmldesign.chapter2.BookParserElements
File: src\xml\Chapter 2\2.2.3.inline.first.xml
Size: 848 bytes
Ælfred2: 0.00465 seconds, 7,172,096 bytes
Crimson: 0.0047 seconds, 6,441,643 bytes
Xerces: 0.0086 seconds, 9,261,056 bytes

Java class: com.wrox.xmldesign.chapter2.BookParserAttributes
File: src\xml\Chapter 2\2.2.3.inline.second.xml
Size: 759 bytes
Ælfred2: 0.0047 seconds, 6,967,296 bytes
Crimson: 0.0039 seconds, 6,909,952 bytes
Xerces: 0.00935 seconds, 9,537,829 bytes

Notes
These examples were run using very tiny input files, so in order to get the memory usage information, they were run 2000 times consecutively rather than the normal 20.

Examples from Chapter 4

The following are the results of running selected examples from *Chapter 4* against the documents that were presented or described for each of those examples in the text of the chapter.

Order Digests (Section 4.2.1)

SAX

Java class: com.wrox.xmldesign.chapter4.OrderDigestSAX

File: src\xml\Chapter 4\4.2.1.1000orders.xml
Size: 749,031 bytes
Ælfred2: 0.13125 seconds, 6,868,992 bytes
Crimson: 0.1172 seconds, 7,193,941 bytes
Xerces: 0.1297 seconds, 9,976,491 bytes

File: src\xml\Chapter 4\4.2.1.10000orders.xml
Size: 7,490,031 bytes
Ælfred2: 1.26955 seconds, 7,021,606 bytes
Crimson: 1.12735 seconds, 7,062,528 bytes
Xerces: 1.1656 seconds, 8,412,856 bytes

File: src\xml\Chapter 4\4.2.1.60000orders.xml
Size: 44,940,031 bytes
Ælfred2: 7.5484 seconds, 6,934,528 bytes
Crimson: 6.7344 seconds, 6,881,280 bytes
Xerces: 6.9492 seconds, 8,073,216 bytes

Notes

Once again, here the most obvious thing is that the memory usage varies very little regardless of the size of the input file, as we would expect with SAX. The only other interesting fact here is that Xerces seems to be a bit more of a memory hog than the other two; it's not by an enormous amount, but it is unquestionably more expensive.

DOM

Java class: com.wrox.xmldesign.chapter4.OrderDigestDOM

File: src\xml\Chapter 4\4.2.1.1000orders.xml
Size: 749,031 bytes
Ælfred2: 1.20155 seconds, 27,526,315 bytes
Crimson: 0.44845 seconds, 13,928,448 bytes
Xerces: 0.4039 seconds, 20,319,346 bytes

File: src\xml\Chapter 4\4.2.1.10000orders.xml
Size: 7,490,031 bytes
Ælfred2: 13.982 seconds, 162,0261,568 bytes
Crimson: 3.9586seconds, 85,338,618 bytes
Xerces: 3.4172 seconds, 115,586,595 bytes

File: src\xml\Chapter 4\4.2.1.60000orders.xml
Size: 44,940,031 bytes
Ælfred2: Failed with OutOfMemoryError
Crimson: Failed with OutOfMemoryError
Xerces: Failed with OutOfMemoryError

Notes

This is more evidence that DOM and large source files aren't a good combination, and also that Ælfred2 is far less optimized than either Crimson or Xerces.

Arithmetic Expressions (Section 4.2.2)

Java class: com.wrox.xmldesign.chapter4.ExpressionDOM

File: src\xml\Chapter 4\4.2.2.expression.xml
Size: 331 bytes
Ælfred2: 0.0047 seconds, 7,651,328 bytes
Crimson: 0.0039 seconds, 7,271,765 bytes
Xerces: 0.0094 seconds, 10,031,104 bytes

Notes

Again, these input files were so small that in order to get memory usage information for them, they were run 2000 times instead of the normal 20.

DOM Adapter (Section 4.2.6)

Java class: com.wrox.xmldesign.chapter4.DOMAdapter

File: src\xml\Chapter 4\4.2.1.1000orders.xml
Size: 749,031 bytes
Ælfred2: fails with a DOM exception
Crimson: 0.4672 seconds, 18,876,826 bytes
Xerces: 0.35935 seconds, 15,863,808 bytes

File: src\xml\Chapter 4\4.2.1.10000orders.xml
Size: 7,490,031 bytes
Ælfred2: fails with a DOM exception
Crimson: 4.05 seconds, 137,439,585 bytes
Xerces: 3.14455 seconds, 97,644,002 bytes

Notes

Ælfred2 failed with a DOM exception for some reason when I tried to run this. The exception class was gnu.xml.dom.DomEx, and the error message was "Parameter or operation isn't supported by this node". I couldn't track it down and fix it, and since the code works fine with Crimson and Xerces, I'm assuming this is a bug in Ælfred2.

Another thing of note here is that while Xerces appeared to be more of a memory hog in an earlier test, it actually ends up requiring significantly less memory than Crimson in this case.

File System DOM (Section 4.3.4)

Java class: com.wrox.xmldesign.chapter4.FileSystemDOM

File: src\xml\Chapter 4\4.3.4.inline.xml
Size: 447 bytes
Ælfred2: 0.0039 seconds, 7,428,096 bytes
Crimson: 0.0031 seconds, 7,596,032 bytes
Xerces: 0.0086 seconds, 9,785,799 bytes

Notes

Once more, since these source files were so small, they were run 2000 times, rather than the normal 20, in order to get the memory usage statistics.

Conclusion

This ends our whirlwind tour of some of the more popular JAXP parser implementations, using our examples as test fodder to put them through their paces. It should be pretty clear at this point that, from what we've seen of Ælfred2's performance and occasionally with Xerces' memory usage, the parser implementation actually does matter. Remember to keep this in mind as you're implementing and stress testing your applications.

XML Design

Handbook

Index

Index

A Guide to the Index

The index is arranged hierarchically, in alphabetical order, with symbols preceding the letter A. Most second-level entries and many third-level entries also occur as first-level entries. This is to ensure that users will find the information they require however they choose to search for it.

D

p2p.wrox.com
The programmer's resource centre

A unique free service from Wrox Press
With the aim of helping programmers to help each other

Wrox Press aims to provide timely and practical information to today's programmer. P2P is a list server offering a host of targeted mailing lists where you can share knowledge with four fellow programmers and find solutions to your problems. Whatever the level of your programming knowledge, and whatever technology you use P2P can provide you with the information you need.

ASP Support for beginners and professionals, including a resource page with hundreds of links, and a popular ASP.NET mailing list.

DATABASES For database programmers, offering support on SQL Server, mySQL, and Oracle.

MOBILE Software development for the mobile market is growing rapidly. We provide lists for the several current standards, including WAP, Windows CE, and Symbian.

JAVA A complete set of Java lists, covering beginners, professionals, and server-side programmers (including JSP, servlets and EJBs)

.NET Microsoft's new OS platform, covering topics such as ASP.NET, C#, and general .NET discussion.

VISUAL BASIC Covers all aspects of VB programming, from programming Office macros to creating components for the .NET platform.

WEB DESIGN As web page requirements become more complex, programmer's are taking a more important role in creating web sites. For these programmers, we offer lists covering technologies such as Flash, Coldfusion, and JavaScript.

XML Covering all aspects of XML, including XSLT and schemas.

OPEN SOURCE Many Open Source topics covered including PHP, Apache, Perl, Linux, Python and more.

FOREIGN LANGUAGE Several lists dedicated to Spanish and German speaking programmers, categories include. NET, Java, XML, PHP and XML

How to subscribe
Simply visit the P2P site, at http://p2p.wrox.com/

WROX PRESS INC.

Wrox writes books for you. Any suggestions, or ideas
about how you want information given in your
ideal book will be studied by our team.
Your comments are always valued at Wrox.

Free phone in USA 800-USE-WROX
Fax (312) 893 8001

UK Tel. (0121) 687 4100   Fax   (0121) 687 4101

NB. If you post the bounce back card below in the UK, please send it to:
Wrox Press Ltd., Arden House, 1102 Warwick Road, Acocks Green, Birmingham. B27 6BH. UK.

Registration Code :   768X4S7R0D8V1KT01

XML Design Handbook - Registration Card

Name _____

Address _____

_____

City _____ State/Region _____

Country _____ Postcode/Zip _____

E-mail _____

Occupation _____

How did you hear about this book?

☐ Book review (name) _____

☐ Advertisement (name) _____

☐ Recommendation _____

☐ Catalog _____

☐ Other _____

Where did you buy this book?

☐ Bookstore (name) _____ City _____

☐ Computer Store (name) _____

☐ Mail Order _____

☐ Other _____

What influenced you in the
purchase of this book?

☐ Cover Design
☐ Contents
☐ Other (please specify) _____

How did you rate the overall
contents of this book?

☐ Excellent   ☐ Good
☐ Average   ☐ Poor

What did you find most useful about this book? _____

What did you find least useful about this book? _____

Please add any additional comments. _____

What other subjects will you buy a computer
book on soon? _____

What is the best computer book you have used this year? _____

*Note: This information will only be used to keep you updated
about new Wrox Press titles and will not be used for any other
purpose or passed to any other third party.*

Check here if you DO NOT want to receive further support for this book. ☐

768X

768X

wrox

PROGRAMMER TO PROGRAMMER™

BUSINESS REPLY MAIL
FIRST CLASS MAIL   PERMIT#64   CHICAGO, IL

POSTAGE WILL BE PAID BY ADDRESSEE

WROX PRESS INC.
29 S. LA SALLE ST.,
SUITE 520
CHICAGO IL 60603-USA

NO POSTAGE
NECESSARY
IF MAILED
IN THE
UNITED STATES